EDEN Annual Conference 2024

Learning in the Age of AI: Towards Imaginative Futures

Concise & Other Papers

Graz, Austria
16 - 18 June 2024

Editors:

Josep M. Duart
Elena Trepule

ISBN: 979-8-3313-0345-7

Printed from e-media with permission by:

Curran Associates, Inc.
57 Morehouse Lane
Red Hook, NY 12571

CURRAN ASSOCIATES INC.
proceedings
.com

Some format issues inherent in the e-media version may also appear in this print version.

For permission requests, please contact the publisher:

European Distance and E-Learning Network (EDEN)
Budapest University of Technology & Economics
H-1111 Budapest, Egry J. u.1.
Hungary

secretariat@eden-online.org

Additional copies of this publication are available from:

Curran Associates, Inc.
57 Morehouse Lane
Red Hook, NY 12571 USA
Phone: 845-758-0400
Fax: 845-758-2633
Email: curran@proceedings.com
Web: www.proceedings.com

EDEN Annual Conference Proceedings

Learning in the Age of AI: Towards Imaginative Futures

EDEN 2024 Annual Conference

hosted by

University of Graz, Graz, Austria

16-18 June 2024

Edited by

Josep M. Duart, Elena Trepulė

on behalf of EDEN Digital Learning Europe

EDEN Annual Conference Proceedings

2024 Annual Conference | Graz, 16-18 June 2024

ISSN: 2707-2819

Published by EDEN Digital Learning Europe

Editors:

Josep M. Duart

Elena Trepulė

Editorial co-ordination:

Gabija Morozovienė

EDEN DLE Secretariat

Kuklase tn 16-12, 13423, Tallinn, Estonia

E-mail: secretariat@eden-europe.eu

https://eden-europe.eu/

Co-funded by the European Union

Funded by the European Union. Views and opinions expressed are however those of the author(s) only and do not necessarily reflect those of the European Union or the European Education and Culture Executive Agency (EACEA). Neither the European Union nor EACEA can be held responsible for them.

Acknowledgement and thanks are given to the Program Committee

Josep M. Duart, EDEN DLE President, Spain

Kathrin Marie Otrel-Cass, Graz University, Austria

Mark Brown, EDEN DLE Vice-President of Strategy and Communication, Ireland

Denise Whitelock, EDEN DLE Vice-President for Research, UK

Sandra Kučina Softić, EDEN DLE Vice-President of Open Professional Collaboration, Croatia

Airina Volungevičienė, Lithuania

Alfredo Soeiro, Portugal

Mart Laanpere, Estonia

Antonella Poce, Italy

Wim E.A. Van Petegem, Belgium

Vlad Mihăescu, Romania

Elena Trepulė, Lithuania

TABLE OF CONTENTS

What does learner-centered pedagogy look like in reimagining the digital classroom of the future?

POSTER ABSTRACTS

What is required to help foster nestedness and integration in the complex digital learning ecosystem?

CONCISE PAPERS

Offline Study in Online Education: Promoting Equity of Access During the Digital Transformation

Christopher Hutton[1], Fiona J. Aiken[2]

[1] School of Environment, Earth and Ecosystem Sciences, The Open University, UK; Christopher.Hutton@open.ac.uk
[2] School of Environment, Earth and Ecosystem Sciences, The Open University, UK; Fiona.Aiken@open.ac.uk

Correspondence: Christopher Hutton: Christopher.Hutton@open.ac.uk

Abstract:

The advent of generative-AI has accelerated digital transformation in distance education, including emerging pedagogies for online and blended settings. Despite numerous advantages, one of the ethical questions posed is how to ensure equity of experience for students with limited, or no online access due to disability, digital poverty, or secure confinement?

At the Open University, UK, distance learning students on Earth and Environment modules study on-screen-only materials; printed packs of these material are therefore provided to those unable to study online. Over 80% of students using print packs as an adjustment for a disability spend over half their study time using them; they blend this with the online materials for interactive content and report it to be effective (Aiken and Hutton, 2023). However, those with no online access are unable to adopt a blended approach and have a much poorer experience (Aiken and Hutton, 2023): it is likely this inequity will increase as more digital technologies are introduced. The problem is compounded by ~75% of students receiving no advice on making the best use of their print pack.

Based on the findings of our previous research (Aiken and Hutton, 2023), we designed an intervention for the academic year 22/23. This involved recruiting and training two Associate Lecturer champions, one on each of our large year 1 ("Science: concepts and practice"; ~1800 students) and year 2 ("Environmental Science" ; ~800 students) modules. Following training and familiarisation with the content of the print packs, the champions provided support and advice to fellow Associate Lecturers through an asynchronous forum and carried out their own evaluation of the print packs. At the conclusion of the academic year, the champions reported on their experiences and evaluation of the packs. There was a high degree of similarity between the two champions' reports, including:

- Recognition of the divide between students able to blend print packs with on-screen study and those entirely reliant on a print pack.
- Recommendations to
  - make print pack materials more readily available to Associate Lecturers, and
  - improve print pack organisation and formatting, particularly for those without online access.

In this session, we will report in more detail on the champions' findings, and on how we have expanded the roles to encompass more Earth and Environmental Science modules for the academic year 23/24. This scaling up is part of a pilot to support a cross-University initiative improving print packs. We are also interested in engaging in discussion on how we can continue to support students equitably if they have limited online access: as generative-AI becomes embedded in our online learning, to what extent can printed materials provide a reasonable adjustment?

How do we promote fairness in digital learning futures?

Keywords: disability; online study; adjustment; digital equity

Reference

Aiken, F.J., and Hutton, C. (2023) *Improving equity of experience in distance education for students with challenges accessing online learning environments*. Paper presented at the European Digital Learning Network Annual Conference 2023, Dublin, Ireland. https://eden-europe.eu/wp-content/uploads/2023/07/EDEN-2023-Annual-Conference-Proceedings.pdf

A Design-based Research Approach to Ethics in Educational Technology: Perspectives of Future Education Professionals

Michaela Kramer[1], Victoria I. Marín[2], Svenja Bedenlier[3]

[1] Department of Educational and Social Sciences, Universität zu Köln, Germany; michaela.kramer@uni-koeln.de
[2] Department of Education Sciences, Universitat de Lleida, Spain; victoria.marin@udl.cat
[3] Department of Education, Friedrich-Alexander-Universität Erlangen-Nürnberg; Germany; svenja.bedenlier@fau.de

Correspondence: Michaela Kramer: michaela.kramer@uni-koeln.de

Abstract:

In the context of digital technologies in education, ethics has always been an important concern. With artificial intelligence fundamentally changing the educational landscape, addressing ethics is even more pressing (Kimmons & Rosenberg, 2022). However, a scarcity of research on the topic was noted in different literature reviews (Kramer et al., 2023; Marín & Tur, 2024). Limited evidence-based work, the predominance of studies at the institutional level, the differences of topic interests in geographic areas and the overrepresentation of specific topics (e.g., data privacy and confidentiality, and academic honesty), are amongst the main findings of those reviews.

Against this backdrop, we seek to explore ethical practices of future education professionals related to decision-making in technology-enhanced learning designs and pursue the following research questions: How do future education professionals think of moral dilemmas and take ethical decisions about digital technology in technology-enhanced learning designs? And how can ethical reflexivity of future educational professionals be promoted?

As a first step of our design-based research approach (Wang & Hannafin, 2005), we revisit the results of our previous reviews (Kramer et al., 2023; Marín & Tur, 2024), to identify specific ethical issues in educational technology and indications of pedagogical strategies at the micro level neglected in previous research. In the design phase, students enrolled in educational technology and media education programs at the Master level in three different universities will adopt the role of partners in research and producers of videos. These videos feature specific moral dilemmas in educational technology. The third phase incorporates a first cycle of implementation and evaluation. Focus groups with other students in Education programs of different contexts and countries, aim at ensuring an interdisciplinary perspective. Focus group participants will be asked to evaluate the videos, explain and justify how they would act in those situations. Results could also feed further cycles to improve the videos, as well as generate design principles for the development of new ones. The videos will be shared as open educational resources, additionally supporting transfer through the creation of open and online training offer on ethics in educational technology (e.g. as microcredentials). The training addresses future and present education professionals of any educational context and country. In our presentation we will introduce the research design and preliminary results.

Keywords: educational technoethics, design-based research, education professionals

Acknowledgments

Victoria I. Marín acknowledges the Grant RYC2019-028398-I funded by MCIN/AEI/ 10.13039/501100011033 and "ESF Investing in your future."

How do we promote fairness in digital learning futures?

References

Kimmons, R., & Rosenberg, J. M. (2022). Trends and topics in educational technology, 2022 edition. *TechTrends, 66*(2), 134-140. https://doi.org/10.1007/s11528-022-00713-0

Kramer, M., Bedenlier, S., & Kammerl, R. (2023). Digitalität, Ethik und Bildung. Ein Narratives Review zur Systematisierung eines internationalen Forschungsfeldes. *MedienPädagogik, 19*. https://dx.doi.org/10.21240/mpaed/jb19/2023.03.05.X

Marín, V. I., & Tur, G. (2024). Ethical Issues in the Use of Technologies in Education Settings: A Scoping Review. Education in the Knowledge Society (EKS), 25, e31301. https://doi.org/10.14201/eks.31301

Wang, F., & Hannafin, M. J. (2005). Design-based research and technology-enhanced learning environments. *Educational Technology Research and Development, 53*(4), 5-23. https://doi.org/10.1007/BF02504682

Promoting Fairness in Digital Learning Futures: Exploring AI Powered Online Academic Support Provision in a Higher Education Context

Lorraine Delaney[1], Mark Brown[2], Eamon Costello[3]

[1] School of Human Development, Institute of Education, Dublin City University, Drumcondra, 9 Dublin, Ireland lorraine.delaney@dcu.ie
[2] School of Policy and Practice, Institute of Education, Dublin City University, Drumcondra, 9 Dublin, Ireland; mark.brown@dcu.ie
[3] School of STEM Education, Innovation and Global Studies, Institute of Education, Dublin City University, Drumcondra, 9 Dublin, Ireland; eamon.costello@dcu.ie

Correspondence: Lorraine Delaney: lorraine.delaney@dcu.ie

Abstract:

This paper examines how AI powered data can be used to enhance fairness of academic support provision to distance university students. The context for this study is Dublin City University (DCU), a dual-mode university with around 1,800 part-time students studying primarily online. In 2018, a decision was taken to pilot the third-party online learning support platform, Studiosity, for online distance students, because they found it difficult to access existing academic support primarily offered during normal office hours.

Little is known about academic help-seeking behaviour in higher education (Netanda et al. 2019, O'Neill & Russell 2019). Within the literature, help-seeking is divided into two categories: *instrumental,* where help-seeking relates to students seeking to solve the problem themselves by asking for explanations of concepts and *expedient*, where students ask for help with something they should be capable of solving themselves (Martin-Arbos et al. 2021). Expedient help-seeking is regarded as less likely to lead to deep learning, and is regarded as of less value (Benzie & Harper 2020, Fong et al. 2023, Gurney & Grossi 2019, Hamilton 2020, Rambiritch 2018). The literature also highlights how students with more cultural/academic capital find it easier to seek help (Bourdieu 1973; 1986, Golann & Darling-Aduana 2020, Lareau 2002, Martin-Arbos et al. 2021).

This study employs an inductive research design, drawing on data collected through Studiosity (2018–2020) who provided monthly reports, powered by AI, on various quantitative (e.g., course level) and qualitative (e.g. the questions students asked) data sets. Quantitative data were analysed using Excel. Content analysis was deemed the most appropriate method of analysing the qualitative data. Ethical approval was obtained for this study from the DCU Research Ethics Committee. This paper explores the experience of two specific groups of students: first-year undergraduate (n= 380) and post-graduate (n=401). All data were anonymised. The research sought to answer the following questions:

- What is the pattern of student cohort engagement with Studiosity?

- What are the implications of this pattern?

- What can we learn from the questions students ask?

Findings reveal that postgraduate students used the service more than first-year undergraduate students (29% against 19%). Postgraduate students tended to engage in expedient help seeking, looking for answers to questions they should, given their postgraduate status, have been able to answer themselves. The evidence from our research indicates that, to support fairness in digital learning futures, institutions could develop their learning support ecosystem in a manner that targets students most at risk of attrition and who are in the early stages of their academic journey and most likely to benefit from academic support over their entire learning journey.

Keywords: University, academic support, help, online, Studiosity.

References

Benzie, H.J.; Harper, R. (2020). Developing student writing in higher education: Digital third- party products in distributed learning environments. *Teach. High. Educ.* 25, 633–647 https://doi.org/10.1080/13562517.2019.1590327

Bourdieu, P. (1973). Cultural Reproduction and Social Reproduction. In *Knowledge, Education and Cultural Change*; Brown, R., Ed.; Tavistock: London, UK.

Bourdieu, P. (1986). The forms of capital. In *Handbook of Theory and Research for the Sociology of Education*; Robinson, J.G., Ed.; Greenwood Press: New York, NY, USA.

Fong, C.J.; Gonzales, C.; Hill-Troglin Cox, C.; Shinn, H.B. (2023). Academic Help-Seeking and Achievement of Postsecondary Students: A Meta-Analytic Investigation. *J. Educ. Psychol.* 115, 1–21.

Golann, J.W.; Darling-Aduana, J. (2020). Toward a multifaceted understanding of Lareau's "sense of entitlement": Bridging sociological and psychological constructs. *Sociol. Compass* 14, e12798. https://doi.org/10.1111/soc4.12798.

Gurney, L.; Grossi, V. (2019). Performing support in higher education: Negotiating conflicting agendas in academic language and learning advisory work. *Higher Education Research Development* 38, 940–953. DOI: 10.1080/07294360.2019.1609916

Hamilton, J. (2020). Learning support literacy: Promoting independent learning skills and effective help-seeking behaviours in HE students. *J. Acad. Lang. Learn.* 14, 69–76. ISSN 1835-5196.

Lareau, A. (2002). Invisible Inequality: Social Class and Childrearing in Black Families and White Families. *Am. Sociol. Rev.* 67, 747–776. https://doi.org/10.2307/3088916.

Martín-Arbós, S.; Castarlenas, E.; Dueñas, J.-M. (2021). Help-Seeking in an Academic Context: A Systematic Review. *Sustainability*, 13, 4460. https://doi.org/10.3390/su13084460.

Netanda, R.S.; Mamabolo, J.; Themane, M. (2019). Do or die: Student support interventions for the survival of distance education institutions in a competitive higher education system. *Stud. High. Educ.* 44, 397–414. https://doi.org/10.1080/03075079.2017.1378632

O'Neill, R.; Russell, A.M.T. (2019). Stop! Grammar time: University students' perceptions of the automated feedback program Grammarly. *Australas. J. Educ. Technol.* 35, 42–56

Rambiritch, A. (2018). A Social Justice Approach to Providing Academic Writing Support. *Educ. Res. Soc. Chang.* 7, 46–60. https://doi.org/10.17159/2221

Decolonial Perspectives on Potentials and Risks of Generative AI in (Language) Education of Immigrant Minority Students

Marion Döll[1], Sabine Guldenschuh[2], Tanja Tajmel[3]

[1] German in the Context of Multilingualism, Europa-Universität Flensburg, Germany; marion.doell@uni-flensburg.de
[2] German in the Context of Multilingualism, Europa-Universität Flensburg, Germany; sabine.guldenschuh@uni-flensburg.de
[3] Centre for Engineering in Society, Gina Cody School of Engineering and Computer Science, Concordia University Montréal, Canada; tanja.tajmel@concordia.ca

Correspondence: Marion Döll: marion.doell@uni-flensburg.de

Abstract:

For several decades now, it seems to be a given that immigrant minority students suffer a – primarily language-based – disadvantage in the educational system of German speaking countries. Analyses of the results of comparative school performance studies such as PISA show that compensatory language support measures have failed to reduce these disadvantages (e.g. Tiele & Rölz 2023). Skutnabb-Kangas (2015) argues that monolingual education systems in multilingual migration societies (such as Germany and Austria) have a discriminatory, linguicist effect on immigrant minority students per se: Monolingualism and the monolingual habitus (Gogolin 1997) inevitably lead to discrimination against multilingual students, as they struggle to convert their (multilingual) resources (Bourdieu 1977) into recognized material or immaterial resources within the established and inflexible monolingual structures (Skutnabb-Kangas 2015). The term linguicism is used to describe this kind of discrimination in connection with (immigrant) language minorities. It is defined as "ideologies, structures and practices which are used to legitimate, effectuate, regulate and reproduce an unequal division of power and resources (both material and immaterial) between groups which are defined on the basis of language." (Skutnabb-Kangas 1988, p. 13) Conceptually, linguicism is linked to the concept of racism, i.e. linguicism is understood as a form of 'new racism' (Balibar 1990), which uses categories of difference other than 'race' to legitimize disadvantages and exclusions. Like racism, linguicism is to be seen as a social relationship or ubiquitous social structure (Rommelspacher 2009), which manifests itself at certain points in the education system in the form of various inferiorizing discourses and practices towards immigrant minority students.

The dynamic developments of the past two years have made teachers and the general public aware of the potential of generative AI technologies for education. Tools such as *ChatGPT* and *DeepL* not only offer a wide range of possibilities for supporting language learning (Huang et al. 2023), but also for reducing language barriers in general educational processes. It is widely known that various inequalities exist and arise in connection with algorithmic bias when using generative AI tools (Baker & Hawn 2021). In addition, discrimination can occur regarding the use of the system, e.g. through the regulation of access to the relevant tools (Huang et al. 2023). This is the starting point for our study, which explores the question of how linguicism (Skutnabb-Kangas 2015) arises and is reproduced in connection with the use of generative AI technologies in (language) education contexts from a decolonial anti-discriminatory perspective at the interdisciplinary intersection of language pedagogy and the sociology of technology. In our contribution, we will use the preliminary results of a critical discourse analysis (Wodak & Meyer 2016) of guidelines and training courses concerning the use of generative AI in education to show how linguicism manifests itself in the use of generative AI technologies in the sense of preventing the reduction of language barriers and, based on this, present initial considerations on how the (re)production of linguicism through AI technologies can be pedagogically addressed at the micro level of the education system.

Keywords: AI, discrimination, language education, language learning, linguicism, postcolonial

How do we promote fairness in digital learning futures?

References

Baker, R. S., & Hawn, A. (2021). Algorithmic Bias in Education. *International Journal of Artificial Intelligence in Education* 32, 1052-1092. :10.1007/s40593-021-00285-9

Balibar, É. (1990). Gibt es einen »Neo-Rassismus«? *Rasse – Klasse – Nation. Ambivalente Identitäten*, 23-38.

Bourdieu, P. (1977). *Outline of a theory of practice*. :10.1017/CBO9780511812507

Gogolin, I. (1997). The "monolingual habitus" as the common feature in teaching in the language of the majority in different countries. *Per Linguam*, 13(2), 38-49. :10.5785/13-2-187

Huang, X., Zou, D., Cheng, G., Chen, X., & Xie, H. (2023). Trends, Research Issues and Applications of Artificial Intelligence in Language Education. *Educational Technology & Society* 26(1), 112-131. :10.30191/ETS.202301_26(1).0009.

Skutnabb-Kangas, T. (1988). Multilingualism and the Education of Minority Children. *Minority education: from shame to struggle* (9-44). :10.21832/9781800418110-002

Skutnabb-Kangas, T. (2015). Linguicism. *The Encyclopedia of Applied Linguistics*. :10.1002/9781405198431.wbeal1460

Rommelspacher, B. (2009). Was ist eigentlich Rassismus? *Rassismuskritik*, Band 1, 25-38.

Tiele, V., & Rölz, M. (2023). Lesekompetenz im Zeitvergleich. *PISA 2022. Kompetenzen in Mathematik, Lesen und Naturwissenschaft am Ende der Pflichtschulzeit im internationalen Vergleich*, 42-44. :10.17888/pisa2022-eb

Wodak, R., & Meyer, M. (Eds.) (2016). *Methods of critical discourse studies.*

Hacking Happier Futures: An AI-Augmented Student Hackathon to Address Affective and Ethical Digital Learning Challenges

Eamon Costello[1], James Brunton[2], Kathrin Marie Otrel-Cass[3], Niels Erik Lyngdorf[4], Mark Brown[5]

[1] School of STEM Education, Innovation and Global Studies, Dublin City University, Ireland; eamon.costello@dcu.ie
[2] School of Psychology, Dublin City University, Ireland; james.brunton@dcu.ie
[3] University of Graz, Austria; kathrin.otrel-cass@uni-graz.at
[4] Aalborg University, Denmark; nel@plan.aau.dk
[5] School of Policy and Practice, Dublin City University, Ireland; mark.brown@dcu.ie

Correspondence: Eamon Costello: eamon.costello@dcu.ie

Abstract:

How can learners stay well in an AI age and navigate the emerging ethical and academic integrity issues? It was these challenges which Dublin City University (DCU) students worked to build collective responses to, in a local event that formed part of the Europe-wide Digital Education Hackathon (DigiEduHack) initiative of the European Commission on November 10-11. The 2023 DigiEduHack hackathon had over 750 students from across Europe who worked over one weekend to explore solutions to existing and future challenges in digital education with local winners going on to compete in a global competition.

Wellbeing and student loneliness are pressing issues, and although loneliness can be a normal part of being an emerging adult, especially during life transitions such as going to college (Kirwan et al, 2023) it is nonetheless imperative that we build learning designs that promote human connection and bring learners together (Beskorsa et al, 2023; Lyngdorf et al, 2023). Current research highlights how students can experience anxiety related to issues of academic integrity and Gen AI as institutions grapple with this phenomenon (Gorichanaz 2023). This hackathon aimed to provide a safe space for students (and staff) to experiment with AI tools outside of their formal coursework. It tackled issues of ethics in AI in education but also explored the creation of connected learning environments for students of which the hackathon itself was an example.

The DCU-hosted hackathon Go Wild to Stay Well: Ensuring Learning Wellbeing an AI Age was a successful deliverable of the Erasmus+ funded Hacking Innovative Pedagogies project led by Graz University with partners in DCU and Aalborg. Participating students pitched and voted on ideas and formed three teams to hack challenges related to ethics in AI education and learning connection and wellbeing. Each team adopted a different GenAI tool as a Companion Learner. Each team also had an Integrity Officer, responsible for scrutinizing and vetting the output of AI-generated content. Ethical issues of AI were explored, and each team appointed an Empathy Officer to help keep people at the heart of their work. The local winning team's solution "EduAI: To encourage the ethical use of AI critically and with integrity in an educational environment" was shortlisted for an award in the newcomer category of the global stage of the competition (EduAI, 2023).

This presentation gives an outline of how the hackathon was organised, run and evaluated via a system of mentors, expert speakers, judges and researchers. We detail our evolving conversations with students about the ethical and critical use of AI and outline how this innovative pedagogy was used in the service of building learning spaces that have intertwined learner and staff wellbeing at their core.

Keywords: AI, hackathons, innovating pedagogies.

How do we promote fairness in digital learning futures?

References

Beskorsa, O., Mendel, I., Fasching, M., Otrel-Cass, K., Costello, E., Lyngdorf, N. E. R., & Brown, M. (2023). University of Graz. https://doi.org/10.25364/9783903374249

Hacking innovative pedagogy: Innovation and digitisation to rewild higher education: a commented atlas.

Gorichanaz, T. (2023). Accused: How students respond to allegations of using ChatGPT on assessments. Learning: Research and Practice, 9(2), 183-196.

Kirwan, E. M., O'Súilleabháin, P. S., Burns, A., Ogoro, M., Allen, E., & Creaven, A. M. (2023). Exploring Loneliness in Emerging Adulthood: A Qualitative Study. Emerging Adulthood, 21676968231194380

Lyngdorf, N. E., Ruggaard, S. T., Otrel-Cass, K., & Costello, E. (2023). The hacking innovative pedagogies (HIP) framework. Aalborg University. ISBN 978-87-89383-90-3 https://doi.org/10.54337/aau602808725

EduAI (2023) "To encourage the ethical use of AI critically and with integrity in an educational environment" https://digieduhack.com/solutions/to-encourage-the-ethical-use-of-ai-critically-and-with-integrity-in-an-educational-environment

Linguistic and Textual Analysis for Museum Education: An Italian Pilot Study

Eliana Maria Torre[1]

[1] Department of Classics, Sapienza University of Rome, Italy; elianamaria.torre@uniroma1.it

Correspondence: Eliana Maria Torre: elianamaria.torre@uniroma1.it

Abstract:

Digital technologies can help museums become agents of social change. This pilot study examines the explanatory texts of the National Roman Museum (MNR) protohistoric section in Rome. The research question is whether the language of text panels and object labels of the protohistoric section of the MNR is culturally accessible, inclusive, and emotionally engaging. Results show room for improvement in the content's readability and engagement. AI can assist in writing more engaging texts and delivering them in personalised digital learning environments.

Museums can be agents of social change, provided their communication strategies are inclusive. They must be "accessible and inclusive, foster diversity and sustainability, and offer varied experiences for education, enjoyment, reflection, and knowledge sharing". Edutainment is, therefore, a step of paramount importance for promoting lifelong learning and active citizenship. Nevertheless, making collections culturally accessible remains challenging, especially considering the vastness of the Italian cultural heritage and the limited resources. Digital technologies can help museum professionals gain precise insight into the characteristics of current text panels and object labels and develop and offer new texts adequate to each visitor's specific needs and interests.

This pilot study examines the explanatory texts of the protohistoric section of the National Roman Museum (MNR) in Rome, Italy, as a necessary preliminary step for its future update. The research question is: Is the language of text panels and object labels of the protohistoric section of the MNR culturally accessible, inclusive, and emotionally engaging? The parameters selected for analysis are:

- Lexical density, indicative of the concentration of information in a text;
- Index of readability, which refers to the presumed level of schooling necessary to understand the texts;
- Frequency of allocutive pronouns as indicative of the level of interaction with users;
- Register, frequency of demonstrative and possessive adjectives and pronouns, anglicisms, polyrematics, and plastisms, predictive of users' emotional involvement.

Italian texts were processed in Tintful and Voyant Tools and compared with their English translations, using also Analyze My Writing for the latter.

The Italian corpus has 16,603 words in total and 3,141 unique word forms. Introductory panels have a subordinate ratio of 92.95, a semantic richness of 68.40, a lexical density of 53.16, and a Gulpease readability index of 52.31. Panels focused on specific aspects of ancient cultures have a subordinate ratio of 100, a semantic richness of 81, a lexical density of 51.33, and a Gulpease readability index of 52.21. Finally, object labels have a subordinate ratio of 92.57, a semantic richness of 73.60, a lexical density of 56.21, and a Gulpease readability index of 63.08. The first two values are in the norm for the Italian language, while the last two are out of the norm. In particular, the Gulpease index shows that these texts are generally quite complex for readers who achieved middle-school education. Allocutive pronouns and anglicisms are absent. The register is always formal. Demonstrative and possessive pronouns and adjectives are 161 in total; polyrematics are 432; plastisms are 3.

The English corpus has 17,283 total words and 2,851 unique word forms, with a lexical density of 56.67 and a Coleman-Liau readability index of 12.01. This shows that texts are pretty complex to read and approachable by 12th graders. Allocutive pronouns are absent, while demonstrative and possessive pronouns and adjectives are 284 in total. The register is always formal.

How do we promote fairness in digital learning futures?

Results show that the content of both corpora is challenging to read and could be more engaging, providing indications for designing more inclusive content. The latest developments in AI are promising in that they could assist professionals in writing more engaging texts and delivering them in personalised digital learning environments.

Keywords: Museum education; Language analysis; Digital technologies

---

References

EUR-Lex (https://eur-lex.europa.eu/legal-content/IT/TXT/PDF/?uri=CELEX:32018H0604(01)).

Farinacci, V. (2020). Comunicazione museale e traduzione: le audioguide del British Museum. In *Memoria, inclusione e fruizione del patrimonio culturale. Primi risultati del progetto Inclusive Memory dell'Università Roma Tre, vol.*(4), pp. 59-70.

Ianich, E. (2006). Analisi di un corpus parallelo inglese-italiano di pubblicazioni dell'OMS: sintassi, lessico e resa della modalità. *Rivista internazionale di tecnica della traduzione / International Journal of Translation*, *9*, 99-121.

ICOM, International Council of Museums (https://icom.museum/en/news/icom-approves-a-new-museum-definition/).

Palmero Aprosio, A., Moretti, G. (2016). Italy goes to Stanford: a collection of CoreNLP modules for Italian. *arXiv preprint arXiv*:1609.06204.

Palmero Aprosio, A., Moretti, G. (2018). Tint 2.0: an All-inclusive Suite for NLP in Italian. *Proceedings of the Fifth Italian Conference on Computational Linguistics (CLiC-it 2018)*, 311-317.

Poce. A. (2017). *Verba Sequentur. Pensiero e scrittura per uno sviluppo critico delle competenze nella scuola secondaria*. Franco Angeli.

Sprugnoli, R., Tonelli, S., Palmero Aprosio, A., Moretti, G. (2018). Analysing the Evolution of Students' Writing Skills and the Impact of Neo-standard Italian with the Help of Computational Linguistics. *Proceedings of the Fifth Italian Conference on Computational Linguistics (CLiC-it 2018)*, 354-359.

The Quality-Link Project: Towards Open Standards for Quality Information and Recognition

Jon Altuna[1], Rimantė Čepauskienė[2], Jochen Ehrenreich[3], Tiago Simões[4], Elena Trepulė[5], Colin Tück[6]

[1] Mondragon University, Spain, jaltuna@mondragon.edu
[2] EDEN Digital Learning Europe, Estonia, rimante.cepauskiene@vdu.lt
[3] DHBW Heilbronn, Germany; jochen.ehrenreich@heilbronn.dhbw.de
[4] European University Foundation, Luxembourg, tiago.simoes@uni-foundation.eu
[5] EDEN Digital Learning Europe, Estonia, elena.trepule@vdu.lt
[6] KIC, Malta, colin@knowledgeinnovation.eu

Correspondence: Jochen Ehrenreich: jochen.ehrenreich@heilbronn.dhbw.de

Abstract:

Quality-Link is an Erasmus+ project committed to empowering stakeholders across the educational spectrum – students, institutions, employers, and recognition information centers alike – with pertinent and exhaustive quality information on courses and micro-credentials. Our aim is that all stakeholders can freely access meaningful data on quality, so they can make informed decisions - e.g. where to study or how to recognise a specific micro-credential.

Currently, metadata on courses or micro-credentials is hard to share and compare within the European Higher Education Area. Even basic information, such as how many courses are offered for different subjects, how many courses are accredited in Europe, is currently not easily available. The project aims to create new organizational, semantic, and technical systems to enable the sharing of basic metadata as well as quality data linked to courses and micro-credentials across educational systems. The project assumes that the first step towards being able to assess quality is enabling anyone to access all relevant quality data about a course or a piece of educational content.

Through rigorous analysis and intensive desk research, the Quality-Link consortium defined five key quality domains, each accompanied by a set of possible indicators

- Content Relevance, Labour Market Demand and Accuracy
- Teaching Methods and Pedagogy
- Accessibility and Inclusivity
- Learner-centred Approach, Satisfaction, and Success
- Institutional Reputation

Currently, metadata on courses or micro-credentials is hard to share and compare within the European Higher Education Area. Even basic information, such as how many courses are offered for different subjects, how many courses are accredited in Europe, is currently not easily available. The project aims to create new organizational, semantic, and technical systems to enable the sharing of basic metadata as well as quality data linked to courses and micro-credentials across educational systems. The project assumes that the first step towards being able to assess quality is enabling anyone to access all relevant quality data about a course or a piece of educational content.

Based on the quality domains and indicators, the Quality-Link consortium is currently gathering feedback from different stakeholders - students first and foremost - to gauge which domains and indicators are the most relevant for making informed decisions.

How do we promote fairness in digital learning futures?

In parallel, the Quality-Link partners are researching existing datasets and standards providing data for the different indicators, to assess the technical feasibility of each indicator. Both aspects combined - relevance and feasibility - will help us decide which indicators to focus on in Quality-Link.

Through the establishment of open standards for (a) course identification, (b) exchange of basic trusted metadata and (c) publication of quality data on micro-credentials and courses, Quality-Link aims to construct an infrastructure capable of aggregating quality data from diverse sources. By collaboration with a Standards Consultation Board, we will ensure that existing standards are used fully and that new standards will build on community ownership and support.

Quality-Link will ultimately pilot and test the aggregation of basic metadata and quality data covering a set of example indicators, and make this data available through an open and freely accessible platform.

This paper presents the initial findings – i.e. the quality domains and indicators, their relevance and feasibility, and a mock-up of the platform envisaged to develop – and outlines Quality-Link's promising potential for the future educational landscape of the EHEA. For further information, please visit https://quality-link.eu/.

Keywords: Open data, interoperability, quality education, micro-credentials, flexible learning pathways

References

Council of the European Union (EU) – Recommendation on a European approach to micro-credentials for lifelong learning and employability, https://data.consilium.europa.eu/doc/document/ST-9237-2022-INIT/en/pdf (June 2022)

QualityLink – Quality Domains and Indicators, https://quality-link.eu/quality-domains-and-indicators/ (February 2024)

QualityLink – Mock-Up of the Platform, https://quality-link.eu/mock-up-of-the-platform/ (March 2024)

Enhancing Student Learning with Custom-Designed AI Study Buddies: The Potential of Large Language Models (LLMs)

Palitha Edirisingha[1], Giasemi Vavoula[2], Terese Bird[3], Gemma Cantlow[4]

[1] School of Education, University of Leicester, UK; pe27@le.ac.uk
[2] Department of Museum Studies, University of Leicester, UK; g.vavoula@leicester.ac.uk
[3] Leicester Medical School, University of Leicester, UK; tmb10@leicester.ac.uk
[4] Department of Museum Studies, University of Leicester, UK; gc250@leicester.ac.uk

Correspondence: Palitha Edirisingha: pe27@le.ac.uk

Abstract:

The potential Artificial intelligence (AI) in Education has been highlighted in recent high-profile reports (eg., Kukulska-Hulme et al., 2023; EDUCAUSE, 2023; Unesco, 2023) and by prominent researchers in AI and educational technology (eg., Sharples, 2022; Lukin et al., 2022; Selwyn, 2024). As AI tools are being taken up 'at scale throughout mainstream schooling and higher education' (Selwyn, 2024, p. 84), arguably following the release of ChatGPT in November 2022, there is widespread concern about the use of these tools by students to generate assessed pieces of work. For example, Wegerif and Major (2024, online) raised the issues surrounding evaluating students' academic writing skills "If AI can be used to complete assignments by generating elegantly framed essays ...". Many educational institutions are currently developing approaches and guidelines to address this issue.

Taking an alternative approach, our project explores the potential of the 'language' aspect of a Large Language Model – ChaptGPT - for creating learning resources by custom-designing GPTs as study buddies. Potentially, these could help create "personal dialogic space[s] of reflection unique for each user" (Wegerif and Major (2024, online). This is based on the recent release of ChatGPT4 that enables users to develop their custom versions of GPTs that can be created for specific purposes. Users can upload a knowledge set to the server, and create a custom GPT that teaches the chosen topics that can be shared with learners. Custom GPTs have significant potential for use in higher education, from developing 'study buddies' to integrate into blended learning solutions and creating whole teaching units, but little is yet known about the breadth and quality of such applications and how they might impact the teaching and learning experience.

We are currently developing six scenarios of use of this GPT Author service at the University of Leicester and test them across three Schools (Education, Medicine, Museum Studies).

The presentation at the conference will outline the methodology and the work-in-progress findings from the project including prototypes of GPT buddies, emerging issues including copyright considerations, and results from alpha testing, and a project evaluation framework.

Keywords: Artificial Intelligence; AI; ChatGPT; Technology-Enhanced Learning; Higher Education

How do we promote fairness in digital learning futures?

References

EDUCAUSE (2023) *EDUCAUSE Horizon Report, 2023: Teaching and Learning Edition*, https://library.educause.edu/resources/2023/5/2023-educause-horizon-report-teaching-and-learning-edition [01.10.2023]

Kukulska-Hulme et al. (2023) *Innovating Pedagogy: exploring new forms of teaching, learning and assessment, to guide educators and policy makers*, Open University and University of Cape Town, https://prismic-io.s3.amazonaws.com/ou-iet/4acfab6d-4e5c-4bbd-9bda-4f15242652f2_Innovating+Pedagogy+2023.pdf [01.10.2023]

Lukin, R. et al., (2022) Empowering educators to be AI-ready, *Computers and Education: Artificial Intelligence,* vol 3, 100076. DOI: https://doi.org/10.1016/j.caeai.2022.100076

Sharples, M. (2022) Automated Essay Writing: An AIED Opinion, *International Journal of Artificial Intelligence* in Education, vol 32:1119–1126. DOI: https://doi.org/10.1007/s40593-022-00300-7

Selwyn, N. (2024) Constructive Criticism? Working with (Rather than Against) the AIED Back-Lash, *International Journal of Artificial Intelligence in Education*, vol 34:84–91. DOI: https://doi.org/10.1007/s40593-023-00344-3

Unesco (2023) *UNESCO survey: Less than 10% of schools and universities have formal guidance on AI*, https://www.unesco.org/en/articles/unesco-survey-less-10-schools-and-universities-have-formal-guidance-ai [12.03.2024]

Wegerif, R., and Major, L. (2024) Generative artificial intelligence and a return to dialogue in education, *BERA Blogpost*, https://www.bera.ac.uk/blog/generative-artificial-intelligence-and-a-return-to-dialogue-in-education, [30.04.2024].

The Forms of Human-Artifacts Interaction: 2D and 3D Digital Twins Models on the Online Repositories of the Main Museums Collections

Diana Di Matteo[1]

[1] Department of Modern Languages and Cultures, University of Genoa, Italy; diana.dimatteo@edu.unige.it

Correspondence: Diana Di Matteo: diana.dimatteo@edu.unige.it; dianadimatteo98@gmail.com

Abstract:

European and International Public cultural heritage institutions are facing the development of advances in both 2D and 3D digitisation publishing on online platforms the digital twins of the most important pieces of art of their collections. The first part of the paper focuses on identifying the main repositories distinguishing between those who use Open Access and those who use Creative Commons. Below there is a list:

1. Sketchfab: it makes use of Open access and CC (Buy Royalty Free 3D models - Sketchfab Store, Explore 3D Models - Sketchfab). Whoever uploads the object decides the licence. For museums, the price is reduced. There are plans such as the basic account that lets upload 10 models per month to put on sale. Then there are also Pro, Premium and Enterprise accounts;

2. Smithsonian: their license is CC0 so people do not need the Smithsonian's permission to use the digital asset in any way. CC0 only applies to copyright, Open Access FAQ | Smithsonian Institution (si.edu);

3. TurboSquid: 3D Archaeology Models - Browse & Download Formats - TurboSquid. TurboSquid has both Open Access with free 3D models and CC for a fee; it is also developing an AI tool for 3D image generation: TurboSquid: AI 3D Generator;

4. 3DArcheoLab: they offer online 3D Museums. For the museums, publishing on the 3D Virtual Museum portal is free of charge. If, on the other hand, a private citizen wants to create a customised online 3D museum, there is a cost, Fabbricazione Digitale: stampa 3D, rilievo 3D, modellazione 3D (3d-archeolab.it);

5. EonXr: CC for a fee, it has 3D models for educational use and allows to download the app to the desktop, EON-XR - Library;

6. CgTrader: Open access and Royalty Free License which allows to use the product without the need to pay royalties for multiple uses. The user cannot resell the model bought in the digital or printed form, but can use it in commercial projects multiple times after paying for it just once. The product remains the property of a seller for further distribution, CGTrader - 3D Models for VR / AR and CG projects;

7. Resurrect3D, University of Rochester: Open access React App (React App (rochester.edu)). Resurrect3D is a browser-based 3D viewer currently in development. It is designed as an open source with a suite of tools designed to facilitate scholarship and research of 3D objects.

The second part of the paper focuses on the possible human-digital artwork interaction within these repositories. The analysis focuses on the activities that the user can do with the digital twins. On Sketchfab the 3D model can be manipulated, zoommed in, rotated. Everyone can create playlists of works or personal databases and download files.

How do we promote fairness in digital learning futures?

On Smithsonian platform the artwork can be downloaded, shared, and reused. On 3DArcheoLab the artifact of the 3D virtual museum can be orbited around, zoomed and shared. In conclusion, all the repositories offer similar possibilities to interact with the digital twin model but the difference lies in the asking price.

Keywords: Cultural Heritage, Museum Collections, Human-Artifacts interaction, 2D/3D models, digital twins, repositories

---

References

Corns, A., Davidson, L., Namberi, S., O'Reilly, R., & Shaw, R. (2024). DEVELOPING ENHANCED AND ENRICHED 3D MODELS OF CULTURAL HERITAGE ASSETS AS PART OF THE EU CO-FUNDED 5DCULTURE PROJECT. *The International Archives of the Photogrammetry, Remote Sensing and Spatial Information Sciences, 48*, 157-164.

ECCO. (2004). *Professional Guidelines: Code of Ethics, European Confederation of Conservator-Restorers'Organizations*. Available at: http://www.ecco-eu.org/fileadmin/user_upload/ECCO_professional_guidelines_III.pdf .

Giovannini E. C. (2023). Digital Transitions for the Use and Reuse of Digital Assets for Museum Collections. In Cannella M., Garozzo A., Morena S. (eds.). *Transizioni. Atti del 44° Convegno Internazionale dei Docenti delle Discipline della Rappresentazione/Transitions. Proceedings of the 44th International Conference of Representation Disciplines Teachers*. Milano: FrancoAngeli, pp. 2755-2766.

Hess, M., Colson, A., & Hindmarch, J. (2018). Capacity building and knowledge exchange of digital technologies in Cultural Heritage Institutions. *Museum International, 70*(1-2), 48-61.

Hess, M., Robson, S., Serpico, M., et al. (2015). Developing 3d Imaging Programmes - Workflow and Quality Control (3DPetrie), *Journal on Computing and Cultural Heritage*, Vol. 9, No. 1, pp. 1:1-1:11. Doi: 10.1145/2786760

Iadanza, E., Maietti, F., Ziri, A. E., Di Giulio, R., Medici, M., Ferrari, F., ... & Turillazzi, B. (2019). Semantic web technologies meet BIM for accessing and understanding cultural heritage. *International Archives of the Photogrammetry, Remote Sensing and Spatial Information Sciences, 42*, 381-388.

Nancarrow, J. H. (2016). Democratizing the digital collection: new players and new pedagogies in three-dimensional cultural heritage. *Museum Worlds, 4*(1), 63-77.

Poce, A. (2020). *Education research in museum settings: methodologies, tools and functions*, Scientifiche Italiane: Napoli.

Romphf, J., Neuman-Donihue, E., Heyworth, G., & Zhu, Y. (2021, November). Resurrect3D: An Open and Customizable Platform for Visualizing and Analyzing Cultural Heritage Artifacts. In *The 26th International Conference on 3D Web Technology*, 1-7.

Statham, N. (2019). Scientific rigour of online platforms for 3D visualization of heritage. *Virtual Archaeology Review, 10*(20), 1-16.

Potential of Artificial Intelligence (AI) for Addressing Injustices of Access to Open Educational Resources (OERs) in the Global South Higher Education

(Funded by University of Leicester Future 100 studentship)

Dilani Abeyrathne[1], Palitha Edirisingha[2]

[1] PhD student, School of Education, University of Leicester, Leicester, UK; whdka1@leicester.ac.uk
[2] Associate Professor, School of Education, University of Leicester, Leicester, UK; pe27@leicester.ac.uk

Correspondence: Dilani Abeyrathne: whdka1@leicester.ac.uk

Abstract:

Open Educational Resources (OERs) - free to access and use educational resources - have been proposed as one of the potential solutions for the educational challenges in the Global South. While there is a good case and hope for OERs to provide opportunities for widening access to higher education, there is an inequality in the level of use of OER between Global South and Global North (de los Acros & Weller, 2018). A range of factors affecting OER adoption in Global South have been identified in the literature.

Artificial Intelligence (AI) appears to make a massive impact on all social systems including education. Generative AI – a technology that can produce variety of contents based on prompts provided by the user- has emerged as a significant topic in educational discussions. Can AI-based solutions might be an answer to some of the challenges that OER field has been facing during last two decades? This study explores the possibility of AI to addressing injustices of OERs in the Global South Higher Education (HE).

The paper focused on the interview data from six stakeholders who are instrumental in promoting OERs in the Global South. The study identified four themes of injustices of OERs in Global South HE: structural, cultural, institutional & governmental and personal. It was then identified from the literature that AI could be used for OER content creation (OERAfrica, 2023; Bozkurt, 2023), curation (Tila & Levy, 2023; Bozkurt, 2023) and localization (OERAfrica, 2023; Bozkurt, 2023).

Therefore, this paper highlights that AI may have the potential uses mainly for the purpose of content creation and related activities, curation and localization. Based on the injustices identified, some of the cultural and personal factors could be addressed through the integration of AI. However, the structural and institutional and governmental factors are beyond the control of AI and yet to be resolved in the Global South HE. We also need to be aware of the biases that may have been built into AI tools which could add to the issues of relevance of OERs for specific cultural contexts.

Keywords: Open Educational Resources, Artificial Intelligence, Global South

How do we promote fairness in digital learning futures?

References

Bozkurt, A. (2023). Generative AI, Synthetic Contents, Open Educational Resources (OER), and Open Educational Practices (OEP): A New Front in the Openness Landscape, *Open Praxis, 15*(3), 178–184. DOI: https://doi.org/10.55982/openpraxis.15.3.579

de los Arcos, B. and Weller, M. (2018). A Tale of Two Globes: Exploring the North/South Divide in Engagement with Open Educational Resources. In: S. Joachim, & H. Ulrich (Eds.) *Open Divide: Critical Studies on Open Access*. Sacramento, CA: Litwin Books.

OERAfrica (2023). Three ways Artificial Intelligence could change how we use Open Educational Resources. https://www.oerafrica.org/

Tila, D., and Levy, D. (2023). Curating OER Content through AI and ChatGPT. Open *Journal of Social Sciences, 11*, 510-527.

Utilizing Chatbots for Automating Examinations in Higher Education: Perceived Fairness, Trust and Learning Outcomes

Katharina Frosch[1], Friederike Lindauer[2], Carmen Winkel[3]

[1] Department of Business and Management, Brandenburg University of Applied Sciences, Germany; frosch@th-brandenburg.de
[2] Transfer Project InNoWest, Brandenburg University of Applied Sciences, Germany; lindauer@th-brandenburg.de
[3] Office of the Vice President for Teaching and International Relations, Brandenburg University of Applied Sciences, Germany; carmen.winkel@th-brandenburg.de

Correspondence: Katharina Frosch: katharina.frosch@th-brandenburg.de

Abstract:

Large Language Models (LLM) are increasingly used to support educational assessment (González-Calatayud et al., 2021), offering a promising approach to addressing challenges associated with scalability, consistency, and personalized feedback that manual assessment implies (Fagbohun et al., 2024).

Pre-configured interfaces for building custom chatbots based on common AI models provide a low-level approach for educators to design their own AI-based examination tools that ask learners questions and provide feedback on the answers. An example of a prototypical application - albeit based on a self-programmed interface - is Nitze's (2024) StudyBuddy, which simulates oral exams. Yet, the extent to which these AI-based exam assistants can autonomously conduct complete exam assessments—creating questions and evaluating and grading responses without manual oversight—is still largely unexplored. Despite the clear advantages, issues related to the quality of the generated content, the precision of assessments, ethical implications, and acceptance among learners persist as significant concerns.

This paper is a proof-of-concept study combined with a field experiment for an AI-based exam assistant based on the StudyBuddy suggested by Nitze (2024). The exam assistant provides students with a set of quiz questions and case studies based on an 80-page reader on topics in organizational behavior, offering personalized feedback and question-by-question scoring ranging from 0 to 100%, along with an overall grade and personalized feedback. To evaluate learning behavior and outcome (in the practice phase), perceived fairness (in the exam phase) and overall learner acceptance, we run a field experiment with N=35 students enrolled in a business management program at a technical university in Germany. They take part in a quiz assignment provided and graded by the exam assistant and subsequently answer a survey with questions based on the Perceived Fairness scale (Sonnleitner & Kovacs, 2020) and the Trust in Automated Systems Test (Wojton et al., 2020). Additionally, the learning outcomes are assessed in a retrospective pre-post design according to Drennan and Hyde (2008). Results will be available by the End of April 2024.

Insights gained from this study will shed light on the question whether custom chatbots can be effectively used for scalable, efficient assessment processes in higher education. As the ready-made interfaces already available require minimal prerequisites and technical skills, they present an accessible opportunity for instructors to develop their own AI-based examination tools, and to ease manual corrections, to guarantee consistent grading and to provide students with individualized, constructive feedback on their solutions even in large courses where personalized feedback would not be possible when manual grading is used.

The results of this study will shed light on whether customised chatbots can be effectively used for scalable, efficient assessment processes in higher education. The readily available interfaces, requiring minimal prerequisites and technical skills, enable educators to develop their own AI-based assessment tools. This would open opportunities for educators to build their own AI-based assessment tools and facilitate manual corrections, ensure consistent grading and provide students with individualised, constructive feedback, even in large courses where personalised feedback would not be possible with manual grading.

Keywords: Examination Automation, Chatbot, Higher Education, Learning Outcomes, Perceived Fairness.

References

Drennan, J., Hyde, A., 2008. Controlling response shift bias: the use of the retrospective pre-test design in the evaluation of a master's programme. *Assessment & Evaluation in Higher Education* 33, 699–709. 10.1080/02602930701773026

Fagbohun, O., Iduwe, N.P., Abdullahi, M., Ifaturoti, A., Nwanna, O.M., 2024. Beyond Traditional Assessment: Exploring the Impact of Large Language Models on Grading Practices. *JAIMLD* 2, 1–8. 10.51219/JAIMLD/oluwole-fagbohun/19

González-Calatayud, V., Prendes-Espinosa, P., Roig-Vila, R., 2021. Artificial Intelligence for Student Assessment: A Systematic Review. Applied Sciences 11, 5467. 10.3390/app11125467

Nitze, A., 2024. Future-proofing Education: A Prototype for Simulating Oral Examinations Using Large Language Models.

Sonnleitner, P., Kovacs, C., 2020. Differences Between Students' and Teachers' Fairness Perceptions: Exploring the Potential of a Self-Administered Questionnaire to Improve Teachers' Assessment Practices. *Front. Educ.* 5:17. 10.3389/feduc.2020.00017

Wojton, H.M., Porter, D., T. Lane, S., Bieber, C., Madhavan, P., 2020. Initial validation of the trust of automated systems test (TOAST). *The Journal of Social Psychology* 160, 735–750. 10.1080/00224545.2020.1749020

Careful and Inclusive Data Practices in Education. A Conceptual Approach

Elisabeth Anna Guenther[1]

[1] Centre for Teacher Education, University of Vienna, Austria; elisabeth.guenther@univie.ac.at

Correspondence: Elisabeth Anna Guenther: elisabeth.guenther@univie.ac.at

Abstract:

This conceptual paper discusses the need and possibilities of careful, inclusive data practices in education. Data practices comprise data generation and data analysis as much as it can manifest itself in platforms or digital tools (Decuypere, 2021). They are both shaped by people as they also influence or mediate people's social practices. In education, this can impact both learning and teaching. The ecology provided by platforms shapes teachers didactical approaches as well as students behaviour and achievements (Decuypere & Hartong, 2022; Förschler et al., 2021; Hartong & Decuypere, 2023). Moreover, data practices carry simultaneously the risk of reproducing inequalities (O'Neil, 2016) or of amplifying feelings of disempowerment (Quinn & Epstein, 2023) while they also carry the promise to enable more inclusive, individualised education. There is a need to implement and expand data practices which will help to reduce the potential risks and strengthen the benefits. Considering the stakes at hand I suggest exploring the potential of careful, inclusive data practices. This concept draws on insights from an ethics of care (Gilligan, 1993; Tronto, 1987, 2015), data feminism (D'Ignazio & Klein, 2020), and data justice (Taylor, 2017). From an ethics of care perspective it is, on the one hand, important to listen to underrepresented voices (Gilligan, 1993) as much as to emphasise the need for competence, for being responsible and for paying attention to the needs of different people (Tronto, 2015). In addition, data feminism and data justice draw attention to the different life experiences of people as well as power dynamics within data practices. Consequently, tackling the power dynamics within current data practices may advance equality and inclusion within this context. Inclusive data practices, furthermore, emphasise the need to both foster a sense of belonging as well as the ability to maintain one's own uniqueness (cf. Shore et al., 2011). My proposition is that careful and inclusive data practices are – ideally – co-created in participatory processes, such as computational empowerment (Dindler et al., 2020). However, to really meet the aim of advancing social justice it is crucial to not only include members of marginalised and underserved communities, but to acknowledge and respect their expertise and interests (Costanza-Chock, 2020; Lee & Soep, 2023).

The overall aim of this work-in-progress conceptual paper is, therefore (1) to highlight some short comings and risks of data practices in education, (2) to conceptualise an alternative – careful, inclusive data practices – and (3) to showcase a potential avenue on how to achieve this alternative in and through education.

Keywords: data practices, inclusion, ethics of care, data feminism, data justice, education

References

Costanza-Chock, S. (2020). *Design justice: Community-led practices to build the worlds we need*. The MIT Press.

Decuypere, M. (2021). The Topologies of Data Practices: A Methodological Introduction. *Journal of New Approaches in Educational Research*, *10*(1), 67. https://doi.org/10.7821/naer.2021.1.650

Decuypere, M., & Hartong, S. (2022). Edunudge. *Learning, Media and Technology*, 1–15. https://doi.org/10.1080/17439884.2022.2086261

D'Ignazio, C., & Klein, L. F. (2020). *Data feminism*. The MIT Press.

Dindler, C., Smith, R., & Iversen, O. S. (2020). Computational empowerment: Participatory design in education. *CoDesign*, *16*(1), 66–80. https://doi.org/10.1080/15710882.2020.1722173

Förschler, A., Hartong, S., Kramer, A., Meister-Scheytt, C., & Junne, J. (2021). Zur (ambivalenten) Wirkmächtigkeit datengetriebener Lernplattformen: Eine Analyse des «Antolin»-Leseförderungsprogramms. *MedienPädagogik: Zeitschrift Für Theorie Und Praxis Der Medienbildung*, *44*, 52–72. https://doi.org/10.21240/mpaed/44/2021.10.28.X

Gilligan, C. (1993). *In a different voice: Psychological theory and women's development*. Harvard University Press.

Hartong, S., & Decuypere, M. (2023). Platformed professional(itie)s and the ongoing digital transformation of education. *Tertium Comparationis*, *29*(1), 1–21. https://doi.org/10.31244/tc.2023.01.01

Lee, C., & Soep, E. (2023). *Code for what? Computer science for storytelling and social justice*. The MIT Press.

O'Neil, C. (2016). *Weapons of math destruction: How big data increases inequality and threatens democracy*. Allen Lane.

Quinn, K., & Epstein, D. (2023). Dimensionalizing privacy to advance the study of digital disempowerment. *Big Data & Society*, *10*(2), 20539517231221739. https://doi.org/10.1177/20539517231221739

Shore, L. M., Randel, A. E., Chung, B. G., Dean, M. A., Holcombe Ehrhart, K., & Singh, G. (2011). Inclusion and Diversity in Work Groups: A Review and Model for Future Research. *Journal of Management*, *37*(4), 1262–1289. https://doi.org/10.1177/0149206310385943

Taylor, L. (2017). What is data justice? The case for connecting digital rights and freedoms globally. *Big Data & Society*, *4*(2), 205395171773633. https://doi.org/10.1177/2053951717736335

Tronto, J. C. (1987). Beyond Gender Difference to a Theory of Care. *Signs*, *12*(4,), 644–663.

Tronto, J. C. (2015). *Who cares? How to reshape a democratic politics*. Cornell Selects, an imprint of Cornell University Press.

Promoting Fairness in Digital Learning Futures: Designing for Inclusion, Equity, and Access Through Open and Distance Learning in the BUKA Project

James Brunton[1]

[1]Dublin City University, Ireland; james.brunton@dcu.ie

Abstract:

As the techno-deterministic trends of the pandemic (Bozkurt et al., 2020; Teräs, Teräs, Arinto, Brunton, Daryono, & Subramaniam) and the 'magic buttonism' (Weller, 2020) of the post-pandemic, digital transformation of Higher Education (HE) period now merge into the era of Generative Artificial Intelligence (GenAI) where academics are invited to bring this new technology into their teaching and assessment without consideration of related ethical questions, how do we continue to promote fairness in digital learning futures? Some answers can be drawn from the Erasmus+ funded BUKA (Advancing Equity and Access to Higher Education Through Open and Distance Learning) project (Teräs & Brunton, 2023). This project was conceived of and began before the pandemic, beginning in early 2020 with the aim of facilitating the use of high quality online and hybrid learning, using open and distance learning approaches, in order to increase inclusion, equity and access in HE. The specific geographic focus of the project was in Malaysia, The Philippines, and Indonesia, where six HE institutions carried out institutional projects, based on local, regional and/or national needs, under the umbrella themes of the project. The institutions were a mix of established open and online learning providers and those that were engaging in development of hybrid and online learning for the first time. The diverse types of institutions coming together in the work of the project was found to be a strength of this project. The development of the institutional projects was supported by capacity building activity organised within the project consortium, which involved two European institutions, TAMK (Finland), and (DCU (Ireland), and six institutions in the target region: WOU and OUM (Malaysia); MSU-IIT and UPOU (The Philippines); UT and UNP (Indonesia). Capacity building focused on online learning design, inclusive learning design, and supporting staff to 'move online'. The pandemic impacted on both the form the capacity building activities took and on the institutional projects themselves as, for example, a planned, intentional move into online learning became an accelerated move to emergency remote teaching for some partners. However, these partners were better placed than others as they were already part of a project community that was underpinned by open approaches to digital, hybrid, online learning. The BUKA project highlights the benefits of community building and staff/capacity building that is based on open education/ODL principles, rather than on typical techno-deterministic narratives. "One can make a persuasive argument that openness acts as a potent catalyst, facilitating and invigorating the process of learning" (Bozkurt et al., 2023, p.77) The project also highlights the power of having projects that support diverse institutional projects, in diverse types of institutions, that have real impact at local, regional, and/or national level. Funding agencies must continue to support community building and capacity building projects that are underpinned by open education/ODL principles so that digital transformation projects, and digital learning futures, aim towards increasing fairness in HE, rather than embracing techno-deterministic narratives and ways of being that increase the digital divide and increase exclusion in HE.

How do we promote fairness in digital learning futures?

Keywords: equity, access, inclusion, capacity building, open and distance learning, inclusive learning design

References

Bozkurt, A; Jung, I; Xiao, J; Vladimirschi, V; Schuwer, R; Egorov, G; Lambert, SR; Al-Freih, M; Pete, J; Olcott Jr., D; Rodes, V; Aranciaga, I; Bali, M; Alvarez Jr., AV; Roberts, J; Pazurek, A; Raffaghelli, JE; Panagiotou, N; de Coëtlogon... Paskevicius, M. (2020). A global outlook to the interruption of education due to COVID-19 Pandemic: Navigating in a time of uncertainty and crisis. *Asian Journal of Distance Education, 15* (1) pp. 1-126. 10.5281/zenodo.3878572

Bozkurt, A., Gjelsvik, T., Adam, T., Asino, T.I., Atenas, J., Bali, M., Blomgren, C., Bond, M., Bonk, C.J., Brown, M., Burgos, D., Conrad, D., Costello, E., Cronin, C., Czerniewicz, L., Deepwell, M., Deimann, M., DeWaard, H.J., Dousay, T.A., Ebner, M., Farrow, R., Gil-Jaurena, I., Havemann, L., Inamorato, A., Irvine, V., Karunanayaka, S.P., Kerres, M., Lambert, S., Lee, K., Makoe, M., Marín, V.I., Mikroyannidis, A., Mishra, S., Naidu, S., Nascimbeni, F., Nichols, M., Olcott, D., Ossiannilsson, E., Otto, D., Padilla Rodriguez, B.C., Paskevicius, M., Roberts, V., Saleem, T., Schuwer, R., Sharma, R.C., Stewart, B., Stracke, C.M., Tait, A., Tlili, A., Ubachs, G., Weidlich, J., Weller, M., Xiao, J. and Zawacki-Richter, O., 2023. Openness in Education as a Praxis: From Individual Testimonials to Collective Voices. *Open Praxis, 15*(2), p.76–112.DOI: https://doi.org/10.55982/openpraxis.15.2.574

Teräs, H., & Brunton, J. (2023). *Reimagining Higher Education: Case Studies on Designing for Inclusion, Equity, and Access in the BUKA Project*. Zenodo. https://doi.org/10.528

The 'Open Educator' as a Force for the Promotion of Fairness In Digital Learning Futures: Charting a Course Using a Competence Conceptual Framework for Open Educational Practices

James Brunton[1], Ulf-Daniel Ehlers[2], Antonio Teixeira[3]

[1] Dublin City University, Ireland; james.brunton@dcu.ie
[2] Baden-Württemberg Cooperative State University, Germany; daniel.ehlers@dhbw-karlsruhe.de
[3] Universidade Aberta, Portugal; antonio.moreira.teixeira.pt@gmail.com

Correspondence: James Brunton: james.brunton@dcu.ie

Abstract:

This paper positions the 'Open Educator' as a force for the promotion of fairness in digital learning futures. The more holistic vision of higher educational futures articulated through the use of an open education lens, made real through the application of related principles at international, national, regional, institutional, unit, and individual level. Here, the focus will be principally on the individual, specifically on how educators can bring a range of OEPs to bear in their teaching and learning work in order to produce a range of beneficial educational and societal outcomes. An educators' competence conceptual framework for open educational practices (OEPs) (Nascimbeni, Burgos, Brunton, & Ehlers, 2024) will be used as a frame to demonstrate the transversal attitude, knowledge, skills that are needed in order to develop competencies relating to engaging in a number of different OEPs. This competency framework was developed as part of the Erasmus+ funded OpenGame project (Padilla-Zea et al. 2022). The framework has a focus on competences relating to OER, such as: use open licences; search for OER; create, revise, and remix OER; and share OER. The framework also has a focus on more complex competences relating to open pedagogy, such as: design open educational experiences; guide students to learn in the open; teach with OER; and implement open assessment The holding of an 'open attitude', and the intentional use of OEPs in teaching and learning practice, can act as a bulwark against the uncritical acceptance of techno-deterministic narratives, for example around the use of Generative Artificial Intelligence (GenAI) in teaching and learning practice and assessment, that more likely lead to more closed and inequitable educational futures.

Keywords: Open education, Open educational resources, OER, OEP, Open pedagogy, Educators' competences

References

Nascimbeni, F., Burgos, D., Brunton, J., and Ehlors U. (2024). A competence framework for educators to boost Open Educational Practices in higher education. *Open Learning: The Journal of Open, Distance and E-Learning, 39(2), 150-169*. https://doi.org/10.1080/02680513.2024.2310538

How do we promote fairness in digital learning futures?

Padilla-Zea, N., Burgos, D., García-Holgado, A., García-Peñalvo, F.J., Harquevaux, M. P., de-la-Higuera, C., Brunton, J., and Tlili, A. (2022) Catch the Open! A Gamified Interactive Immersion Into Open Educational Practices for Higher Education Educators. *Front. Psychol. 13*(812091). doi: 10.3389/fpsyg.2022.812091

The Possibilities and Challenges of Process-Driven Assessment Design in an Environment of Pervasive AI

Sukaina Walji[1]

[1] Centre for Innovation in Learning and Teaching, University of Cape Town, South Africa; Sukaina.Walji@uct.ac.za

Correspondence: Sukaina Walji: Sukaina.Walji@uct.ac.za

Abstract:

Assessment designs in higher education contexts have been shifting to more flexible, learner-centred approaches, aligning well with professional fields where competency with tools, like coding software, is now expected. Assessment designers need to make decisions about appropriate access to tools and resources, which are used as supports or scaffolds. The notion of "cognitive offloading" is a useful way of understanding the role of such supports in the enactment of an assessment event. Variously defined as "the use of physical action to alter the information processing requirements of a task so as to reduce cognitive demand" (Risko and Gilbert, 2016), other ideas related to "cognitive offloading" include reference to "scaffolding technologies" (Pitura & Chang, 2023).

The use of external tools or devices to manage one's mental workload is not new, and includes computing software and calculators, language translation tools, note-taking software or mindmapping tools (Dawson, 2020, Lodge et al., 2023b). For educators, cognitive offloading in assessment design involves a tradeoff between what is required to be demonstrated by a human as an essential skill, while acknowledging that the ability to use external tools is part of future human capability (Lodge et al. 2023c). In these cases the ability to deploy tools becomes a learning outcome itself with students given guidance on when and how to use these tools (Dawson, 2020). However the availability of general purpose Artificial Intelligence (AI) technologies enables students to use AI tools in ways that potentially circumvent assessment blueprints designed to ensure that students achieve learning outcomes without a support or scaffold. The widespread availability of AI tools that enable the "cognitive offloading" of tasks therefore poses challenges for assessors in determining the validity of student work (Dawson, 2020).

Detecting, banning or restricting AI tools is at best a short-term stop gap measure and increasingly unfeasible (Lodge et al, 2023a) and harmful to marginalised students (Liang et al, 2023). Given the capability of AI tools, many assessments now require reconsideration of what is worth assessing. Assessment designers need to consider the capabilities human professionals will need once technology can take on tasks that were traditionally human (Fawns & Schuwirth, 2023). The dilemma lies in designing assessments that ensure the validity of judgments and also allow for the use of AI tools. One response is to consider the process by which that product was generated to be more important in relation to assessing outcomes than any final output (Lodge et al, 2023a). This approach to establishing "audit trails of progress" can contribute to assessment integrity in the context of contract cheating, where this requirement to show progress is difficult to obtain (French et al., 2023). The same digital tools that enable "cognitive offloading" can potentially capture digital footprints of an assessment development process including feedback, iteration, reflection and self-evaluation stages. Such moves may contribute to more learner-centred and inclusive approaches to assessments (Tai et al., 2023). This conceptual paper analyses existing frameworks and proposes emergent approaches to AI-enabled assessment designs in higher education contexts that take a process-oriented approach for inclusive assessment outcomes.

Keywords: Artificial Intelligence, Assessment, Cognitive Offloading, Scaffolding

References

Dawson, P. (2020). Cognitive offloading and assessment. In M. Bearman, P. Dawson, R. Ajjawi, J. Tai, & D. Boud (Eds.), *Re-imagining university assessment in a digital world* (pp. 37–48). Springer International Publishing. https://doi.org/10.1007/978-3-030-41956-1_4

Fawns, T., & Schuwirth, L. (2023). Rethinking the value proposition of assessment at a time of rapid development in generative artificial intelligence. *Medical Education*. 1-3. https://doi.org/10.1111/medu.15259

French, S., Dickerson, A., & Mulder, R. A. (2023). A review of the benefits and drawbacks of high-stakes final examinations in higher education. *Higher Education*. https://doi.org/10.1007/s10734-023-01148-z

Liang, W., Yuksekgonul, M., Mao, Y., Wu, E., & Zou, J. (2023). GPT detectors are biased against non-native English writers. *Patterns*, *4*(7), 100779. https://doi.org/10.1016/j.patter.2023.100779

Lodge, J. M., Howard, S., Bearman, M., Dawson, P, & Associates (2023a). Assessment reform for the age of Artificial Intelligence. Tertiary Education Quality and Standards Agency.

Lodge, J. M., Thompson, K., & Corrin, L. (2023b). Mapping out a research agenda for generative artificial intelligence in tertiary education. *Australasian Journal of Educational Technology*, *39*(1), 1–8. https://doi.org/10.14742/ajet.8695

Lodge, J. M., Yang, S., Furze, L., & Dawson, P. (2023c). It's not like a calculator, so what is the relationship between learners and generative artificial intelligence? *Learning: Research and Practice*, *9*(2), 117-124. https://doi.org/10.1080/23735082.2023.2261106

Pitura, J., & Chang, H. (2023). Tools for Scaffolding the Development of L2 Speaking in English-medium Higher Education: Lessons from Poland and Australia. *Theory and Practice of Second Language Acquisition*, *9*(2). https://doi.org/10.31261/TAPSLA.12816

Risko, E. F., & Gilbert, S. J. (2016). Cognitive offloading. *Trends in Cognitive Sciences*, *20*(9), 676–688. https://doi.org/10.1016/j.tics.2016.07.002

Tai, J., Ajjawi, R., Bearman, M., Boud, D., Dawson, P., & Jorre de St Jorre, T. (2023). Assessment for inclusion: Rethinking contemporary strategies in assessment design. *Higher Education Research & Development*, *42*(2), 483-497. https://doi.org/10.1080/07294360.2022.2057451

Open Access Publishing – It's a Great Idea (In Theory)

Tom Farrelly[1], Eamon Costello[2], Tony Murphy[3]

[1] Munster Technological University, Ireland; tom.farrelly@staff.ittralee.ie
[2] Dublin City University, Ireland; eamon.costello@dcu.ie
[3] South East Technological University, Ireland; tony.j.murphy@setu.ie

Correspondence: Tom Farrelly: tom.farrelly@staff.ittralee.ie

Abstract:

Over the past decade, there has been a noticeable surge in interest towards open-access practices and the impact that they can have on educational practices at both institutional and national levels in terms of accessibility and teaching affordances (Weller et al. 2015). This heightened interest has led to the development of policies at national and supranational levels, coinciding with mandates from major funding organisations requiring research findings to be publicly accessible (Coalition S, 2023; European Commission, n.d.; Wellcome Trust, 2024). However, while national and institutional initiatives appear commendable and ambitious, the practical implementation may not fully align (Anderson, 2020; Author's Ref; Kipphut-Smith et al. 2018).

To explore this, we conducted a comprehensive internet search incorporating two interconnected elements. Firstly, we assessed the open access landscape across 36 universities in Ireland and the UK, focusing on five key criteria: (1) the presence of a university policy on open access, (2) the nature and quantity of agreements with open-access publishers, (3) existence of a support team for open access initiatives, (4) availability of a university-owned open access publishing platform, and (5) establishment of an institutional repository for open access materials. Additionally, we checked if these policies were documented on ROARMAP and if the institutional repository was listed on Open Access DOAR.

While the evaluation of policies, agreements, and organisational structures signalled a positive commitment to fostering open practices within institutions in the second phase of the project, our primary focus was on determining if these commitments translated into tangible hiring practices. We believe job descriptions for academic and research positions could reflect the institution's mission statements and objectives. To delve deeper, we manually reviewed over 650 academic job postings from 36 universities in Ireland and the UK between late December 2022 and mid-January 2023. We repeated this process across the same universities in March and early April 2024, examining over 700 job advertisements. Our objective was to evaluate the extent to which open access was explicitly mentioned as a requirement or desirable attribute for potential lecturers and researchers. Unfortunately, our analysis revealed minimal evidence of a robust commitment to open access solely based on the content of these job advertisements. This paper asks us to consider how we can promote fairness in digital learning futures if a commitment to openness is apparently not highly valued in terms of career development, thus acting as a disincentive to become an open educator.

Keywords: Open Access Practices; Institutional Policies; Funding Mandates; Research Accessibility; Hiring Practices

How do we promote fairness in digital learning futures?

References

Anderson, R. (2020, March 12). Measuring the success of transformative agreements. *Scholarly Kitchen*. Retrieved from https://scholarlykitchen.sspnet.org/2020/03/12/measuring-the-success-of-transformative-agreements/

Author's reference [Redacted for Review Process]

Coalition S. (2023). *Five years of Plan S: A journey towards full and immediate open access*. Retrieved from https://www.coalition-s.org/blog/five-years-of-plan-s-a-journey-towards-full-and-immediate-open-access/

European Commission. (n.d.). *Open Science*. Retrieved from https://rea.ec.europa.eu/open-science_en

Kipphut-Smith, S., Boock, M., Chapman, K. and Hooper, W.M. (2018). Measuring Open Access Policy Compliance: Results of a Survey. *Journal of Librarianship and Scholarly Communication*, 6(General Issue), eP2247. https://doi.org/10.7710/2162-3309.2247

Wellcome Trust. (2024). *Open access policy guidance*. Retrieved from https://wellcome.org/grant-funding/guidance/open-access-guidance/open-access-policy

Weller, M., de los Arcos, B., Farrow, R., Pitt, B. and McAndrew, P. (2015) The impact of OER on teaching and learning practice. *Open Praxis*, 7(4) October–December 2015, pp. 351–361(ISSN 2304-070X

Integrating GenAI Asynchronous Collaborative Learning into an Academic Course

Lilach Gal[1]

[1]Faculty of Instructional Technologies, Holon Institute of Technology, Israel; Lilachg@hit.ac.il

Correspondence: Lilach Gal: Lilachg@hit.ac.il

Abstract:

The rise of Generative AI (GenAI) tools emphasizes the need to reconsider their integration into learning curricula(Baidoo-Anu & Owusu Ansah, 2023), with research highlighting their transformative impact on academic teaching and learning. A case study at the Holon Institute of Technology (HIT) in Israel demonstrates the incorporation of GenAI tools into an asynchronous online course aimed at fostering critical thinking. This course, part of HIT's Instructional Technologies Faculty curriculum, combines real-world challenges with teamwork and project-based learning. Specifically, the course "Information Literacy in the Internet Environment," studied in the 2nd year of the undergraduate program, enhances students' ability to locate online learning materials and their awareness of digital tools. It utilizes short video content for self-learning and practical assignments to address real-world needs (Gal & Israel-Fishelson, 2020), Additionally, practical assignments are included, where students must apply the acquired knowledge to address real-world needs (Kohen-Vacs & Amzalag, 2021).

Following the emergence of GenAI and in line with the pedagogical philosophy of the Learning Technologies Faculty management (Kurtz et al., 2023), the course's foundations and format were maintained. Simultaneously, outdated course materials were refreshed, and a significant layer addressing GenAI, with a focus on information retrieval capabilities, was added. Consequently, two learning units [see Figure 1] have been adapted to content related to GenAI. The first unit covers topics such as understanding GenAI and its different types, distinguishing between a search engine and an AI-based chatbot, and principles for writing a prompt. The second unit explores the wide array of tools available to information professionals, featuring a live demonstration of a popular tool as a basis for a collaborative task. As part of this task, students are required to choose an AI tool from a provided list. They must register, gain in-depth and informed experience with the chosen tool, and evaluate it based on a detailed criteria list set by the faculty. This evaluation involves applying the tool to a topic relevant to their academic studies as information retrieval content. From the list of criteria, students must select two that the tool implements well, providing reasoning and examples of optimal implementation. Additionally, they must identify two criteria that the tool does not seem to implement at all, providing detailed explanations along with evidence and recommendations for potential improvements and how these would enhance its capabilities.

What is required to help foster nestedness and integration in the complex digital learning ecosystem?

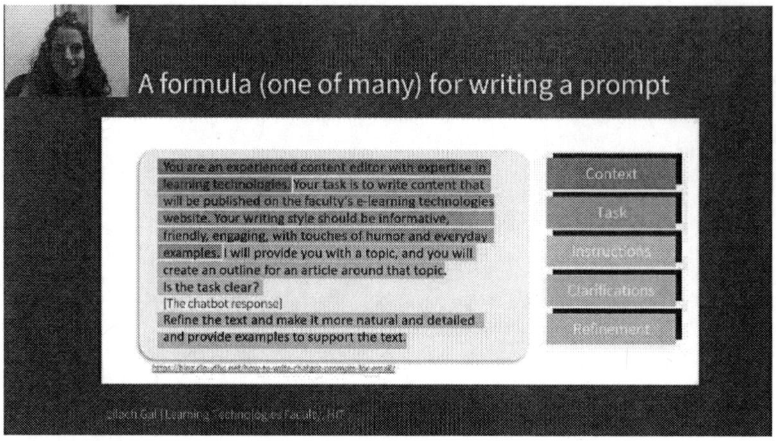

Figure 1. Screenshot from the learning unit

The rationale behind the design of this task is based on the need to provide students with the opportunity to gain experience in an academic setting, recognizing that their professional world is dynamic and constantly changing, thus equipping them with the ability to adapt even outside the walls of academia. Additionally, the task cultivates their ability to think critically about the implications of GenAI in the field of information science. During the conference presentation, we will share results and examples of student's work and offer suggestions for refining and enhancing their potential about the given assignment.

Keywords: Generative Ai, Critical Thinking, Project-Based Learning, Collaborative Learning, Authentic Learning, Learning technologies

References

Baidoo-Anu, D., & Owusu Ansah, L. (2023). Education in the era of generative artificial intelligence (ai): understanding the potential benefits of chatgpt in promoting teaching and learning. *SSRN Electronic Journal*, *7*(December), 52–62. https://doi.org/10.2139/ssrn.4337484

Gal, L., & Israel-Fishelson, R. (2020). Enhancing students virtual engagement using asynchronous workshop: COVID-19 case study. *EdMedia + Innovate Learning*, *2020*(1), 31–36.

Kohen-Vacs, D., & Amzalag, M. (2021). Alternative approach for evaluation adapted for times of emergent conditions. *29th International Conference on Computers in Education Conference, ICCE 2021 - Proceedings*, *1*, 599–607.

Kurtz, G., Amzalag, M., Barak-Medina, E., Gal, E., Kohen-Vacs, D., Shaked, N., Zailer, G., & Zaguri, Y. (2023). *Higher education and generative ai (genai) in israel: opportunities, challenges and recommendations*. https://facultyprojects.telem-hit.net/HigherEducationGenAI/En/

Promoting Social Inclusion: AI-Enhanced Learning Experience for Emoji Interaction to Older Adults

Meital Amzalag[1], Liraz Cohen[2], Stav Eini[3], Dan Kohen-Vacs[4]

[1234] Faculty of Instructional Technologies, Holon Institute of Technology (HIT), Israel
[1] mrkohen@hit.ac.il
[2] lirazcohen69@gmail.com
[3] staveini38@gmail.com
[4] mrkohen@hit.ac.il

Correspondence: Dan Kohen-Vacs: mrkohen@hit.ac.il

Abstract:

Over the last two decades, Mobile and Seamless Learning (MSL) has gained attention for its role in promoting continuous learning across diverse contexts and adapting to flexible educational conditions (Kohen-Vacs & Amzalag, 2023). MSL can be exercised among older adults to familiarize them with skills potentially offering alleviation from risks of social exclusion. In this sense, often older adults lack the capabilities to use Instant Messengers(IM) for exercising texting encompassed by emoji symbols incorporated to emphasize their feelings and emotions. To tackle this issue and enhance social inclusion, we introduce the Senior Emoji Trainer (SEmoT), a mobile web application designed to provide AI-enhanced learning for adults over 65 interested in incorporating emoji language into their IM practices. Developed as a graduation project at the Faculty of Instructional Technologies at the Holon Institute of Technology in Israel, SEmoT offers a realistic IM environment akin to Social Network Services (SNS). Through this application, older adults can engage in learning experiences, practicing texting with emoji language in various conversational contexts with virtual actors (Figure 1). SEmoT aims to facilitate the integration of emoji language into IM practices, promoting a more inclusive digital experience for older adults.

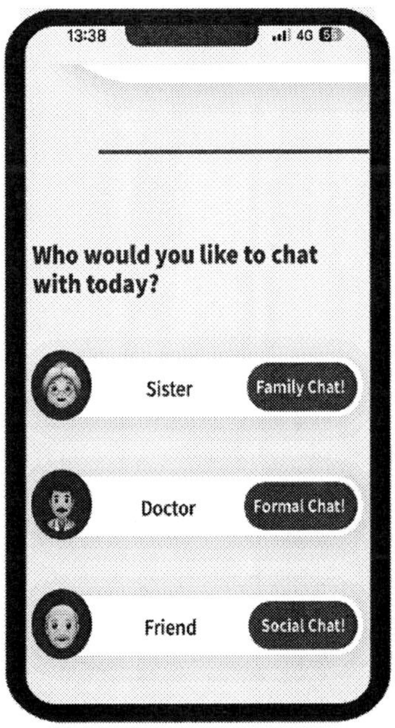

Figure 1. SEmoT application offers educational IM with various types of virtual actors

What is required to help foster nestedness and integration in the complex digital learning ecosystem?

SEmoT's UI and UX aspects are tailored to facilitate a convenient use aligned to typical challenges among older adults, creating an environment conducive to their needs. Its development included integration of the application with OpenAI API. Resulting in an AI-supported functionality leveraging capabilities of Natural Language Processing (NLP) exploited for conducting educational opportunities adapted for the requirements of the older adults. There, conversation is incorporated with emojis used for reflecting various conversational contexts with virtual actors. This learning approach aims to address the authentic requirements of older adults, fostering social inclusion. An experiment involving 30 participants, aged above 60 (average age 69.5), utilized SEmoT to teach emoji language through a questionnaire. The findings indicate positive perceptions of the application's effectiveness, educational feedback, and UX/UI offerings. These promising results motivate our ongoing efforts to further enhance and refine SEmoT's educational features. Accordingly, we emphasize the promising potential of AI-enhanced learning also for older adults sometimes showing challenges with challenges related to the use of upcoming technologies (Kurtz et al., 2023). Future work aims to expand Mobile Seamless Learning (MSL) definitions to encompass artificial intelligence capabilities, enriching the learning experience for older adults.

Keywords: AI-enhanced learning, Senior Emoji Trainer (SEmoT), Mobile Seamless Learning (MSL), Older Adults, User Experience (UX)

References

Kohen-Vacs, D., & Amzalag, M. (2023). Re-embracing MSL approaches in realities of emergent conditions. *Research & Practice in Technology Enhanced Learning*, 18.

Kurtz, G., Amzalag, M., Barak-Medina, E., Gal, E., Kohen-Vacs, D., Shaked, N., Zailer, G., & Zaguri, Y. (2023). *Higher education and generative ai (genai) in Israel: opportunities, challenges and recommendations*. https://facultyprojects.telem-hit.net/HigherEducationGenAI/En/

What is required to help foster nestedness and integration in the complex digital learning ecosystem?

Can "Smart Import" Create Smart Learning Content?

Jue Wang Szilas[1], Patrizia Birchler Emery[2]

[1] Centre for Continuing and Distance Education, University of Geneva, Switzerland; jue.wangszilas@unige.ch
[2] Centre for Continuing and Distance Education, University of Geneva, Switzerland; patrizia.birchler@unige.ch

Correspondence: Jue Wang Szilas: jue.wangszilas@unige.ch

Abstract:

This paper explores the transformative impact of the "Smart Import" AI engine, a new feature introduced by the H5P team, on the creation of interactive text-based learning content. As instructional designers working in University continuing education, the authors embarked on an experiential journey to gain insights into the capabilities and limitations of this innovative tool.

After a compelling demo session with the H5P team, the authors were provided with a temporary account to test Smart Import's functionality with colleagues. Choosing a 30-minute YouTube video of a presentation previously delivered by one of them, the authors utilized Smart Import to convert the video into recorded text. Subsequently, the original transcript has been proofread and corrected as needed. Smart Import then generated eight different learning activities based on this text, which were distributed to colleagues for completion and feedback.

The findings revealed that Smart Import effectively generated powerful text-based learning activities, primarily enhancing the learning of declarative knowledge. It notably improved the mastery and understanding of key concepts by increasing their frequency within the activities. However, limitations were identified, for example the inability to generate open-ended questions requiring critical thinking, or incorporate in-depth distractors in multiple-choice questions, or facilitate collaborative learning. Additionally, the current version of the tool only supports English language resources, with other languages yet to be developed.

Through this trial, the authors explored the benefits of an AI engine, recognizing its potential to significantly increase productivity in creating interactive text-based learning content and enhance accessibility. Simultaneously, the authors gained a clearer understanding of potential risks, particularly concerns about stifling creativity and the necessity for human intervention to maintain pedagogical integrity.

The authors call for a discussion on key questions: To what extent will interactive learning content created by AI tools be credible in an academic environment? What aspects of instructional design are most practically helped by AI engines? How can a balance between automation and creativity be achieved in learning content design? When integrating AI tools such as Smart Import into instructional design, where can human roles not be replaced by AI? With this specific case, the authors of this paper hope to prompt educators and researchers to think about the evolving role of AI in shaping the future of intelligent learning content creation. We want a world in which knowledge is created by humans. But is it already too late for that?

Keywords: AI engine, Smart Import, H5P, Instructional Design, Learning Activities

What is required to help foster nestedness and integration in the complex digital learning ecosystem?

References

Farrelly, T., & Baker, N. (2023). Generative artificial intelligence: Implications and considerations for higher education practice. *Education Sciences, 13*(11), 1109.

García-Peñalvo, F. J., Llorens Largo, F., & Vidal, J. (2023). The new reality of education in the face of advances in generative artificial intelligence.

Shumailov, I., Shumaylov, Z., Zhao, Y., Gal, Y., Papernot, N., & Anderson, R. (2023). The curse of recursion: Training on generated data makes models forget. *arXiv preprint arXiv:2305.17493*.

ANNEMISSELBROOK. (2023, November 22). H5P software trial of the feature 'Smart Import' using AI technology [Blog post https://blogs.northampton.ac.uk/learntech/2023/11/22/h5p-software-trial-of-the-feature-smart-import-using-ai-technology/].

BERSIN, J. (2023, April 21). EdTech Is Going Crazy For AI [Blog post https://joshbersin.com/2023/04/edtech-is-going-crazy-for-ai/].

Lindsay, R. (2023, November 10). Embracing Interactive Learning - H5P at the University of Liverpool [Blog post https://www.liverpool.ac.uk/centre-for-innovation-in-education/blog/general/embracing-interactive-learning-h5p-uol/].

O'Donnell, F. (2023). Let AI automatically create learning activities [Blog post https://teachnet.ie/let-ai-automatically-create-learning-activities/].

Zhgenti, S., & Holmes, W. (2023, July 24). Generative AI and Education: Adopting a Critical Approach [Blog post https://botpopuli.net/generative-ai-and-education-adopting-a-critical-approach/].

Wladawsky-Berger, I. (2023, September 28). The Critical Value of Human-Created Knowledge to the Future of Generative AI [Blog post https://blog.irvingwb.com/blog/2023/09/the-critical-value-of-human-created-knowledge-to-generative-ai.html].

Packer, H. (2023, July 4). UK universities set out plans to use AI in teaching [Newspaper article https://thepienews.com/news/uk-universities-ai-teaching/]

What is required to help foster nestedness and integration in the complex digital learning ecosystem?

You & I - and AI: Enhancing the Quality of an Online Course

Hanne Kristin Dypedal[1]

[1] NLA University College, Norway; handyp@nla.no

Correspondence: Hanne Kristin Dypedal: handyp@nla.no

Abstract:

The surge in interest for online courses necessitates innovative approaches to overcome the initial barriers faced by academicians transitioning from traditional classroom settings. This project, conducted in Spring 2024, therefore explores a collaboration between a subject matter expert, an instructional designer specializing in online pedagogy, and generative AI, to enhance the quality of an online philosophy course (Ex.phil) within an intensive five days-framework.

Within the scope of this collaborative endeavor, we grounded our approach in the TPACK framework to ensure a structured integration of technology with pedagogical and content knowledge. Grounded in the TPACK framework, this project explored the collaborative innovation, uniting the academic's depth of content knowledge, the instructional designer's digital didactic strategies, and AI's data-driven insights, with the aim of achieving a synergy that can efficiently elevate course quality.

Building upon this theoretical foundation, this action research intervention focuses on three critical areas identified as pivotal for online course quality: user-centered structure, student-active learning, and opportunities for social interaction(Garrels & Zemliansky, 2022). Both a potential student group and an expert group graded the course pre and post-intervention, using a validated questionnaire.

Translating these principles into practice, our presentation will unfold the practical outcomes, showcasing our experiences from utilizing AI to elevate the quality of the online course. We will also share concrete examples of the course both pre- and post-intervention. These comparative snapshots will illustrate the transformative impact of our multidisciplinary approach. We delve into the key factors that contributed to our success, the challenges we faced, and the valuable lessons learned throughout the collaboration. Further, we reflect on how this type of partnership can effectively harness diverse expertise to enhance the quality of online courses in the future, and how a digital learning expert can be the bridge between a traditional educator and the new AI technology as a tool in online learning.

Keywords: Online teaching, higher education, AI in Education, Learner-Centered Design, Instructional design, digital pedagogy

References

Garrels, V., & Zemliansky, P. (2022). Improving Student Engagement in Online Courses through Interactive and User-Centered Course Design: Practical Strategies. *Nordic Journal of Digital Literacy*, vol 17(2), 112-122. https://doi.org/10.18261/njdl.17.2.3

Challenges and Opportunities of Integrating GPT in a Faculty Development Centre

Laura Cattaneo-Molteni[1], Hervé Platteaux[2], Christiane Caneva[3]

[1 2 3]Service for university didactics and digital skills, Academic Affairs Directorate, University of Freiburg, Switzerland
[1] laura.molteni@unifr.ch
[2] herve.platteaux@unifr.ch
[3] cristiane.caneva@unifr.ch

Correspondence: Christiane Caneva: christiane.caneva@unifr.ch

Abstract:

AI chatbots are being used in a variety of sectors and can provide immediate assistance to users, answering questions and providing explanations and additional resources on specific topics. While their use in various fields has been known for a number of years, the possibility of creating Generative Pretrained Transformers (GPTs) tailored to one's specific needs is a more recent development that is attracting interest in higher education circles (Labadze et al., 2023). Higher education institutions are wondering about the opportunities, challenges, potential limitations, concerns and prospects associated with the use of AI chatbots in educational settings (Selwyn, 2024). At the University of Fribourg (Switzerland), a bilingual institution with five faculties, the Faculty Development Centre is investigating the usefulness of developing a GPT to assist and meet the needs of the center's pedagogical and techno-pedagogical advisors. A GPT was designed to assist them supporting teachers in developing their didactic and digital skills, in two languages and with faculties that have different didactic and pedagogical approaches. In this presentation, we will share our experiences in creating our GPT, the challenges we encountered (pedagogical, technical, ethical, legal, etc.) and the usefulness perceived by the members of our team, with a view to eventually integrating the GPT into everyday tasks. For example, we think about: analysing and structuring a training course, creating learning content, creating quizzes that can be integrated into existing learning platforms, etc. While this study seeks to explore the potential benefits of AI chatbots in higher education more generally, our areas of interest are the personalisation of content and the skills that need to be developed, as highlighted in the meta-analysis conducted by Bond et al. (2024). How can AI benefit higher education? What are the specific training requirements for the successful integration of AI into university teaching practices? To what extent can AI facilitate innovation and personalisation of teaching across disciplinary boundaries? Finally, what specific challenges need to be considered when using AI to develop teaching strategies based on data generated by educators themselves?

Keywords: AI chatbots; Higher education; GPT development; Pedagogical support

What is required to help foster nestedness and integration in the complex digital learning ecosystem?

References

Bond, M., Khosravi, H., De Laat, M., Bergdahl, N., Negrea, V., Oxley, E., Pham, P., Chong, S. W., & Siemens, G. (2024). A meta systematic review of artificial intelligence in higher education: A call for increased ethics, collaboration, and rigour. *International Journal of Educational Technology in Higher Education, 21*(1), 4. https://doi.org/10.1186/s41239-023-00436-z

Labadze, L., Grigolia, M., & Machaidze, L. (2023). Role of AI chatbots in education: Systematic literature review. *International Journal of Educational Technology in Higher Education, 20*(1), 56. https://doi.org/10.1186/s41239-023-00426-1

Selwyn, N. (2024). On the Limits of Artificial Intelligence (AI) in Education. *Nordisk Tidsskrift for Pedagogikk Og Kritikk*, 10(1), Article 1. https://doi.org/10.23865/ntpk.v10.6062

What is required to help foster nestedness and integration in the complex digital learning ecosystem?

AI Assistant for the Assessment of Asynchronous Video Tests

Xavier Mas Garcia[1], Josep Antoni Martinez-Aceituno[2]

[1] eLearning Center, Universitat Oberta de Catalunya, Spain; xmas@uoc.edu
[2] eLearning Center, Universitat Oberta de Catalunya, Spain; jmartineza@uoc.edu

Correspondence: Josep Antoni Martinez-Aceituno: jmartineza@uoc.edu

Abstract:

The Universitat Oberta de Catalunya (UOC) prioritizes mitigating misuse of AI in education as part of its strategy to integrate AI into its teaching processes. One initiative includes Proofs of Concept (PoC) to explore AI's application in education, such as the "AI Assistant for the assessment of asynchronous video tests." This AI Assistant supports teaching staff by automating transcripts and generating pre-assessment reports, thus expediting the assessment process and reducing workload. Additionally, UOC employs asynchronous oral tests to ensure student identity and authorship credibility, further safeguarding against fraudulent AI use. These measures are being tested for potential wider application across more courses.

Mass access to generative AI has challenged the learning methodologies and assessment systems applied to date at universities. Teaching staff and institutions identify as their main concern the threat posed by the fraudulent and mass use of this technology by students for their learning assignments and assessment tests (Chan, C.K., 2023; Toba, H. et al, 2024). Preventing and avoiding these misuses in order to continue guaranteeing a sound and reliable learning process and assessment is the UOC's (Universitat Oberta de Catalunya) main priority as part of its strategy for adopting AI in its teaching activity in the short and medium term. One of the actions in this adoption strategy is performing Proofs of Concept (PoC) on teaching uses of AI. This involves testing various uses of AI to validate or refute hypotheses about their application to teaching. The "AI Assistant for the assessment of asynchronous video tests" is one such test, its approach being to test a use designed to support teaching staff in an online assessment process.

In its continuous assessment process, the UOC has incorporated, as an action, holding asynchronous oral tests in bachelor's degree courses that may have several classroom groups of 50-60 students each. The incorporation of oral tests is part of a strategy designed to increase the credibility of tests regarding the identity and authorship of students and to ensure that they have been answered without a fraudulent use of AI. Specifically, it consists of the teaching staff preparing a set of assessment questions that are then randomly distributed among the students. The students access an assessment environment at the time chosen by them within a defined time slot and, upon access, the system asks them one of the questions and each student has 5-10 minutes to answer it. The system stores a recording of each test, and teaching staff can view the recordings to assess the tests using the rubric prepared for that purpose. The recordings also make it possible for the assessing teacher and a second reviewing teacher to view them again for a second assessment in the event of claims from students.

Under the PoC presented, AI is incorporated as an assistant in this process. On the one hand, an automated transcript of the recording of the test is generated by Open AI's Whisper application using a self-developed API; and on the other, a pre-assessment report based on the test rubric is generated with ChatGPT, also through an API. Having these two text-based documents allows teaching staff to speed up the assessment process and reduce the associated workload, because the assessment can be made without having to view the video every time. The PoC validation of this hypothesis has allowed the UOC to consider carrying out real pilot tests to extend this type of test to a greater number of courses with large numbers of enrolled students.

Keywords: AI teaching assistance, online assessment, video test, ChatGPT, higher education

What is required to help foster nestedness and integration in the complex digital learning ecosystem?

References

Chan, C.K. (2023). Is AI Changing the Rules of Academic Misconduct? An In-depth Look at Students' Perceptions of 'AI-giarism'. ArXiv, abs/2306.03358.

Toba, H., Karnalim, O., Johan, M.C., Tada, T., Djajalaksana, Y.M., Vivaldy, T. (2024). Inappropriate Benefits and Identification of ChatGPT Misuse in Programming Tests: A Controlled Experiment. In: Auer, M.E., Cukierman, U.R., Vendrell Vidal, E., Tovar Caro, E. (eds) *Towards a Hybrid, Flexible and Socially Engaged Higher Education*. ICL 2023. Lecture Notes in Networks and Systems, vol 899. Springer, Cham. https://doi.org/10.1007/978-3-031-51979-6_54

Meeting Labor Market Demands: Exploring Online Micro-credentials for Soft Skills Development

Carles Bruguera[1], Carme Pagès[2], Mitchell Peters[3], Àngels Fitó [4]

[1234] Universitat Oberta de Catalunya (UOC), Spain
[1] cbruguerat@uoc.edu
[2] cpagesserra@uoc.edu
[3] mjosephp@uoc.edu
[4] afitob@uoc.edu

Correspondence: Carles Bruguera: cbruguerat@uoc.edu

Abstract:

Data from over four million online job vacancies in Spain show an increasing demand for soft skills in today's labor market across disciplines. Teamwork, problem-solving, adaptation to changes, or creativity are now essential qualities sought by employers across various industries, alongside technical expertise. This poses a significant challenge, as traditional educational systems struggle to adequately prepare individuals with the necessary soft skills required for their professional development within organizations. Consequently, there is a noticeable demand from the workforce for innovative training solutions coming from higher education institutions, especially among all learning providers, to address this context. This paper explores the potential of online micro-credentials, a novel learning approach that awards credentials after short educational experiences, as a viable solution to bridging the soft skills gap in the workforce given its focus on lifelong learners that are already working. Using a qualitative methods approach, our study analyzes and synthesizes insights gathered from 80 in-depth interviews with key stakeholders in the labor market. According to the results, employers generally view online micro-credentials as a feasible and flexible way for professionals to engage in training, allowing them to participate at their convenience without disrupting their schedules. However, employers underscore various challenges associated with online micro-credentials in soft skills that distance education must take into consideration: training in soft skills entails a transformation in professionals' attitudes or behaviors, posing a challenge for educational course design; there is a tension between substantial learning outcomes and course length; longer duration of training is associated with higher reliability in acquiring certain soft skills, even in short-term courses; a practical application of learned skills is perceived as crucial for the soft skill development even in online settings; there is a lack of novel forms of soft skill assessment and evaluation in online settings; a key aspect for employers to recognize the value of micro-credentials. In conclusion, to fully harness the potential of micro-credentials in bridging the widening skills gap in the workforce, particularly in the context of online education, we advocate for strategic initiatives with a practical orientation. This involves integrating insights from the labor market into curriculum development processes, implementing some innovative course design involving practical instances and fostering collaboration between industry stakeholders and online education providers. Through these efforts, micro-credentials tailored to soft skills development can be designed and implemented in settings that closely resemble real-life scenarios.

Keywords: Micro-credentials, soft skills, labor market, distance education.

References

Babbie, E.R. (2016) The Practice of Social Research. 14th Edition, Cengage Learning, Belmont.

What is required to help foster nestedness and integration in the complex digital learning ecosystem?

Bakule, M., Czesana, V., Havlickova, V., Kriechel, B., Rasovec, T., & Wilson, R. (2016). Developing skills foresights, scenarios and forecasts: guide to anticipating and matching skills and jobs. Luxemburgo: Publications Office of the European Union, 2.

Boyatzis, R. E. (1998). Transforming qualitative information: Thematic analysis and code development. Sage.

Brown, M., & Nic-Giolla-Mhichil, M. (2022). Unboxing micro-credentials: an inside, upside and downside view (Descifrando las microcredenciales: en qué consisten, ventajas e inconvenientes). Culture and Education, 34(4), 938-973.

Cedefop (2023). Microcredentials for labour market education and training: microcredentials and evolving qualifications systems. Luxembourg: Publications Office. Cedefop research paper, No 89. http://data.europa.eu/doi/10.2801/566352

Dicce, R. P., & Ewers, M. C. (2020). Becoming Linked In: Leveraging Professional Networks for Elite Surveys and Interviews. Geographical Review, 110(1–2), 160–171. https://doi.org/10.1111/gere.12346

Fereday, J and Eimear Muir-Cochrane, A. 2006. Demonstrating rigor using thematic analysis: A hybrid approach of inductive and deductive coding and theme development. International Journal of Qualitative Methods, 5(1): 80–92. http://journals.sagepub.com/doi/ pdf/10.1177/160940690600500107. DOI: https://doi.org/10.1177/160940690600500107

JRC-IPTS (2020) For-Learn online foresight guide: an A to Z of foresight http://forlearn.jrc.ec.europa.eu/guide/A1_key-terms/foresight.htm [accessed 24.6.2014].

Kiiskilä, P., Kukkonen, A., & Pirkkalainen, H. (2023). Are micro-credentials valuable for students? Perspective on verifiable digital credentials. SN Computer Science, 4(4), 366.

Kozłowski, A., Kaliszewski, A., Dąbrowski, J., & Klimek, H. (2021). Virtual network sampling method using LinkedIn. MethodsX, 8, 101393.

Manual, F. Empowered Futures for the 2030 Agenda (2018). UNDP Global Centre for Public Service Excellence, Singapore.

Pirkkalainen, H., Sood, I., Padron Napoles, C., Kukkonen, A., & Camilleri, A. (2023). How might micro-credentials influence institutions and empower learners in higher education?. Educational Research, 65(1), 40-63.

Thi Ngoc Ha, N., Spittle, M., Watt, A., & Van Dyke, N. (2023). A systematic literature review of micro-credentials in higher education: a non-zero-sum game. Higher Education Research & Development, 42(6), 1527-1548.

Twining, P, Heller, RS, Nussbaum, M and Tsai, C-C. 2017. Some guidance on conducting and reporting qualitative studies. Computers & Education, 106: A1–A9. DOI: https://doi.org/10.1016/j. compedu.2016.12.002

Štefanić, J., & Šimić, D. (2021). An overview of skills foresight methods. In Central European Conference on Information and Intelligent Systems (pp. 283-289). Faculty of Organization and Informatics Varazdin.

Varadarajan, S., Koh, J. H. L., & Daniel, B. K. (2023). A systematic review of the opportunities and challenges of micro-credentials for multiple stakeholders: learners, employers, higher education institutions and government. International Journal of Educational Technology in Higher Education, 20(1), 13.

GenAI: N^3 - The Missing Link: Gen AI and Staff Engagement in Higher Education

Ken Mccarthy[1], Hazel Farrell[2]

[1] South East Technological University, Ireland; ken.mccarthy@setu.ie
[2] South East Technological University, Ireland; hazel.farrell@setu.ie

Correspondence: Ken Mccarthy: ken.mccarthy@setu.ie

Abstract:

The emergence of Gen AI on the higher education landscape has proven exhilarating, or even liberating for some, but intimidating and threatening for others who may feel both overwhelmed by the rapidity of technological advancements and the colossal amount of information being released daily. The standard university approach has been to provide staff with training opportunities, usage guidelines focused on academic integrity, and resources to help them to engage with Gen AI. While this may appear to be robust, a distinctive gap has emerged in the lack of staff engagement with these supports and consequently with Gen AI.

While obvious reasons behind this include fear of the unknown and the 'head-in-the-sand' cohort continuing to bask in the comfort of pre-Gen AI pedagogical practices, further explorations revealed several key factors, the most prominent of which was a lack of time to engage effectively with the training and resources. Others felt a lack of relevance to their discipline while more have expressed concerns about the ethics, integrity, and the cost of generative AI platforms.

To address some of these concerns this paper presents the approach being adopted by the GenAI: N-TUTORR National Network (GenAI:N^3) which has been established across the seven partners of the Irish N-TUTORR programme (National Technological University Transformation for Recovery and Resilience). The programme partners are the five new technological universities (ATU, MTU, SETU, TU Dublin, TUS) and the two remaining institutes of technology (Dundalk IT, IADT).

The focus of the network has been on the opportunities to improve educational practices and enhance learning experiences that Gen AI provides by scaffolding educators to ensure the effective application and understanding of these tools. In practice this takes the form of regular meetings of the network and a shared space of curated resources and case studies. The network lead in each of the seven partners is funded to develop local resources and activities along with their contribution to the national network and proposed project outputs.

The proposed outputs consist of a collaborative multi-location hackathon on using Gen AI in education that will be held during October 2024. A crowd-sourced digital book of case studies, practices, and examples of novel usage of Gen AI in higher education that will be published in December 2024, and the development of a workshop format called AI Play that will provide an opportunity to explore the limitations and capabilities of the technology in a collaborative context.

This multi-faceted approach will be highlighted in this short paper, and it will illustrate the innovative space designed for educators to interact with the technology.

Unlocking Potential: Nudging Growth Mindsets Through AI-Informed Teaching and Learning

Anita L. Campbell[1]

[1]Academic Support Programme for Engineering; & Centre for Research in Engineering Education, University of Cape Town, South Africa; anita.campbell@uct.ac.za

Correspondence: Anita Campbell: anita.campbell@uct.ac.za

Abstract:

As educators embrace generative AI, the conventional approach to student assignments undergoes a paradigm shift. Moving beyond the confines of summative assessments, particularly in large courses such as first-year mathematics, I advocate for a transition towards formative assessments that prioritize process over product. This re-evaluation encourages educators to deepen the learning journey for students rather than merely assessing the final outcome. By leveraging generative AI, we can create dynamic, personalized assessments that adapt to individual learning styles and nudge students towards their self-care goals (e.g. sleep, movement, nutrition), fostering a more holistic understanding of student progress.

Central to my argument is the infusion of growth mindset principles into AI-informed teaching and learning practices. Generative AI provides a unique platform to embed these principles, cultivating a positive and resilient mindset among students. Drawing on the insights from my PhD studies (Campbell, Craig & Collier-Reed, 2020), the mere integration of AI is insufficient to guarantee the success of growth mindset-informed changes. Hence, this submission proposes guidelines for effectively incorporating growth mindset principles into AI-informed educational practices.

The potential benefits of integrating growth mindset principles with generative AI extend beyond academic outcomes. By nurturing a mindset that embraces challenges and values effort, students are better prepared for the demands of lifelong learning. Generative AI, when harnessed with a growth mindset approach, becomes a powerful tool in developing adaptable, resilient learners capable of navigating the uncertainties of the future (Michel-Villarreal et al., 2023).

However, while the potential of generative AI is vast, ethical considerations, privacy concerns, and the risk of perpetuating biases demand careful scrutiny. This submission encourages a balanced exploration, urging educators to navigate the landscape of generative AI with mindfulness and a commitment to ethical practices.

The collaborative relationship between educators and AI is not about replacing human intuition but amplifying it. Generative AI serves as a support system, offering insights, automating routine tasks, and providing valuable feedback. In this symbiotic relationship, educators are empowered to focus on fostering creativity, critical thinking, and interpersonal skills — elements that define the essence of holistic education. Establishing an institutional-wide culture that values learning goals (e.g. personal transformation) over performance goals (e.g. valuing only high grades) is key.

Keywords: Generative AI; Formative assessments; Growth mindset; Personalized learning; Ethical AI; Educator-AI collaboration

What is required to help foster nestedness and integration in the complex digital learning ecosystem?

References

Campbell, A., Craig, T., & Collier-Reed, B. (2020). A framework for using learning theories to inform 'growth mindset' activities. *International Journal of Mathematical Education in Science and Technology, 51*(1), 26-43. https://doi.org/10.1080/0020739X.2018.1562118

Michel-Villarreal, R., Vilalta-Perdomo, E., Salinas-Navarro, D. E., Thierry-Aguilera, R., Gerardou, F. S. (2023). Challenges and opportunities of generative AI for higher education as explained by ChatGPT. *Education Sciences, 13*, 856. https://doi.org/10.3390/educsci13090856

What is required to help foster nestedness and integration in the complex digital learning ecosystem?

What Schools Can Learn from Virtual Schools (and Online Universities)

Paul Bacsich[1], Charlotte Doody[2], Jonathan Lloyd[3], Margaret Korosec[4]

[1] Matic Media Ltd, Managing Director, UK; paul@matic-media.co.uk
[2] Matic Media Ltd, Researcher, UK; charlotte_doody@hotmail.com
[3] The Pilgrims' School, Head of Digital Learning, UK; jonathan.a.lloyd@gmail.com
[4] University of Leeds, UK, Dean of Online and Digital Education, M.D.Korosec@leeds.ac.uk

Correspondence: Paul Bacsich: paul@matic-media.co.uk

Abstract:

This paper describes interim results from a small ongoing study project involving experts on virtual schools and virtual universities.

The fundamental question the study asks is:

- Why is the education sector (schools in particular) not learning lessons (resilience, LMS use, etc.) from the growing community of virtual schools?

This question is best answered by splitting the answering process into several more detailed objectives:

1. To understand the reasons why so many overview reports – e.g. OECD (2023) and European Commission (2024) – largely ignore virtual schools (VISCED 2011, Open Education Wiki 2024) and the positive implications of their practice for the wider education sector. Since one of the key reasons seems to be the custom for such overview reports to focus primarily on research literature rather than grey literature, this leads to the need for #2 below.

2. To scope and understand better the research community that is generating research material on virtual schools (articles in peer-reviewed journals, and monographs), in order to understand the degree to which it interpenetrates the "conventional" education research community, especially at elite (and thus opinion-forming) levels. Investigations so far suggest that the research community looking at virtual schools is very small especially outside the US (Johnson et al 2023) – this in turn leads to #3 below.

3. To develop ways by which more case studies of individual virtual schools and groups of them can be generated, suitable for publication in research journals. This relates to theme 2 on nestedness/ integration. However, to avoid "false negatives", a check has to be done to make sure that there are not virtual schools "hiding in plain sight". This leads to #4.

4. To investigate the full range of virtual schools: full-time (essentially replacing a f2f school), part-time ("supplemental virtual school") teaching one or more subjects online to students at a f2f school, both visible (e.g. a separate organisation or visible department) and invisible (a group within a school teaching some subjects online to students in other schools).

The fundamental question can be split also by considering:

- Which subsectors of the education sector have the most to learn from virtual schools?

What is required to help foster nestedness and integration in the complex digital learning ecosystem?

Initial considerations suggest that the university sector (f2f or online) will be reluctant to learn. Our contention is that the most promising area is upper secondary schools (grades 11-12 in many countries). The paper will look at a case study in a particular country (Sixth Form providers in United Kingdom/England) where upper secondary is a liminal zone with aspects of both school-level and tertiary-level education.

This case study leads on to a further but related issue

- What aspects of how universities run (especially online universities) could be usefully adopted by the schools sector? This also relates to the issue of whether a country should have unified support for all education providers – on the whole countries do not, but NRENs often take a more unified approach (GÉANT 2023).

This will encompass areas including group and regional procurement, LMS selection and use, AI use, and staff training/certification.

Keywords: Virtual schools; Hybrid schools; online universities

---

References

COL (2020). *Towards More Resilient Schooling: Possible Models for the Future*. Burnaby: Commonwealth of Learning.

European Commission. (2024). *Scenarios for the future of school education in the EU: A Foresight Study*. Brussels: Publications Office of the European Union.

Ferdig, R. & Kennedy, K. (2018). *Handbook of research on K-12 online and blended learning (2nd edition)*. Pittsburgh: ETC Press.

GÉANT (2023). *Compendium 2022 of National Research and Education Networks in Europe*. Brussels: GÉANT.

Johnson, C. et al. (2023). "Online Teaching in K-12 Education in the United States: A Systematic Review". *Review of Educational Research* vol. 93 no. 3 pp. 353-411.

Lee, Y.F. & Lee, L.S. (2023). *Trends and Issues of Promoting Digital Learning in High-Digital-Competitiveness Countries: Country Reports and International Comparison*. Taichung: National Taiwan Normal University and Ministry of Education Taiwan.

OECD (2023). *Country Digital Education Ecosystems and Governance: A Companion to Digital Education Outlook 2023*. Paris: OECD.

Open Education Wiki (2024). Virtual schools. http://openeducation.wiki/wiki/Virtual_school

VISCED (2011). *Virtual schools and colleges: providing alternatives for successful learning: Volumes 1 and 2*. Roosbeek: ATiT bvba.

Empowering Mathematics Personalisation for Dyslexic and Colour-Blind Students through MIT App Inventor with GenAI Integration

Muhammad H. Al Omoush[1], Tracey Mehigan[2]

[1,2] Faculty of Engineering and Computing, Dublin City University, Dublin, Ireland
[1] Muhammad.menazelalomoush2@mail.dcu.ie
[2] Tracey.mehigan@dcu.ie

Correspondence: Muhammad H. Al Omoush: Muhammad.menazelalomoush2@mail.dcu.ie

Abstract:

MIT App Inventor[1] is a user-friendly visual programming platform designed to facilitate building mobile phone and tablet applications (apps) through an interactive interface. It allows users to design the graphical user interface (GUI) and program functionalities for apps without extensive coding knowledge (Mir & Llueca, 2020).

The Universal Design for Learning (UDL) principles include multiple means of engagement, representation, and action and expression, ensuring that instructional methods are flexible and diverse to effectively meet all learners' needs (CAST, 2018). Therefore, designing and developing educational apps aligning with these principles can potentially support students' education (Rao et al., 2021).

In this concise paper, the authors investigate the development of an educational app (chatbot) using the MIT App Inventor platform, focusing on mathematics accessibility tailored for students with dyslexia and colour blindness. The personalised chatbot offers assistance and guidance in mathematics learning for primary education students. Integration of generative AI enriches the chatbot's capabilities, enabling dynamic interactions and customised learning experiences. This app incorporates features to accommodate diverse learners, specifically emphasising engagement and accessibility, aligning with the (UDL) principles.

The chatbot is equipped with advanced capabilities such as speech-to-text (STT) and text-to-speech (TTS) (Trivedi et al., 2018), enabling seamless interaction through both spoken and written communication. Moreover, the OpenAI API is used for generative AI integration to generate natural responses, while key parameters such as temperature, tokens limit, and logit bias[2] (Finnie-Ansley et al., 2022; Wu et al., 2023) are managed to optimise the chatbot's performance. Temperature regulates the diversity of generated text, while the token limit ensures responses remain coherent and relevant within a reasonable length by limiting the maximum number of words or symbols it can process in a single interaction. Logit bias steers conversations towards relevant topics or specific answers like yes or no (Chung et al., 2023).

Additionally, an integrated accessibility tool enhances the user experience for dyslexic and colour-blind students by allowing control over background colour, font size, colour, and type. For smartphones equipped with an accelerometer, an extra feature enables users to control background colour by simply shaking the device, with shaking sensitivity dictating colour selection intensity for a personalised experience.

Figure 1 presents the initial vision of the chatbot through MIT App Inventor's Graphical Interface Editor, representing the app's layout, while Figure 2 shows part of the chatbot's coding blocks through a block-based programming interface. These components highlight MIT App Inventor's robustness in empowering users to create dynamic and interactive mobile applications, including chatbots.

What is required to help foster nestedness and integration in the complex digital learning ecosystem?

---

1 https://appinventor.mit.edu/about-us

2 https://platform.openai.com/docs/api-reference/chat/create#chat-create-logit_bias

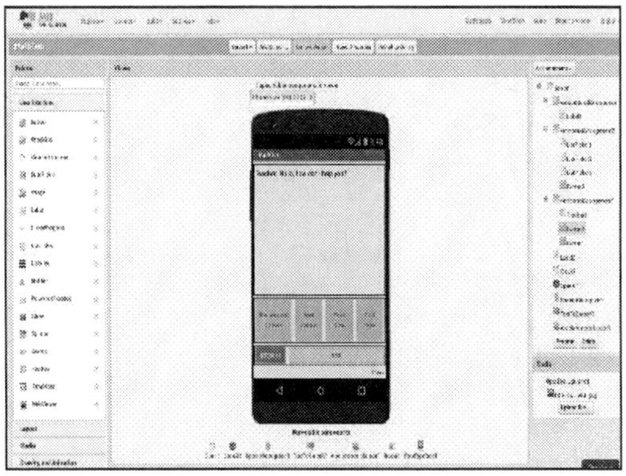

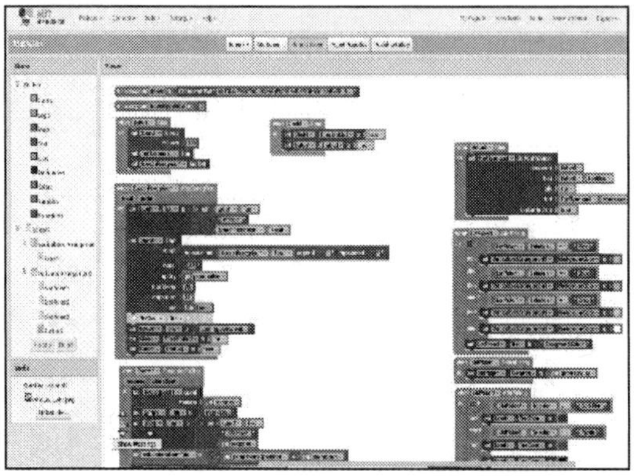

Figure 1: MIT App Inventor graphical interface editor

Figure 2: The coding blocks page

Tokens spent during response generation can be translated into meaningful metrics aligned with student learning and interaction with the app. These metrics can include measuring the depth of engagement, the richness of content (conversation), and the overall effectiveness of the learning experience. For example, tokens spent could correlate with the complexity and coherence of responses generated by the chatbot, reflecting the depth of understanding and relevance to student queries. By monitoring the tokens spent during generation, educators and developers can gain valuable insights to enhance the learning journey and foster meaningful interactions within the app.

This app demonstrates the potential of technology in fostering inclusive educational experiences through the use of MIT App Inventor and the integration of generative AI. By adhering to UDL principles and aiming to enhance accessibility, the app aims to empower learners of all abilities to succeed in mathematics education, regardless of any challenges they may face.

Keywords: MIT App Inventor, Dyslexia, Colour blindness, Chatbot, Mathematics, Universal Design for Learning (UDL).

Acknowledgement

This work was conducted with the financial support of the Science Foundation Ireland Centre for Research Training in Digitally-Enhanced Reality (d-real) under Grant No. 18/CRT/6224.

References

CAST (2018). Universal Design for Learning Guidelines version 2.2. Retrieved from http://udlguidelines.cast.org

Chung, J. J. Y., Kamar, E., & Amershi, S. (2023). *Increasing diversity while maintaining accuracy: Text data generation with large language models and human interventions.*

Finnie-Ansley, J., Denny, P., Becker, B. A., Luxton-Reilly, A., & Prather, J. (2022). *The robots are coming: Exploring the implications of openai codex on introductory programming. In Proceedings of the 24th Australasian Computing Education Conference (pp. 10–19).*

What is required to help foster nestedness and integration in the complex digital learning ecosystem?

Mir, S. B., & Llueca, G. F. (2020). *Introduction to programming using mobile phones and MIT app inventor. IEEE Revista Iberoamericana de Tecnologías Del Aprendizaje, 15(3), 192–201.*

Rao, K., Torres, C., & Smith, S. J. (2021). Digital tools and UDL-based instructional strategies to support students with disabilities online. *Journal of Special Education Technology, 36(2), 105-112.*

Trivedi, A., Pant, N., Shah, P., Sonik, S., & Agrawal, S. (2018). *Speech to text and text to speech recognition systems-Areview. IOSR J. Comput. Eng, 20*(2), 36-43.

Wu, Y., Jia, F., Zhang, S., Wu, Q., Li, H., Zhu, E., ... & Wang, C. (2023). *An empirical study on challenging math problem solving with gpt-4. arXiv preprint arXiv:2306.01337.*

What is required to help foster nestedness and integration in the complex digital learning ecosystem?

Digital Transformation: A Systems Thinking View for Sustainable Change in Higher Education

Margaret Korosec[1]

[1] University of Leeds, Dean of Online and Digital Education, UK, M.D.Korosec@leeds.ac.uk

Correspondence: Dr Margaret Korosec: M.D.Korosec@leeds.ac.uk

Abstract:

How do we acknowledge, leverage, and sustain a complex digital learning ecosystem that is adaptive to AI in education whilst ensuring a suitable foundation? This concise paper presentation explores a human-centred design approach applied to the broader system within which higher education operates. Drawing on insights from developing sustainable online education portfolios in higher education in the UK and US, this presentation will share considerations to enable AI to be embedded in the educational systems. It will reflect insights from work undertaken that identified interrelations within a complex system as well as implications of dependencies.

The primary question is:

- Can we learn lessons of agility to introduce AI in education by drawing on insights from intentionally designed online universities as compared to introducing online education into historically campus-based universities?

This will be explored through the following case studies:

5. A fully online US-based institution designed from inception as non-campus based able to scale rapidly and adapt to emerging technology applicable to learning, teaching and assessment.

6. A campus university based in the United Kingdom that established a separate unit to facilitate a growing online degree portfolio.

7. A campus university based in the United Kingdom that approached an online portfolio through existing systems and processes.

8. The implications and opportunities of these scenarios will highlight transferrable strategic and tactical considerations for embedding AI in education. This relates to theme 1 of the conference "What is required to help foster nestedness and integration in the complex digital learning ecosystem?"

Keywords: Digital transformation; online education; emergent technology; organisational systems; systems thinking.

References

Benavides, L.M.C., Tamayo Arias, J.A., Arango Serna, M.D., Branch Bedoya, J.W. and Burgos, D., (2020). Digital transformation in higher education institutions: A systematic literature review. Sensors, 20(11), p.3291.

What is required to help foster nestedness and integration in the complex digital learning ecosystem?

Chow, A. S. & Croxton, R.A. (2017). Designing a responsive e-learning infrastructure: Systemic change in higher education. *American Journal of Distance Education, vol 31*(1), 20-42.

Dasgupta, M., Gupta, R. K. & Sahay, A. (2011). Linking technological innovation, technology strategy and organisational factors. *Global Business Review, vol 12*(2), 257-277.

Hall, G. E. & Hord, S. M. (2011). *Implementing change: patterns, principles, and potholes.* Pearson.

Tamim, S. R. (2020). Analyzing the complexities of online education systems: A systems thinking perspective. *TechTrends, vol 64,* 740-750. :10.1007/s11528-020-00538-9

Reflecting on the Present and Futures of Professional Associations in Open and Digital Education: New Times, New Actors and New Challenges

António Moreira Teixeira[1], Morten Flate Paulsen[2]

[1] Laboratório de Educação a Distância e eLearning, Universidade Aberta, Portugal; Antonio.Teixeira@uab.pt
[2] NooA – the Nordic open online Academy, Norway; mfp@nooa.no

Correspondence: António Moreira Teixeira: Antonio.Teixeira@uab.pt

Abstract:

Driven by advancements in technology, changes in pedagogical approaches, and shifts in societal needs, the field of open, distance and digital education (ODDE) has been transforming substantially in recent years. There is a global shift towards more accessible, flexible, and personalized learning experiences that leverage the power of digital technologies to meet the ever more diverse needs and complex trajectories of learners in the 21st century. At the same time, the possibilities offered by new digital technologies are leading to a datafication of educational processes which raises major challenges to the educational systems. The impact of the SARS-CoV-2 pandemic and the phenomena of Emergency Remote Teaching has certainly accelerated this movement and pushed educational institutions worldwide to engage in their digital transformation. As a result, technology-enhanced practices are now mainstream. Especially in Europe, public policies are also contributing to this change of the institutional landscape. Because the field of practice in ODDE is growing rapidly, increased professional support is needed to ensure good quality standards and effective regulation. The pandemic crisis has demonstrated how professional associations have contributed successfully in widening access of the education community to reliable information, good practices, specialised research output as well as mentoring and guidance. As recently stated by Ms Stefania Giannini, UNESCO Assistant Director-General for Education, "education must not only adapt to these changes but also ensure more just, inclusive and sustainable digital futures. To achieve this shared goal, collaboration with all stakeholders is key."[1] With the emergence of such powerful and disruptive technologies as Generative Artificial Intelligence (GenAI) the need for collaboration across the field of ODDE has become paramount given the complexity of the scientific, pedagogic and ethical challenges it brings about as well as the high risks involved not only for the professional community, but for society at large. In this challenging new post-pandemic context, how are traditional professional associations in the field of ODDE managing to represent the new practitioners and new researchers and responding to their increasingly complex and diverse needs and profiles? In this paper we describe the changing field of research and practice in ODDE, analyse the new emerging challenges it brings to professional associations and discuss how these are actively preparing to meet them successfully. We focus our analysis particularly on the experiences of EDEN, ICDE, EADL and NADE. The paper explores how these professional associations are enhancing inclusivity, widening their outreach and increasing the diversity of their membership, but also expanding professional development opportunities, by providing frequent webinars on current trends, technologies, and methodologies in ODDE or by developing specialized certifications that acknowledge expertise in emerging areas. The paper analyses also how traditional professional associations in ODDE are fostering community, promoting research and innovation on a more sustainable way, advocating for policy changes and playing a more active role in decision-making, integrating technology, and providing tailored support, as mentorship programmes. Finally, we identify an

[1] https://www.unesco.org/en/articles/unesco-and-partners-explore-digital-futures-education

What is required to help foster nestedness and integration in the complex digital learning ecosystem?

awareness amongst professional associations of the importance of networking and collaborating together for preserving their rich common legacy.

Keywords: Open Education; Digital Education; Professional Associations; Learning Futures

References

Olcott, D. Jr., Arnold, D. & Blaschke, L. (2023). Leadership 2030: Renewed visions and empowered choices for European university leaders. *European Journal of Open, Distance and E-Learning, 25*(1) 74-92. https://doi.org/10.2478/eurodl-2023-0006

Paulsen, M.F. (2024). *The dawn of online education: The first decade of my online education world, 1980-1990.* Kragerø, Norway: NooA.

Paulsen, M.F. (2024). *Early adaptors of online learning: The second decade of my online education world 1990-2000.* Kragerø, Norway: NooA.

Paulsen, M.. (2023). Thirty Years of ICDE. A selection of ICDE anecdotes from My Online Education World: 1980 - 2020.

Pelletier, K., Robert, J., Muscanell, N., McCormack, M., Reeves, J., Reeves, J., Arbino, N., Grajek, S., Birdwell, w.T., Liu, D., Mandernach, J., Moore, A., Porcaro, A., Rutledge, R. & Zimmern, J. (2023). *2023 EDUCAUSE Horizon Report Teaching and Learning Edition*. Boulder, CO: EDUCAUSE23. https://library.educause.edu/-/media/files/library/2023/4/2023hrteachinglearning.pdf?

Moreira Teixeira, A., Arnold, D., & Andone, D. (2023). Pre-Visions: First Results of the EDEN Fellows Survey on the Futures of Learning. 2023 Ubiquity Proceedings, *3*(1): 318-325. DOI: https://doi.org/10.5334/uproc.103

Teixeira, A., Bates, T., & Mota, J. (2019). What future(s) for distance education universities? Towards an open network-based approach. *RIED. Revista Iberoamericana de Educación a Distancia*, *22*(1), 107-126. doi: 10.5944/ried.22.1.22288

Raising Awareness on the Need for Digital Competencies in the Academic Community

Zrinka Popić[1], Gorana Urukalo Čorkalo[2], Sandra Kučina Softić[3]

[123] University of Zagreb University Computing Centre, Croatia
[1] zrinka.popic@srce.hr
[2] gorana.urukalo.corkalo@srce.hr
[3] sskucina@srce.hr

Correspondence: Sandra Kučina Softić, sskucina@srce.hr

Abstract:

Today, in the digital age, acquiring new competencies is more necessary than ever, and digital competencies are becoming one of the key skills for lifelong learning. The European Commission emphasizes the importance of acquiring new knowledge, skills, and competencies, and has developed a range of frameworks, self-assessment tools, and educational programs that describe different dimensions of digital competencies and help users assess their level of competence and identify needs for further education and training. Acquiring digital competencies encourages lifelong learning and personal and professional development of individuals, enabling them to adapt to the demands and challenges they face throughout life and career. The University of Zagreb University Computing Centre (SRCE), provides high-quality and diverse educational and training programs in the area of ICT application, as well as professional and specialized knowledge related to information and communication technologies, e-infrastructure and services SRCE provides to the academic and research community. Recognizing the need to align with European standards, SRCE has further improved its educational and training programs by allocating areas and levels of digital competencies that participants can achieve by attending a particular educational program. Areas and levels of digital competences are defined based on the European Framework for Digital Competence of Educators (DigCompEdu) and the European Framework for Digital Competence for Citizens (DigComp), considering the diversity of SRCE educational and training programs and allow users to more easily perceive the digital competencies they have, which they want to upgrade, and which they lack. Accordingly, SRCE is in the process of setting up packages with specified educational activities related to the particular field and particular users (teachers, students, researchers...). Such packages will enable users to acquire the specific digital competencies they need and can find easily in one place all information about training and educational programs in a transparent manner. The goal of aligning the area and level of digital competences to SRCE educational and training programs was to raise awareness among all interested parties, especially the academic and research community, about the importance of acquiring digital competencies needed in teaching, research, learning, or daily life. This approach to the preparation and definition of SRCE's educational program concept allows for the creation of high-quality programs and better planning of new ones.

In this presentation, we will explain why it is important to assign areas and levels of digital competencies to educational activities, as well as how specific frameworks for digital competencies were chosen. The experiences gained and the method of application can also be applied to other educational programs.

Keywords: digital competencies, lifelong learning, academic community

What is required to help foster nestedness and integration in the complex digital learning ecosystem?

References

European Commission, Directorate-General for Education, Youth, Sport and Culture, (2023). *Digital education action plan 2021-2027 : key enabling factors for successful digital education and training*, Publications Office of the European Union. https://data.europa.eu/doi/10.2766/548454

European Commission, Directorate-General for Employment, Social Affairs and Inclusion, (2016). EU digital competence framework for citizens, Publications Office. https://data.europa.eu/doi/10.2767/00458

European Commission, Joint Research Centre, Redecker, C., Punie, Y. (2017). European framework for the digital competence of educators : DigCompEdu, (Y.Punie,editor) Publications Office. https://data.europa.eu/doi/10.2760/159770

Kučina Softić, S. (2020). Digitalne kompetencije nastavnika za primjenu e-učenja u visokom obrazovanju (Disertacija). Zagreb: Sveučilište u Zagrebu, Filozofski fakultet. Preuzeto s https://urn.nsk.hr/urn:nbn:hr:131:543198

Use of Artificial Intelligence in Light of AI Literacy and AI Anxiety Among Hungarian Higher Education Students – A Pilot Study

László Horváth[1]

[1] Institute of Education, ELTE Eötvös Loránd University, Budapest, Hungary; horvath.laszlo@ppk.elte.hu

Correspondence: László Horváth: horvath.laszlo@ppk.elte.hu

Abstract:

Artificial intelligence (AI) is rapidly spreading in different sectors of society, and higher education is no exception. The potential of AI in higher education (e.g. personalized learning, automate tasks, data analysis etc.) is not without its risks (Chen et al., 2020). The widespread adoption of AI in higher education raises questions about its impact on student learning, the potential for algorithmic bias, and ethical concerns surrounding its use (Zawacki-Richter et al. 2019). To fully understand the complex dynamics at play, this research aims to understand the current landscape of AI adoption among Hungarian university students. This study focuses on validating established instruments for measuring AI literacy (Hornberger et al., 2022) and AI anxiety (Li & Huang, 2020) in a Hungarian university student sample. along with a custom-developed section to understand patterns of AI usage within this specific population. In our research, we would like to explore the connection between students' AI literacy, AI anxiety and the use of AI solutions. Furthermore, we would like to explore the main purposes and motivations behind their use of AI, including their perceptions regarding ethical use.

The data gathering is ongoing, but preliminary results are based on 79 respondents (83,3% are female) who are representing various disciplines (e.g. agriculture: 20.8%; humanities: 19.4%; economic sciences: 22.2%), mostly from BA/BSc programmes (69%), full-time studies (77.1%). Around 1/3 of respondents had some preliminary training or qualifications in the field of computer science. After closing the data-gathering process, we will assess the reliability of our scales and use confirmatory factor analysis to establish the factor structure from previous research.

According to the preliminary results, respondents haven't used AI solutions for creating programme code, generating feedback on their own or others' work, creating transcriptions of audio or checking AI-generated content or plagiarism. The most prominent uses regarding studies are information and idea gathering for assignments or presentations, supporting their learning by using AI to explain difficult concepts or outright creating longer texts. Use outside of studies (e.g. work, hobby) include translation (e.g. deepl.com) and language learning (e.g. Duolingo). The main reason to use AI is to spare time (M=3.94 on a scale of 1-5). On a scale of 0-100 respondents rated how ethical they perceive the way their classmates use AI. The average (M=63.97) raises concerns regarding academic misconduct. Regarding AI literacy we used a multiple-choice test with 10 items. On average, respondents achieved 4 correct answers (SD=1.78) which can be considered low. Finally, respondents voiced their concerns and anxieties regarding AI, especially highlighting issues of algorithmic bias, loss of jobs, and concerns about data privacy. Overall, the correlation between respondents' AI literacy and their level of AI anxiety is not significant (p=.32), while the connection between the level of AI anxiety and the perceived ethical use of AI by classmates shows a medium negative correlation (p=.026; r=-0.365).

Further analysis and interpretation of the results is necessary to be able to fully answer our research questions.

Keywords: artificial intelligence, AI literacy, AI anxiety, higher education

What is required to help foster nestedness and integration in the complex digital learning ecosystem?

References

Chen, L., Chen, P., & Lin, Z. (2020). Artificial intelligence in education: A review. *IEEE Access: Practical Innovations, Open Solutions, 8,* 75264–75278. https://doi.org/10.1109/access.2020.2988510

Hornberger, M., Bewersdorff, A., & Nerdel, C. (2023). What do university students know about Artificial Intelligence? Development and validation of an AI literacy test. *Computers and Education: Artificial Intelligence, 5*(100165), 100165. https://doi.org/10.1016/j.caeai.2023.100165

Li, J., & Huang, J.-S. (2020). Dimensions of artificial intelligence anxiety based on the integrated fear acquisition theory. *Technology in Society, 63*(101410), 101410. https://doi.org/10.1016/j.techsoc.2020.101410

Zawacki-Richter, O., Marín, V. I., Bond, M., & Gouverneur, F. (2019). Systematic review of research on artificial intelligence applications in higher education – where are the educators? *International Journal of Educational Technology in Higher Education, 16*(1). https://doi.org/10.1186/s41239-019-0171-0

Development of a Design Guide for Micro-Credentials and Creation of a Learning Community: Design-Based Research

Amaia Arroyo Sagasta[1]; Jon Altuna Iraola[2]; Jon Aldazabal Basauri[3]; Ander Elkoro Ugarteburu[4]

[1 2 3 4] Mondragon University, Spain
[1] aarroyo@mondragon.edu
[2] jaltuna@mondragon.edu
[3] jaldazabal@mondragon.edu
[4] aelkoro@mondragon.edu

Correspondence: Amaia Arroyo Sagasta: aarroyo@mondragon.edu

Abstract:

The implementation of micro-credentials at Mondragon University (MU) began with the Erasmus+ MicroCredX project, which aimed to establish an institutional strategy for short-term education and facilitate its exchange between universities in the consortium. The project was named 'Micro-Credentials Exchange' (MicroCredX, 2021). DHBW Heilbronn and DHBW Heidenheim, along with Digital Learning Europe (EDEN), Knowledge Innovation Center (KIC), Tampere University of Applied Sciences, FH Joanneum, Universitat Oberta de Catalunya (UOC), and Mondragon University (MU). In the ever-changing landscape of higher education and the evolving world of work, it is crucial for academic institutions to align the development of micro-credentials with their institutional strategic plan and the demands of the labour market (Shapiro, Andersen & Nedergaard, 2021). The MicroCredX project prioritised the development of an institutional strategy. At MU, the strategy was developed not only at the macro level. Actions were taken to develop the strategy at the micro and meso levels. These actions focused on creating a design guide for micro-credentials.

At the micro level, the purpose of this manual is to provide a clear foundation for professionals involved in micro-credential design. The guide was developed by individuals with diverse profiles, led by someone with a technopedagogical background and a focus on educational design. The following are the key points covered in the design guide:

- Introduction: brief definition of micro-credentials and typologies.
- Organisation and structure: macro structure (objective, learning outcomes...) and micro structure didactic sequencing.
- Digital certificate: brief explanation.
- Types: massive open online course (MOOC), hybrid online, face-to-face, external practices, laboratory practices or recognition of work experience.
- Technopedagogical criteria (Arroyo Sagasta, 2023): characteristics of the digital environment to support the learning experience.
- Linguistic criteria: quality assurance aspects.
- Accessibility criteria: didactic and technical aspects related to Universal Design for Learning (UDL).
- Treatment of gender: the importance of ensuring a gender perspective.
- Platforms: possibilities and barriers of Moodle and EdX.
- Quality: Internal Quality Assurance Systems (IQAS) of faculties and European criteria and guidelines set out in the European Quality Assurance Framework for Higher Education (2015).
- Micro-credentials step-by-step: checklist for design.

What is required to help foster nestedness and integration in the complex digital learning ecosystem?

A design-based research (DBR) methodology (Reimann, 2013) was used at the meso level with a twofold objective: to test the points developed in the guide and to involve the community in the micro-credentials strategy. Two sessions were held with an average of 40 participants from all MU faculties. During the first session, the design guide was presented, and feedback was collected on areas for improvement. After revising the guide based on the feedback received, a second participatory session was held to compare the design process with the guide.

The design process was collaborative, involving end users of the manual in the improvements of the guide. This resulted in a useful product that was adapted to the needs of the community. Additionally, promoting community participation in the design of micro-credentials strengthened ownership of the strategy. Therefore, it can be concluded that this project resulted in the development of a specific framework and a participatory guide for the design of micro-credentials, as well as the creation of a community of practice to share experiences and promote the growth of micro-credentials in MU.

Keywords: micro-credentials, strategy, learning design, design-based research, community of practice.

References

Arroyo Sagasta, A. (2023). *Teknopedagogia praktikoa. Teknologia digitalak hezkuntzan integratzeko ereduak eta diseinu didaktiko digitala*. UEU. Bilbo.

European Association for Quality Assurance in Higher Education. (2015). Standards and Guidelines for Quality Assurance in the European Higher Education Area (ESG). Recuperado de: https://www.enqa.eu/wp-content/uploads/2015/11/ESG_2015.pdf

Reimann, P. (2013). Design-based research—Designing as research. In R. Luckin, S. Puntambekar, P. Goodyear, B.L. Grabowski, J. Underwood, & N. Winters (Eds.), *Handbook of Design in Educational Technology* (pp. 44-52). Routledge. https://doi.org/10.4324/9780203075227

Shapiro, H., Andersen, T. & Nedergaard, K. (2021). *European approach to micro-credentials: output of the micro-credentials higher education consultation group: final report*. Publications Office of the European Union. https://data.europa.eu/doi/10.2766/30863

Integrated Course Projects: Applying Academic Knowledge in Real-life Challenges in Teacher Education

Mart Laanpere[1], Hans Põldoja[2]

[1] Tallinn University, Estonia; mart.laanpere@tlu.ee
[2] Tallinn University, Estonia; hans@tlu.ee

Correspondence: Mart Laanpere: mart.laanpere@tlu.ee

Abstract:

A generally positive trend towards more evidence- and research-based teacher education focus could often result with increasing the gap between theory and practice of teaching (Sjølie, 2014). Furthermore, the theory-driven approach might decrease coherence of teacher education and increase disconnection between various sub-domains of disciplinary knowledge (Liliedahl et al, 2020). To address these issues, we designed the final course project jointly for three different courses, expecting the teacher education students to integrate the newly acquired knowledge from three different courses in a single project that they continue working on over the period of two semesters. This approach combines the ideas and practices of multidisciplinary teaching (Doyle & Bozzone, 2018), Project-Based Learning and service education. While multidisciplinary teaching and Project-Based Learning are quite well-known and widely used approaches in teacher education, the service education has been more known in the circles of religious education. In our teacher education context, we interpret service education in line with Bringle et al (2006) as "*a credit-bearing learning activity in which students participate in an organised service activity that addresses the identified needs of a community*". Every year we identify another common topic on which a specific target group is lacking some learning, training or guidance materials and our masters' students are expected to provide a solution to this need by integrating their knowledge from two courses: Learning Environments and Instructional Design. These courses are taught by different lecturers, using quite contrasting approaches. While the Learning Environments course is focusing on research-informed exploration of various instructional technologies, platforms and tools, Instructional Design course follows one specific theoretical model to address all stages of the design process. The third course, Digital Learning Resources is taught in the next semester, and it engages the students in hands-on activities of developing various types of resources (interactive videos, e-tests, presentations, adaptive learning paths). For the last five years, the students did not have to create a separate coursework for these three courses, instead they were working with the same team on the same collaborative project that integrated the knowledge and skills from three domains.

In 2021, the common topic for student projects was digital competence of elderly people. In 2022, the students were radically updating and redesigning an outdated e-textbook for 10th grade on data literacy. This academic year, we assigned all informatics teacher education students to design, prototype and develop a set of learning resources on Artificial Intelligence, as it is so recent topic in education and there are no relevant learning resources available in the community of Estonian school teachers and their students.

This paper reports on action report exercise that was carried out during 2023 autumn semester with a group of 38 informatics teacher education students. We describe the formation of groups, selection of topics and target groups, methods of integrating and assessing the knowledge from three different domains in the collaboration process as well as in the final product. We describe the benefits and challenges of replacing the separate course work with an integrated service-learning project.

What is required to help foster nestedness and integration in the complex digital learning ecosystem?

Keywords: Project-based learning, multidisciplinary learning, coherence, teacher education, service learning

References

Bringle, R.G., Hatcher, J.A., & McIntosh, R. (2006). Analyzing Morton's Typology of Service Paradigms and Integrity. *Michigan Journal of Community Service-Learning, 13*, 5-15.

Doyle, M., & Bozzone, D. (2018). 'Multidisciplinary Teaching Providing Undergraduates with the Skills to integrate knowledge and tackle "Big" questions. *The Journal of the Center for Interdisciplinary Teaching & Learning*, vol. 7, no. 1, pp. 12-17.

Lilliedahl, J., Wikman, T., Hansén, S.-E. (2020). Coherence within Teacher Education: Swedish Lessons. In *International Perspectives on Knowledge Integration: Theory, Research, and Good Practice in Pre-service Teacher and Higher Education* (pp. 291–312). https://doi.org/10.1163/9789004429499_013

Sjølie, E. (2014). The role of theory in teacher education: reconsidered from a student teacher perspective. *Journal of Curriculum Studies*, 46(6), 729–750. https://doi.org/10.1080/00220272.2013.871754

Navigating the Digital Frontier: Post-Digital Literacy and Its Implications for Language Education

Elke Höfler[1]

[1] University of Graz, Austria; elke.hoefler@uni-graz.at

Correspondence: Elke Höfler: elke.hoefler@uni-graz.at

Abstract:

The term 'post-digital' is used to describe an era or condition where digital technologies are deeply embedded in everyday life to the extent that the distinction between digital and non-digital becomes less relevant. This represents a shift from viewing digital and physical worlds as separate entities to understanding them as integrated and interdependent. In the context of post-digitality, digital technologies are so pervasive and indispensable that they are taken for granted. The focus shifts to how they are intertwined with social, cultural, and material practices (Cramer 2014).

Post-digital literacy is a critical concept that has significant implications for the educational system. With the increasing integration of digital technologies in education, it is essential to understand the nuances of post-digital literacy and its impact on teaching and learning (languages) (Council of Europe 2020). Post-digital literacy refers to the ability to navigate and make sense of the complex and interconnected digital and physical world we live in today (Knox, 2019). It goes beyond traditional literacy skills and encompasses the ability to critically evaluate digital technologies, to understand their impact on society, and to use them effectively and ethically (Siemens 2005; Döbeli Honegger 2016).

In this talk focusing on post-digital literacy and language learning, ten key implications will be explored. These implications encompass a shift in pedagogical approaches to incorporate digital technologies meaningfully (Hofer & Grandgenett 2012; Koehler & Mishra 2009; Martin 2015), a redefinition of the teacher's role as a facilitator of learning (Barrot 2021; Codreanu & Combe 2020), the need for innovative assessment methods that measure real-world application of knowledge (Ollivier 2018), a curriculum redesign to integrate digital literacy seamlessly Bundesministerium für Bildung, Wissenschaft und Forshcung 2024), the creation of adaptable learning environments that foster collaboration and critical thinking (Lamb et al. 2022), the transformation of students into active participants in the learning process (Weich & Macgilchrist 2023), an awareness of the societal impact of technology integration (Couldry & Hepp 2023), an emphasis on ethical considerations in using digital tools (Caws et al. 2021; Ollivier 2018; Ollivier 2021), a broader view of education's role in preparing students for a complex world, and a focus on sustainability in utilizing digital technologies (Blessiger et al. 2023).

By addressing these implications, educators can enhance language learning experiences, equip students with essential post-digital literacy skills, and prepare them to thrive in a digitally interconnected society.

Keywords: Post-digital literacy, language education, language learning, language teaching.

References

Barrot, J. S. (2021). Social media as a language learning environment: A systematic review of the literature (2008-2019). *Computer Assisted Language Learning*. https://doi.org/10.1080/09588221.2021.1883673.

What is required to help foster nestedness and integration in the complex digital learning ecosystem?

Blessiger, P., Singh, A., Raimi, L., & Patnaik, S. (2023). Higher education for sustainability in a post-digital world. University World News. https://www.universityworldnews.com/post.php?story=20230325073852586.

Bundesministerium für Bildung, Wissenschaft und Forschung (2024). *Grundsatzerlass Medienbildung, Aktualisierung, Information der Schulen*, https://rundschreiben.bmbwf.gv.at/rundschreiben/?id=1308#01.

Caws, C., Hamel, M.-J., & Jeanneau, C., & Ollivier, C. (2021). Formation en langues et littératie numérique en contextes ouverts – Une approche socio-interactionnelle. *Editions des archives contemporaines*. https://doi.org/10.17184/eac.9782813003911.

Codreanu, T., & Combe, C. (2020). Vlogs, video publishing, and informal language learning. In M. Dressman & R. W. Stadler (Eds.), *The Handbook of Informal Language Learning* (pp. 153-168). Wiley Blackwell.

Council of Europe. (2020). *Common European Framework of Reference for Languages: Learning, teaching, assessment – Companion volume*. Strasbourg: Council of Europe Publishing.

Couldry, N., & Hepp, A. (2023). Die mediale Konstruktion der Wirklichkeit. In N. Couldry & A. Hepp (Eds.), *Die Konstruktion der Wirklichkeit: Eine Theorie der Mediatisierung und Datafizierung* (pp. 21-45). Springer.

Cramer, F. (2014). What is 'Post-digital'? In Post-Digital Research (pp. 12-26). Meson Press.

Döbeli Honegger, B. (2016). *Mehr als 0 und 1. Schule in einer digitalisierten Welt*. hep.

Hofer, M., & Grandgenett, N. (2012). TPACK development in teacher education. *Journal of Research on Technology in* Education, 45(1), 83–106. https://doi.org/10.1080/15391523.2012.10782598.

Koehler, M. J., & Mishra, P. (2009). What is Technological Pedagogical Content Knowledge (TPACK)? *Contemporary Issues in Technology and Teacher Education, 9*(1), 60-70.

Knox, J. (2019). What does the 'Postdigital' mean for education? Three critical perspectives on the digital, with implications for educational research and practice. *Postdigital Science and Education, 1*(3), 357-370.

Lamb J., Carvalho L., Gallagher M., & Knox J. (2022). The Postdigital Learning Spaces of Higher Education. *Postdigit Sci Educ.4*(1):1–12. https://doi.org./10.1007/s42438-021-00279-9.

Martin, B. (2015). Successful implementation of TPACK in teacher preparation programs. *International Journal on Integrating Technology in Education, 4*(1), 17-26. https://doi.org/10.5121/ijite.2015.4102.

Ollivier, C. (2018). *Towards a socio-interactional approach to foster autonomy in language learners and users. E-lang project 'Digital literacy for the teaching and learning of language'*. European Centre for Modern Languages.

Ollivier, C. (2021). e-lang citoyen: Un cadre didactique et des fiches de tâches pour l'apprenant-citoyen usager des langues et du numérique. *Courriel européen des langues, 45*, 6–7. https://www.france-education-international.fr/document/cel-juin2021.

Siemens, G. (2005). Connectivism: A learning theory for the digital age. *International Journal of Instructional Technology and Distance Learning, 2*(1), 3-10.

Weich, A., & Macgilchrist, F. (Eds.) (2023). *Postdigital Participation in Education How Contemporary Media Constellations Shape Participation*. Palgrave MacMillan.

Embracing Change: The Journey of Digital Transformation at the National University of Maldives

Marcelo Maina[1], Nati Cabrera[2], Lourdes Guàrdia[3], Albert Sangrà[4]

[1 2 3 4] Faculty of Psychology and Education Sciences , Universitat Oberta de Catalunya, Spain
[1] mmaina@uoc.edu
[2] ncabrera@uoc.edu
[3] lguardia, asangra@uoc.edu
[4] asangra@uoc.edu

Correspondence: Marcelo Maina: mmaina@uoc.edu

Abstract:

Digital Transformation (DT) poses a significant challenge in the realm of higher education. This paper interprets DT as an ongoing process necessitating universities to foster continuous modifications in their culture, workforce, and technology (Bygstad, Øvrelid, Ludvigsen et al., 2022). The objective is to develop models and strategies that are adaptable to the evolving needs of education (JISC, 2023).

The paper discusses various aspects such as organizational changes to facilitate knowledge creation, innovation, management, and utilization; the imperative for a cultural shift within the organization, complemented by suitable communication and training strategies; the necessity for robust technological infrastructure to meet the technological challenges; and the critical need for clear leadership that steers the institution and its people towards digital literacy and maturity (Martin & Xie, 2022). We present the DT journey undertaken by the National University of Maldives, primarily through the hybridization of its educational model, as part of a Capacity Building Erasmus+ project.

The process began with a comprehensive institutional and situational diagnostic assessment to identify the key elements that necessitated evolution and transformation for a successful digital overhaul. This was followed by simultaneous discussions at the decision-making level, aimed at fostering a shared understanding of the implementation of hybrid learning. This included the formulation of a policy, a clear roadmap, and actionable steps. The institution then concentrated on leveraging the skills and competencies of key stakeholders, which was integral to the definition and adoption of an approach deeply rooted within the institution. Our presentation will delve into the co-design process and the implementation of a comprehensive training program tailored for academic and senior-level staff.

We will conclude our presentation by highlighting the key outcomes and the transformative impact of the project. The primary results encompass the development of a novel educational model steering towards a bi-modal university, the restructuring of crucial organizational units to align with the requirements of the new model, and the technological upgrades implemented following these new demands.

The successful implementation of the project has had impacts on various levels. At the organizational level, it has reinforced the central role of the Center for Educational Technology and Excellence in providing training and support to teachers, increased the digitalization of the library, and adapted the quality assurance framework to accommodate new digital teaching modes. On the professional development front, a hands-on, modular training program has been adopted, focusing on hybrid course design and digital transformation (DT) adoption. The pilot program trained seven senior-level staff members (decision-makers) in leadership roles that enable digital transformation, and 44 teachers in redesigning their courses for hybrid learning. Lastly, on the technology level, the

What is required to help foster nestedness and integration in the complex digital learning ecosystem?

institutional Moodle platform has been updated and consolidated, an e-facilitation room for online remote teaching has been set up, and an e-studio for video lectures and narrated presentations has been established.

The project has laid the groundwork for an ongoing digital transformation process, steered by the roadmap and bolstered by an agreed-upon policy. Indeed, the initiated process possesses the capability to adapt to upcoming shifts in context, needs, and emerging opportunities. This adaptability is a pivotal asset of the digital transformation journey, enabling the institution to maintain its relevance and responsiveness in a swiftly changing digital environment. It's not merely about the integration of new technologies, but also about nurturing a culture of continuous learning and adaptation.

Keywords: digital transformation, blended learning, digital leadership, teacher development, higher education, distributed leadership

References

JISC (2023). Framework for digital transformation in higher education. https://shorturl.at/bBE59

Bygstad, B., Øvrelid, E., Ludvigsen, S., & Dæhlen, M. (2022). From dual digitalization to digital learning space: Exploring the digital transformation of higher education. *Computers & Education, 182*, 104463. https://doi.org/10.1016/j.compedu.2022.104463

Martin, F. & Xie, K. (2022, September 27). Digital Transformation in Higher Education: 7 Areas for Enhancing Digital Learning. *Educause Review*. https://shorturl.at/gpZ15

Fostering Learning of "GenAI-Augmented Designers" for Enhancing Instructional Technologies

Nohar Raz Fogel[1], Dan Kohen-Vacs[1]

[1] Faculty of Instructional Technologies, Holon Institute of Technology (HIT), Israel; nohar@hit.ac.il
[2] Faculty of Instructional Technologies, Holon Institute of Technology (HIT), Israel; mrkohen@hit.ac.il

Correspondence: Nohar Raz Fogel, nohar@hit.ac.il

Abstract:

This paper presents recent advancements integrated into mandatory undergraduate courses focused on User Experience (UX) and User Interface (UI) studies at the Faculty of Instructional Technologies, Holon Institute of Technology in Israel. Renowned for pioneering efforts in meeting the demand for skilled professionals in advanced learning technologies, the faculty comprises three interconnected branches of studies. The branches target learning and training, technological development, and design. The synergy between these branches is crucial for cultivating excellence in learning and development practitioners. The faculty, acknowledging significant global strides in Artificial Intelligence (AI) and Generative AI (GenAI), addresses these developments across its branches of study (Kurtz et al, 2023). Specifically, this paper explores transformations in design-focused courses, elucidating changes resulting from GenAI integration into the undergraduate program's core components. The curricula now encourage Project-Based collaboration among students, leveraging GenAI to enhance creativity and critique (Shi et al., 2023). Furthermore, a methodology emphasizing requirement discovery and stakeholder detection optimizes concepts into vibrant artifacts tailored to realistic settings (Forsgren & Schröder, 2023). Illustrated in Figure 1, the workflow across design branch courses emphasizes collaborative Project-Based modes enriched by GenAI, reflecting the evolution and innovation within the instructional landscape.

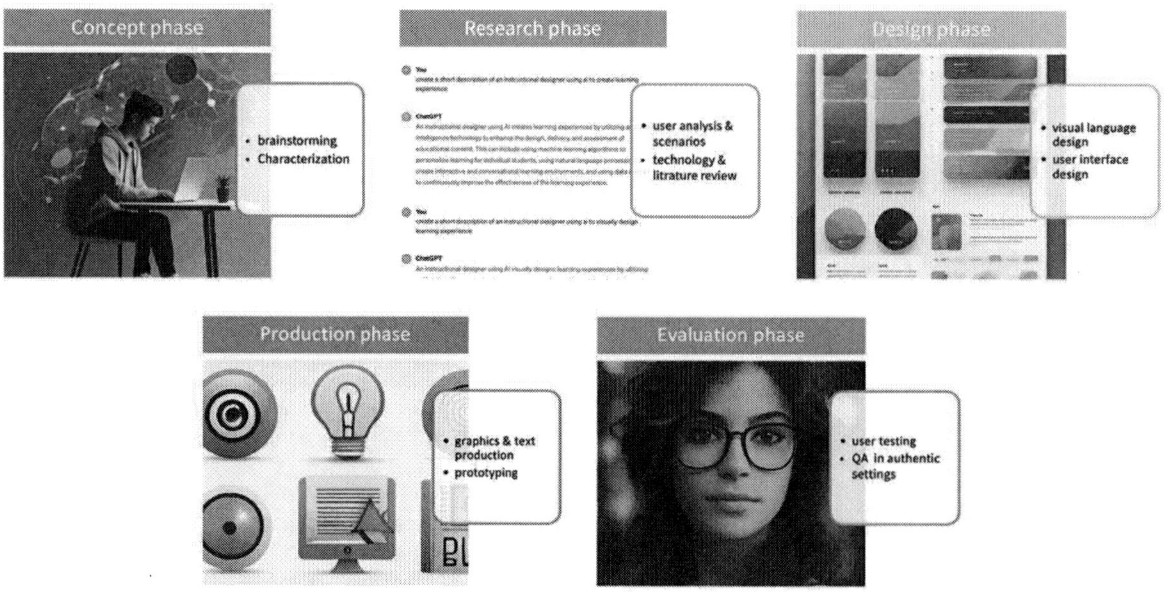

Figure 1. Phases of a workflow for design courses exercised with GenAI-Augmented practices

As illustrated the workflow includes brainstorming and research supported by AI prompting used for consultation purposes followed by design and production exercised with GenAI tools capable to offer facilitation of the design process. The workflow commences with brainstorming targeting the graphical concept followed by a research phase enabling students to support their visual concepts by previous ones used as exemplars. Next, students shift to the actual design followed to its mature to a production state. Finally, students conduct an evaluation occasionally exercised in a peer assessment mode. In some cases, the workflow is iteratively as students are required to refine and further mature their outcomes. Subsequently, GenAI supports students in creating a visual language that is coherent, efficient, and appealing and effectively serves educational purposes. Furthermore, GenAI is employed by students to translate their visual language seamlessly into effective UIs. In subsequent stages, GenAI is instrumental in achieving optimized integration within the technological solutions developed by students. While working on using GenAI, students are frequently tasked with employing GenAI in prompt writing activities, which we consider alternative forms of representation catering to various desired outcomes, including visual language aligned with the desired design styling. Our preliminary insights suggest that educational activities involving GenAI prompt writing tasks significantly enhance students' skills and knowledge in design-related domains. We underscore this approach as a valuable contribution to a community of educators seeking innovative ways to integrate GenAI-augmented design instruction for educational purposes.

Keywords: Artificial Intelligence (AI), Generative AI (GenAI), Instructional Technologies, Design Courses, User Experience(UX), User Interface (UI)

References

Forsgren, J., & Schröder, H. (2023). Can AI perform the work of human designers?: A qualitative study on the impact of AI on digital design professions.

Kurtz, G., Amzalag, M., Barak-Medina, E., Gal, E., Kohen-Vacs, D., Shaked, N., Zailer, G., & Zaguri, Y. (2023). *Higher education and generative ai (genai) in israel: opportunities, challenges and recommendations*. https://facultyprojects.telem-hit.net/HigherEducationGenAI/En/

Shi, J., Jain, R., Doh, H., Suzuki, R., & Ramani, K. (2023). An HCI-Centric Survey and Taxonomy of Human-Generative-AI Interactions. *arXiv preprint arXiv:2310.07127*.conditions. *Research & Practice in Technology Enhanced Learning*, 18.

Evaluating Video-Enhanced Learning in Higher Education: A Case Study Approach

Yanay Zaguri[1], Gila Kurtz[2], Noa Felman Weiner[3], Ariel Berliner[4]

[1 2 3 4] Holon Institute of Technology (HIT), Israel
[1] yanayz@hit.ac.il
[2] gilaku@hit.ac.il
[3] noafelman@gmail.com
[4] ariel.berliner@gmail.com

Correspondence: Gila Kurtz: Gilaku@hit.ac.il

Abstract:

Videos have long been a staple in educational technology, yet the advent of the "Crash Course" format marks a relatively recent innovation. These videos offer concise lessons through dynamic audio-visual presentations, aiming to quickly and in a fun way topics to learners. Currently, Crash Course stands as one of the most celebrated educational channels on the YouTube platform, boasting 15 million subscribers and nearly 1.9 billion views as of October 1, 2023 (Anderson, 2020; Marsh & Johnson, 2020), according to data from socialblade.com (https://socialblade.com/youtube/user/crashcourse). This study delves into the perceptions of undergraduate students at the Faculty of Instructional Technologies at HIT concerning the impact of ten Crash Course videos, specifically designed for their course, on their learning journey. The course, titled "Basics of Characterization and Development of Learning Units," aimed to equip students with fundamental skills in crafting targeted educational content. It was structured around ten approximately 15-minute videos, employing the flipped classroom model. In this model, students engage with the video content and complete comprehension questions before class, setting the stage for in-depth discussions and practical exercises during the lesson (Long et al., 2016). Data was gathered through an online questionnaire distributed across ten sessions throughout the course duration, querying students on their comfort with video-based learning, content internalization, and interest in utilizing similar video resources in future studies. Additional inquiries focused on their sentiments towards the learning process itself, with data collection spanning from February to May 2023. The findings reveal a generally positive reception towards the learning experience afforded by Crash Course videos, though they also highlight certain challenges that merit attention for future video development. The use of Crash Course videos is identified as a novel educational approach that fosters engagement, experiential learning, and an element of surprise, aligning with the technological era and evolving student demographics both within and beyond academia. Overall, the study suggests a favorable evaluation of student learning experiences, indicating a significant and distinctive educational process. However, it also points to the existence of "growing pains" within this emerging video-based educational domain. These findings spotlight the potential of Crash Course videos as a focal point for future educational endeavors, offering insights into the continued evolution and integration of such content into tailored learning experiences.

Link to course videos (Hebrew with subtitles
https://www.youtube.com/playlist?list=PLBKMVlYcUgyYh97iWkGTReGT3u5ZRV5Sv

Keywords: Video-Enhances Learning, Higher Education, Learning

What does learner-centered pedagogy look like in reimagining the digital classroom of the future?

References

Bannan-Ritland, B. (2003). The role of design in research: The integrative learning design framework. *Anderson, C. M. L. (2020). A Crash Course in Liberal Education: An Analysis of Civically Engaged Edutainment Videos (Doctoral dissertation, Clemson University).*

Long, T., Logan, J., Waugh, M. (2016). Students' Perceptions of the Value of Using Videos as a Pre-class Learning Experience in the Flipped Classroom. TechTrends, 60, 245–252. https://doi.org/10.1007/s11528-016-0045-4.

Marsh, A., & Johnson, B. (2020). Crash Course History of Science: Popular Science for General Education?. Isis, 111(3), 588-594

Hacking the Big Idea on Tackling Assessment in the Age of Artificial Intelligence (AI) at the Atlantic Technological University (ATU) with a Challenge-Based Learning Toolkit

Carina Ginty[1], Noreen Henry[2]

[1] Atlantic Technological University (ATU), Ireland; carina.ginty@atu.ie
[2] Atlantic Technological University (ATU), Ireland; noreen.henry@atu.ie

Correspondence: Carina Ginty: carina.ginty@atu.ie

Abstract:

This paper will share an assessment hackathon activation toolkit and a collection of assessment briefs derived from a one-day assessment hackathon in Atlantic Technological University (ATU) Ireland supported by N-TUTORR Transforming Learning programme. The hackathon involved 100+ colleagues and student leaders who undertook a challenge-based learning experience, to hack a big idea on tackling assessment in the age of Artificial Intelligence (AI).

A book of big ideas was produced as an output from this learning event. The publication provides insights and approaches for educators to re-imagine their assessment strategies and consider new teaching and learning approaches to support engagement with generative artificial intelligence technologies. Generative AI focuses on creating new and original content, chat responses, designs, or synthetic data. It is particularly valuable for problem-solving and promoting creativity. As the use of ChatGPT and Generative AI becomes increasingly popular, it is vital to understand its impact on higher education and identify strategies that may address potential risks (Wang, 2023).

N-TUTORR is a national programme of work designed to enable and leverage digital transformations to achieve sustainable and long-lasting change in the higher education student experience. The project is structured as 4 streams delivering 10+ work packages across 6 themes. The Student Empowerment Stream is transforming the student experience through learner empowerment. A standout work package, 'Building an academy for education for sustainability, leadership and employability' includes the development of a TU sector 'Student Digital Backpack' (MyDigitalBackpack.ie). the creation of a digital and sustainable futures student champions and a fellowship programme supporting student partnership.

Keywords: Assessment, Hackathon, Artificial Intelligence, Academic Integrity, Digital Learning, Student Partnership, Curriculum Design.

Summary

This session will share an assessment hackathon activation toolkit and a collection of assessment briefs derived from a one-day assessment hackathon in Atlantic Technological University (ATU) Ireland, where 100+ colleagues and student leaders undertook a challenge-based learning experience, to hack a big idea on tackling assessment in the age of Artificial Intelligence (AI).

A book of big ideas was produced as an output from this learning event. The publication provides insights and approaches for educators to re-imagine their assessment strategies and consider new teaching and learning approaches to support engagement with generative artificial intelligence technologies. Generative AI focuses on creating new and original content, chat responses, designs, or synthetic data. It is particularly valuable for problem-solving and promoting creativity. As the use of ChatGPT and Generative AI becomes increasingly popular, it is vital to understand its impact on higher education and identify strategies that may address potential risks (Wang, 2023).

The ATU Assessment Hackathon was coordinated by the N-TUTORR Project Office and the Teaching and Learning Centre teams. From the beginning, the aim of this learning event was to provide a first-hand experience of a Challenge Based Learning (CBL) hackathon for academic staff to support them in implementing a similar approach and to facilitate teams of educators on learning about designing authentic and sustainable assessments in the age of AI.

This paper presentation will present the hackathon methodology and resources plus a sample from the collection of nineteen assessment briefs generated from ATU education hackathon teams. The assessment briefs are grouped under four categories:

Category 1: Education Principles

Category 2: Guiding Principles

Category 3: Assessment Method

Category 4: Lesson Plan

Under the category of Education Principles, the briefs explore developing a culture of academic integrity and ethical practices in students and staff, plus project-based learning on AI.

The Guiding Principles category, covers sound advice on when and how it is appropriate for students to use AI in assessments and embracing the opportunities that AI offers to support the development of students' foundational knowledge, understanding, skills, critical engagement, and self-expression.

On Assessment Methods, a guiding framework is presented that supports best practice in use of AI in relation to Blooms Taxonomy, and designing rubrics that students can use to critically evaluate the quality of AI-generated assessments.

The Lesson Plan category, presents approaches on how to investigate language models that can support and develop on assessment in response to the current and future working environment, acknowledging the challenges of plagiarism. Further briefs explore rethinking and rewriting programme or module learning outcomes in the age of AI and creating an assessment and feedback method, which develops sustainable critical thinking skills. A complete listing of the assessment briefs is available on page 30-31 and includes the full team names.

This publication also provides the tools and resources used to drive the hackathon and the outputs delivered on the day. The ATU assessment hackathon toolkit includes: a Lego Serious Play activity; a Hackathon CBL Game Card; a Learning Outcomes & Activities Game Card; A to Z Assessments deck of cards; a Padlet collaborative board; and a suite of nineteen assessment briefs presented in a series of engaging information cards (see Chapter 4 in the ATU Assessment Hackathon Big Ideas book).

The learning event was supported by the ATU N-TUTORR Transforming Learning project. N-TUTORR is a national programme of work designed to enable and leverage digital transformations to achieve sustainable and long-lasting change in the higher education technological university sector in Ireland (see ATU.ie/NTUTORR).

The big book of assessment ideas is available to download at
https://issuu.com/atlantictechnologicaluniversity/docs/atu_assessment_hackathon_flipbook

References

Association of master trainers in the Lego serious play (2019), The Lego serious play method. Available from: https://seriousplay.training/lego-serious-play/

Flus, M. and Hurst, A. (2021), 'Design at hackathons: New opportunities for design research'. Design Science [Online], 7 (4). Available from: https://doi.org/10.1017/dsj.2021.1

What does learner-centered pedagogy look like in reimagining the digital classroom of the future?

Gilly Salmon (2020), Carpe Diem – A team based approach to learning design. Available from: https://www.gillysalmon.com/carpe-diem.html

Lego (2023), LSP Method. Available from https://www.lspmethod.com/lsp-method-book/

The Challenge Institute (2018), Challenge Based Learning in a Post-Truth World. Available from: https://www.challengebasedlearning.org/

N-TUTORR Transforming Learning at ATU (2024). Available from https://ATU.ie/NTUTORR

University College London (UCL) (2022), Hackathon | Our World in Crisis | UCL Engineering Welcome Festival 2022. Available from: https://www.ucl.ac.uk/engineering/events/2022/sep/hackathon-our- world-crisis-ucl-engineering-welcome-festival-2022

Wang, T. (2023). Navigating Generative AI (ChatGPT) in Higher Education: Opportunities and Challenges. In: Anutariya, C., Liu, D., Kinshuk, Tlili, A., Yang, J., Chang, M. (eds) Smart Learning for A Sustainable Society. ICSLE 2023. Lecture Notes in Educational Technology. Springer, Singapore. https://doi.org/10.1007/978-981-99-5961-7_28

Transforming the Student Experience through Learner Empowerment in the Technological University Sector in Ireland with N-TUTORR

Carina Ginty[1], Moira Maguire[2]

[1] Atlantic Technological University (ATU), Ireland; carina.ginty@atu.ie
[2] Dundlak Institute of Technology (DKIT), Ireland; moira.maguire@dkit.ie

Correspondence: Carina Ginty: carina.ginty@atu.ie

Abstract:

Ireland's technological sector, combining five new technological universities and two institutes of technology, have formed a partnership to develop and deliver on the National Technological University Transformation for Recovery and Resilience (NTUTORR) programme in 2023 and 2024. This programme, which is EU funded (40 million euro) and overseen by the Higher Education Authority (HEA) Ireland, utilises the national scale and scope of the technological university sector to deliver a best-practice suite of initiatives and opportunities for the learner, for staff development and supported by necessary enabling technologies.

N-TUTORR is a national programme of work designed to enable and leverage digital transformations to achieve sustainable and long-lasting change in the higher education student experience. The project is structured as 4 streams delivering 10+ work packages across 6 themes. The Student Empowerment Stream is transforming the student experience through learner empowerment. A standout work package, 'Building an academy for education for sustainability, leadership and employability' includes the development of a TU sector 'Student Digital Backpack' (MyDigitalBackpack.ie). the creation of a digital and sustainable futures student champions and a fellowship programme supporting student partnership.

Keywords: Digital Learning, Student Empowerment, Digital Skills, Sustainable Development Goals, Student Partnership.

Summary

Ireland's technological sector, combining five new technological universities and two institutes of technology, have formed a partnership to develop and deliver on the National Technological University Transformation for Recovery and Resilience (NTUTORR) programme in 2023 and 2024. This programme, which is EU funded (40 million euro) and overseen by the Higher Education Authority (HEA) Ireland, utilises the national scale and scope of the technological university sector to deliver a best-practice suite of initiatives and opportunities for the learner, for staff development and supported by necessary enabling technologies.

N-TUTORR is a national programme of work designed to enable and leverage digital transformations to achieve sustainable and long-lasting change in the higher education student experience. The project is structured as 4 streams delivering 10+ work packages across 6 themes. The Student Empowerment Stream is transforming the student experience through learner empowerment. A standout work package, 'Building an academy for education for sustainability, leadership and employability' includes the development of a TU sector 'Student Digital Backpack'

(MyDigitalBackpack.ie). the creation of a digital and sustainable futures student champions and a fellowship programme supporting student partnership.

Student-staff partnerships can be difficult to define, and there are numerous attempts to describe them in the literature. However, a commonly used definition is a collaborative, reciprocal process through which all participants have the opportunity to contribute equally, although not necessarily in the same ways, to curricular or pedagogical conceptualisation, decision making, implementation, investigation, or analysis (Cook-Sather et al., 2014, p.6-7 cited in Carroll, Ginty & Maguire 2023).

The Student Digital Backpack (mydigitalbackpack.ie), is a Virtual Learning Environment (VLE) platform for students across the Technological University (TU) sector (ATU, MTU, SETU, TUS, TU Dublin, DKIT and IADT) to complete short non-accredited courses and gain digital badges. The collaboratively developed and adapted courses provide students with additional skills to complement their existing programmes of study. They include: Digital Discovery; Sustainable Development Goals; Civic Engagement; Academic Integrity; and Gender Based Violence on Campus.

The Digital and Sustainable Futures Student Champion Programme offers 100 students across 5 universities and 2 institutes of technology the opportunity to learn and develop skills in one of the key N-TUTORR priority areas (Academic Integrity, Digital Transformation, Equality, Diversity & Inclusion, Education for Sustainability, Universal Design for Learning) in addition to developing leadership, collaboration and communication skills. The conference presentation will discuss:

- the open education principles and practices (Bali, 2022; Cronin, 2020) that have underpinned the development journey of the Student Digital Backpack to date and learnings from the pilot experience across the sector.
- the role of the student champions in developing the digital backpack.
- the student champion digital engagement initiatives that are transforming the learning and teaching experience at a local and national level.

The Partners in Innovation and Change Fellowship Programme includes 130 projects from across the technological university sector in Ireland awarded funding grants (5,000 euro per project) in 2023-24 to transform learning on programmes of study or through student services available on campus or off campus. Each fellowship project supports student empowerment and involves a collaboration between learners and staff, and focuses on enhancing the experience of students at technological universities across all of N-TUTORR's core themes. A catalogue of the 130 project proposals is available at https://issuu.com/atlantictechnologicaluniversity/docs/postcards_flipbook1. Student empowerment happens in HE when students are given the power to make decisions and drive change and innovation in their university. When Students are empowered to make decisions it will enhance the learning, teaching or assessment experience at the university. N-TUTORR funding provided the enabler for this opportunity and a vehicle to create a culture of student Empowerment across the Irish technological higher education sector.

Finally, this paper presentation will demonstrate how this work package is aligning with the sustainable development goals and empowering students to learn and develop skills focused on global priorities and challenges.

What does learner-centered pedagogy look like in reimagining the digital classroom of the future?

References

Bali, M. (2022). Outside-In: Entangled Openness as Subversion Influencing Emergent Change. OTESSA Journal, 1(1). DOI: https://doi.org/10.18357/otessaj.2022.1.1.25

Carroll. S., Ginty, C., Maguire, M. (2023): Transforming Learning Together: The Power of Student-staff Partnerships in Higher Education

Cronin, C. (2020). Open education: Walking a critical path. In D. Conrad & P. Prinsloo (Eds.), Open(ing) education: Theory and practice. Brill. doi: 10.1163/9789004422988_002

Ginty, C., Maguire, M., (2024) Empowering students and transforming learning in Ireland through a Digital and Sustainable Futures Student Champion Programme and a Student Digital Backpack. OER 2024 at MTU, Ireland https://www.oer2024.co.uk/. Learn more about Student Digital Backpack (SDB) at https://www.atu.ie/sites/default/files/2023-12/sdb-info-sheet-v3.pdf

Ginty, C., (2023), Choosing Sustainable Futures: The N-TUTORR Project and Student Empowerment in the Irish Technological University Sector in Ireland. Panel member and chaired by Prof. Gilly Salmon on Truly Transforming Higher Education. Beyond Tradition, Beyond Our Wildest Dreams. OEB Berlin 2023, https://oeb.global/conference.

Ginty, C., Maguire, M., (2023) Transforming the Student Experience in Ireland through Learner Empowerment with N-TUTORR. Gasta Proceedings from EDEN International Conference, DCU, Ireland. Available at https://www.youtube.com/watch?v=RhaW0cxVf7g

Maguire, M. & Ginty, C. (2023). Students as Partners and leaders in digital transformation: Student empowerment and the N-TUTORR project. Digital Education Conference 2023, December. SETU, Waterford.

The Importance of Online Social Interaction for Distance and Commuter Students

Susan Pawley[1], Cath Brown[2]

[1] School of Mathematics and Statistics, The Open University, UK; susan.pawley@open.ac.uk
[2] School of Mathematics and Statistics, The Open University, UK; cath.brown@open.ac.uk

Correspondence: Susan Pawley: susan.pawley@open.ac.uk

Abstract:

It is widely recognised that students can feel anxious when they start university; Bradshaw & Mann (2021) describe the high incidence of new undergraduates feeling terrified at the start of their studies, even if they appeared to be confident students compared to their peers. The feelings of trepidation, anxiety and distress can be more prevalent in distance learning and commuter students, who have reduced opportunities for interactions with their peers and report higher levels of perceived loneliness (Ali and Smith, 2015). Barber et al (2019) suggests that a growth mindset and resilience are particularly useful to the distance learner and that these can be developed through connecting with their peers in online communities. Social interaction and community on online courses can also be seen to improve the achievement of students (Kurucay and Innan, 2017) and help them to find their course more satisfying (Gunawarda and Zittle, 1997). Gaining a sense of community online can be perceived as harder than in the face-to-face environment; one issue can be a lack of social presence, which is needed for students to relate to each other and to intuitively feel that those they are interacting with are real human beings (Kear, 2010). With universities placing more reliance on "chatbots" and other AI methods to offer advice and help to students, can this cast doubt on the authenticity of asynchronous and text-based peer to peer interactions, which are the main forms of communication for distance learners?

In order to assess how important community is for our undergraduate distance learning students, we surveyed them about their feelings and experiences of community. Highlights include: the difference between desired and perceived community and where the principal focus of community lies. In an attempt to foster a meaningful online community between students we organised some online social activities. This aimed to enhance the student experience by facilitating direct and synchronous interaction which allowed them to form guaranteed human connections with their immediate peers. We planned events that were inclusive and accessible to all, and not dependent on academic knowledge or attainment. We also promoted social interaction by encouraging "social media" type posts on our "student buddies" forum, which is traditionally used for informal peer mentoring from students further through their degree, alongside introducing more opportunities for student interaction during some online tutorials.

Our presentation will focus on discussing key findings of the survey and how the students engage within these social activities.

Keywords: online, distance learners, interaction, social, community, belonging.

References

Ali, A., & Smith, D. (2015). Comparing social isolation effects on students attrition in online versus face-to-face courses in computer literacy. *Issues in Informing Science and Information Technology*, 12, 11-20.

What does learner-centered pedagogy look like in reimagining the digital classroom of the future?

Barber, W., Van Oostveen, R. & Childs, E. (2019). Situating resilience, grit and growth mindset as constructs of social presence in the fully online learning community model (FOLC). *European Conference on e-Learning. Kidmore End: Academic Conferences International Limited*

Bradshaw, N.-A., & Mann, T. (2021). Welcoming students to the mathematics community: obstacles to "belonging". *MSOR Connections*, 19(2).

Gunawardena, C., & Zittle, F. (1997) Social presence as a predictor of satisfaction within a computer-mediated conferencing environment. *American Journal of Distance Education*, 11(3), 8-26.

Kear, K. (2010). Social presence in online learning communities. *Proceedings of the 7th International Conference on Networked Learning*.

Kurucay, M., & Inan, F.A. (2017). Examining the effects of learner-learner interactions on satisfaction and learning in an online undergraduate course. *Computers and education*, 115, 20–37.

Support for Students Taking Remote Examinations

Cath Brown[1], Susan Pawley[2]

[1] School of Mathematics and Statistics, The Open University, UK; cath.brown@open.ac.uk
[2] School of Mathematics and Statistics, The Open University, UK; susan.pawley@open.ac.uk

Correspondence: Cath Brown: cath.brown@open.ac.uk

Abstract:

Academic misconduct in online examinations is a source of ongoing concern from regulatory bodies (QAA 2022, 2023); this originally related to contract cheating such as essay mills, but more recently the prime concern has been use of generative AI. Scripts produced by generative AI may be harder to detect due to it not producing a set output each time, and detection processes to date are not reliable (Weber-Wulff *et al* 2023). Noorbehbahani *et al's* (2022) review discusses the reasons for cheating, and highlights perceptions of lack of support, and unpreparedness as contributing factors. Offering greater support, appropriate practice and making expectations clear for students will not eliminate academic misconduct, but they potentially contribute to a reduction in cheating behaviours.

Additionally, students experiencing anxiety in online examination situations is an established issue. Common concerns for students taking online tests from home included internet or power disconnection and being disturbed by others at home. Arora *et al* (2021) highlight the anxiety about the unknown nature of online examinations. Whilst not all anxieties can be eliminated, reducing the unfamiliarity, giving opportunities to practice the technical side and timing are likely to reduce anxiety and hence partially address issues with underperformance.

To address some of these issues, we offered students the opportunity to sit a timed unseen remote mock examination which was fully marked, thus replicating at least partially the circumstances of the actual examination Students also receive specimen answers, short videos going through the questions and discussing exam technique, and the opportunity to attend drop-in sessions to discuss any queries.

In addition to improving student performance and reducing their likelihood of using AI, the hope is that students' improved awareness of examination demands will promote more effective preparation in future modules, leading to improved degree outcomes.

This talk presents the data, including the relationship between taking the mock examination and student performance, and the feedback collected from a questionnaire after the actual examination.

Keywords: remote examination, online examination, assessment, distance learners

References

Arora, S., Chaudhary, P. & Singh, R.K. (2021). Impact of coronavirus and online exam anxiety on self-efficacy: the moderating role of coping strategy, *Interactive technology and smart education*, 18(3), 475–492. Doi: https://doi.org/10.1108/ITSE-08-2020-0158.

Noorbehbahani, F., Mohammadi, A. & Aminazadeh, M. (2022). A systematic review of research on cheating in online exams from 2010 to 2021, *Education and information technologies*, 27(6), 8413–8460. Doi: https://doi.org/10.1007/s10639-022-10927-7.

Surahman, E. & Wang, T. (2022). Academic dishonesty and trustworthy assessment in online learning: A systematic literature review, *Journal of Computer Assisted Learning*, 38(6), 1535–1553. Doi: https://doi.org/10.1111/jcal.12708.

QAA. (2022). Contracting to cheat in Higher Education. Contracting to Cheat in Higher Education (qaa.ac.uk)

QAA (2023). Reconsidering assesment for the Chat GPT era. Reconsidering assessment for the Chat GPT era: QAA advice on developing sustainable assessment strategies

Weber-Wulff, D., Anohina-Naumeca, A., Bjelobaba, S. *et al.*(2023). Testing of detection tools for AI-generated text. *International Journal for Educational Integrity*, 19, 26. Doi: https://doi.org/10.1007/s40979-023-00146-z

Let Us Talk About Operations: Interactive Oral Assessment in the Era of Generative AI

Colum A. Foley [1], James Byrne[2]

[1] DCU Business School, Dublin City University, Ireland; colum.foley@dcu.ie
[2] DCU Business School, Dublin City University, Ireland; james.byrne@dcu.ie

Correspondence: colum.foley@dcu.ie

Abstract:

Recent advances in generative AI have turned the spotlight on assessment in academic activity. Interactive oral assessments can be used as an alternative to assessing written submissions, making it difficult for students to rely upon generative AI. This paper addresses the introduction of this method as a pilot in Dublin City University Business School in assignments for two modules as part of a fully online MSc suite. The assessments took the form of eight-minute assessment conversations between tutor and student in a predetermined scenario, building on the knowledge of these post-experience students to gain insights into how contemporary tools and techniques can be efficiently and effectively employed. The conversations were led by a series of prompts, seeking to capture the student's ability to critically assess and to orally express their analysis with clarity. Results indicate that the outcome was a success both as an assessment technique and a learner experience.

Keywords: Interactive oral assessment, Generative AI, Operations management

Introduction

Interactive oral assessments are a dynamic alternative to traditional written exams, providing a platform for students to articulate their understanding verbally. This method assesses not only the content knowledge but also communication skills, critical thinking, and the ability to respond to questions in real-time. The assessment takes the form of a conversation around the subject area where the student is presented with a scenario based around the programme and both the student and the examiner assume pre-determined roles to conduct the conversation. In DCU the IOA process is guided by a community of practice which meets to discuss and advise projects with colleagues on a weekly basis. This COP has guided the use of the process on a pilot basis this year on module MT5228 Operational Change Management.

Interactive oral assessments demonstrate potential to develop graduate attributes such as critical thinking, professional communication, and collaborative skills in students through authentic simulation of workplace scenarios (Tan et. al 2021). Interactive oral assessment has been introduced to two modules related to operations management in DCU Business School. Student feedback was captured through survey and semi-structured interview regarding the introduction of this form of assessment towards understanding the effectiveness of such an approach, and to aid with future improvements.
The study set out to gather student feedback on the introduction of interactive oral assessment on two masters' modules. This aims to direct the faculty towards informing future improvements. This is one of a few pilot assessments utilizing interactive oral assessment in the faculty. In using this method and gathering student feedback to assess its suitability in the operations management domain, the research will assist in designing assessments across the faculty going forward, particularly at a time when we have just launched a new MSc in Management (Operations and Supply Chain)

https://business.dcu.ie/course/msc-in-management-operations-and-supply-chain/ with Interactive Oral Assessment being planned as a component of at least two new modules ("Simulation for Decision Making" and "Sustainable Transport and Logistics").

This study is supported by members of the DCU Interactive Oral Community of Practice (CoP), and it is expected that the outputs of this study will provide an aid in informing the community of best practice in relation to interactive oral assessment in relation to the operations management domain.

A small group of DCU academics across all five faculties are using interactive oral assessments as a viable alternative to traditional assessments. They meet weekly as part of a community of practice (CoP). The CoP is led by TEU in collaboration with Griffith University. Griffith University has extensive experience, and a body of evidence-based research to show that interactive orals are an authentic assessment approach that effectively helps prepare students for employment, and when used as part of strategically designed integrated assessment, promotes academic integrity.

This short 2 min. video provides a quick introduction to the approach through the voices of both students and academics involved in the initiative.

A TEU Interactive Oral User Guide is also available to support academics wishing to use this approach.

An exciting enhancement to the DCU Interactive Oral CoP is a shared Interactive Oral CoP with Griffith University and Charles Sturt University in Australia. The first meeting was held on 24th November 2021, hosted by the TEU. At a two hour meeting over twenty academics (eight from DCU) presented vignettes of their use of interactive oral across all disciplines. This shared CoP will continue to meet twice a year to collaborate and share experience and research in this space.

Colleagues who may be interested in joining the IO Community of Practice, please contact Lily (lily.girme@dcu.ie) to be added to the CoP list.

Figure 1. Interactive Oral Assessment DCU Community of Practice

Hypothesis

The research has implications regarding assessing the pilot introduction of interactive oral assessment as a suitable assessment technique for assessment in modules relating to Operations Management, in the era of threats to academic integrity from generative artificial intelligence, as evidenced generally by Newell (2023).

- Research question: The pilot introduction of Interactive Oral Assessment in relation to Operations Management modules has been an effective approach in assessing students
- Null Hypothesis (H0): The pilot introduction of Interactive Oral Assessment in relation to Operations Management modules has not been an effective approach in assessing students

Methods

A mixed methods approach was utilised. A pre-developed questionnaire was disseminated to students who took part in the interactive oral assessment on the two operations management related modules, followed by semi-structured interviews with a random subset of this cohort. The survey took approximately 10 minutes to complete, and interviews lasted 15 minutes. The research questionnaire used was a tried and tested instrument used extensively in geographical locations where this method of assessment has been employed for many years, with

success and adopted in consultation with the DCU Teaching Enhancement Unit to elicit its effectiveness in this environment.
A research questionnaire previously employed successfully in DCU was used, with approval from the DCU Research Ethics Committee, see Ward et al, (2023). The purpose of conducting qualitative interviews was to drill down at a more granular level, to elicit how this application has examined student learning, and if it is robust. Interviewing students has been applied in the past effectively in relation to assessing techniques to support their studies, see Hratastinski and Aghaee (2012), and a similar approach was taken in this case.

Results

Among the findings were that students found that the assessment met the needs of the module.

Table 1. In your opinion did the interactive oral assessment meet the needs of the module(i.e. assess what was required as was stated in the module learning outcomes)

	Percentage	Count
Yes	100%	5
No	0	0

All students found the method appropriate.

Table 2. Rank how you felt the following supports were in helping you prepare for the Interactive Oral Assessment (5 Extremely Useful, 1 Not Useful)

	Not Useful 1	Slightly Useful 2	Moderately Useful 3	Very Useful 4	Extremely Useful 5
Rubric	0	0	2	3	0
Interactive Oral Exemplar	0	0	2	3	0
Class Discussion using Assessment Brief	0	0	1	4	0
Exemplar in conjunction with rubric in class with Lecturer	0	0	1	4	0

.

Supports were a help in preparing for the assessment. Students felt they were either very useful or moderately useful.

What does learner-centered pedagogy look like in reimagining the digital classroom of the future?

Table 3. What did you like most about the assessment on this module?

I thought it was a welcome change of assignment and the opportunity to develop a different skill set.
The Video Meeting
Face to face is interesting.

Students found the face-to-face nature of the assessment rewarding.

Themes that emerged from qualitative interviews included that this method of assessment was fair and equitable. Students felt it encouraged them to perform with integrity and refrain from plagiarism. It came across as a refreshing alternative to traditional assessments. They did feel however that too many topics were covered in the assessment.

Conclusions

Benefits of Interactive Oral Assessments

Enhanced Critical Thinking: Oral assessments require students to think on their feet, fostering critical thinking skills and counteract the possibility of plagiarism which has intensified with the advent of generative AI. In alignment with Vygotsky's social constructivist theory, learning is a social process and discussion plays a central role in cognitive development (Vygotsky, 1978).

Robust Assessment Method: In both programmes we found the examination method to be robust. It gave a fair, authentic reflection of the student's ability allowing for clarification in the event of misunderstanding.

Improved Communication Skills: Students developed the verbal communication skills that are crucial in most professions. Gulikers, Bastiaens, and Kirschner (2004) highlight the fact that authentic assessments, like oral exams, prepare students in a more realistic way for real-world tasks.

Immediate Feedback: Both examiners found that they could provide instant feedback, explaining errors to students enabling them to learn as they go . This supports Nicol and Macfarlane-Dick's (2006) principles of good feedback practice, which highlight the importance of timely and constructive feedback.

Challenges and Solutions

- Interactive oral assessments can be time consuming and subject to bias.
- To mitigate these issues, detailed rubrics and training for examiners can help ensure consistency and fairness (Race, 2001).
- We attempted to examine too many topics in the allocated time, this was not necessary as the process was sufficiently robust to narrow the range.
- Utilizing a detailed rubric was very effective in ensuring accuracy and equity

References

Black, P., & Wiliam, D. (1998). Assessment and classroom learning. Assessment in Education: principles, policy & practice, 5(1), 7-74.

Bloom, B. S. (1956). Taxonomy of Educational Objectives, Handbook I: Cognitive Domain. New York: David McKay Company. Inc., 1956. 207 pp.

Chin Pei Tan, Dora Howes, Rendell K. W. Tan & Karina M. Dancza (2022) Developing interactive oral assessments to foster graduate attributes in higher education, Assessment & Evaluation in Higher Education, 47:8, 1183-1199, DOI: 10.1080/02602938.2021.2020722

Dewey, J. (1930). Democracy and education: An introduction to the philosophy of education. New York: Macmillan.

Dewey, J. (1986, September). Experience and education. In The educational forum (Vol. 50, No. 3, pp. 241-252). Taylor & Francis Group.

Gulikers, J. T., Bastiaens, T. J., & Kirschner, P. A. (2004). A five-dimensional framework for authentic assessment. Educational technology research and development, 52(3), 67-86.

Hrastinski, S., Aghaee, N.M. How are campus students using social media to support their studies? An explorative interview study. Educ Inf Technol 17, 451–464 (2012). https://doi-org.dcu.idm.oclc.org/10.1007/s10639-011-9169-5

Jopp, R. (2020). A case study of a technology enhanced learning initiative that supports authentic assessment. Teaching in Higher Education, 25(8), 942-958.

Kolb, D. A. (2014). Experiential learning: Experience as the source of learning and development. FT press.

Lange, C., Costley, J., & Han, S. L. (2016). Informal cooperative learning in small groups: The effect of scaffolding on participation. Issues in Educational Research, 26(2), 260-279.

Newell, S. J. (2023). Employing the interactive oral to mitigate threats to academic integrity from ChatGPT. Scholarship of Teaching and Learning in Psychology. Advance online publication. https://doi.org/10.1037/stl0000371

Ní Bheoláin, R., Lowney, R. & O'Riordan, F. (2020). Students as partners in assessment (SaPiA): a literature scoping review.: Dublin City University. https://doi.org/10.5281/zenodo.4270579

Nicol, D. J., & Macfarlane-Dick, D. (2006). Formative assessment and self-regulated learning: A model and seven principles of good feedback practice. Studies in higher education, 31(2), 199-218.

Pearce, J. & Chiavaroli, N. (2020). 'Prompting Candidates in Oral Assessment Contexts: A Taxonomy and Guiding Principles', Journal of Medical Education and Curricular Development, Volume 7: 1-4, https://doi.org/10.1177/2382120520948881

Race, P. (2001). The lecturer's toolkit: a practical guide to learning, teaching & assessment. Psychology Press.

Rittel, H. W., & Webber, M. M. (1974). Wicked problems. Man-made. Futures, 26(1), 272-280

Rogers, Carl R. (1969)."Freedom to Learn." Charles Merrill,

Sotiriadou, P., Logan, D., Daly, A. & Guest, R. (2020) 'The role of authentic assessment to preserve academic integrity and promote skill development and employability', Studies in Higher Education, 45:11, 2132-2148, https://doi.org/10.1080/03075079.2019.1582015

Sotiriadou, P., Logan, D., Daly, A., & Guest, R. (2020). The role of authentic assessment to preserve academic integrity and promote skill development and employability. Studies in Higher Education, 45(11), 2132-2148.

Vygotsky, L. S., & Cole, M. (1978). Mind in society: Development of higher psychological processes. Harvard university press.

What does learner-centered pedagogy look like in reimagining the digital classroom of the future?

Ward, M., O'Riordan, F., Logan-Fleming, D., Cooke, D., Concannon-Gibney, T., , M. & Watkins, N. (2023) Interactive oral assessment case studies: An innovative, academically rigorous, authentic assessment approach, Innovations in Education and Teaching International, DOI: 10.1080/14703297.2023.2251967

Psychology 101 for AI: What Should be Personalized in Designing AI-Powered Learning Assistants?

Eran Barak-Medina[1]

[1] Faculty of Instructional Technologies, Holon Institute of Technology, Israel; eranba@hit.ac.il

Correspondence: Eran Barak-Medina; eranba@hit.ac.il

Abstract:

When Large Language Models (LLMs) will not be solely reactive and start being proactive, it might have a profound effect on learning. Proactive AI-powered learning assistants could support learners by making highly accurate personalized adjustments and interventions that will help learners gain skills and knowledge more efficiently. While human teachers and mentors have psychological and communication skills that allow them to adjust themselves to learners and personalize their approach, AI learning assistants will do so only if designed to.

So, what do developers of AI-powered learning assistants should consider if they want their product to be able to personalize the interaction between the system and the learner in a way that truly supports learners? Principles for achieving this could be drawn from the psychology of motivation and the psychology of learning. From the existing knowledge in the psychology of motivation, concepts such as the type of motivation that drives the learner best (external, introjected, identified, intrinsic) could be identified by the AI learning assistant to adjust the way it interacts with the learner. The psychology of learning could help pinpoint variables that can help the AI learning assistant characterize the learner's learning preferences and types of learning objects that are most effective to the learner (through text, video, dialogue, etc.). It can also study and help the learner reveal his learning habits profile, such as the optimal length of his learning sessions, times of day most suitable for learning, and more. By collecting the data from interacting with the learner, reflecting the data to the learner, and helping him by advising on learning goals, learning plan and schedule, and motivating the learner through personalized interventions, AI-powered learning assistants might revolutionize self-regulated and self-directed learning.

This speculative presentation tries to examine the possibilities that upcoming developments in AI and specifically LLMs could offer the field of learning and start the "groundwork" for harnessing the technological developments for learning purposes by drafting guidelines for designing the interaction between AI and learners.

Keywords: Generative Ai, Critical Thinking, Project-Based Learning, Collaborative Learning, Authentic Learning, Learning technologies

References

Agnes, Kukulska-Hulme., Helen, Lee. (2020). Intelligent assistants in language learning: an analysis of features and limitations.

Eleni, Zalavra., Kyparissia, Papanikolaou., Yannis, Dimitriadis., Cleo, Sgouropoulou. (2022). Personalising learning: towards a coherent learning design framework. doi: 10.1109/ICALT55010.2022.00030

Elizabeth, Lameier., Lauren, Reinerman-Jones., Michael, W., Boyce., Elizabeth, Biddle. (2017). Assessing Motivation to Individualize Reinforcement and Reinforcers for an Intelligent Tutor. doi: 10.1007/978-3-319-58625-0_12

Junhua, Xiao., Qingchun, Bai. (2022). iTutor: Promoting AI Guided Knowledge Interaction in Online Learning. doi: 10.1109/ISET55194.2022.00061

Luiz, Felippe, S., Rodrigues., Seiji, Isotani. (2023). When Personalized Gamification meets Computing Education: A Multidimensional Approach to Motivate Students to Learn. doi: 10.5753/ctd.2023.229916

Mascha-Lea, Fersch., Sigurd, Schacht., Betiel, Woldai., Charlotte, Kätzel., Sophie, Henne. (2022). Digital Learning Assistants in Higher Education Environments: A Qualitative Focus Group Study. doi: 10.22492/issn.2435-9467.2022.28

Watkins, R., & Barak-Medina, E. (2023, November 26). AI's Influence on Human Creative Agency. https://doi.org/10.31219/osf.io/md5ef

Using Advanced Learning Technologies to Boost Sustainability Education: The Role of AI-based Chatbots

Maximilian Bollow[1], Katharina Frosch[2], Angelina Grunz[3], Svenja Hädicke[4], Rabina Judge[5], Olga Levina[6]

[123456] Department of Business and Management, Brandenburg University of Applied Sciences, Germany
[1] maximilian.bollow@th-brandenburg.de
[2] frosch@th-brandenburg.de
[3] grunza@th-brandenburg.de
[4] haedicke@th-brandenburg.de
[7] judge@th-brandenburg.de
[6] levina@th-brandenburg.de

Correspondence: Katharina Frosch: katharina.frosch@th-brandenburg.de

Abstract:

In the face of the 2030 Agenda of the United Nations, the everchanging knowledge base of sustainability and the related learning become vital. This applies especially to the field of sustainable digitalization. The literature provides gaps in the combination of sustainable digitalization with learning, due to the rapid developments and innovations in this field.

AI-based Chatbots could be a solution to rapidly build knowledge in this fast-evolving field, as they are able to draw upon a large body of recent knowledge and allow personalized, individual learning. They are created to understand questions and respond to users via text, voice, or avatar in an interactive manner to facilitate learning (Al-Abdullatif, 2023). Thus, AI-based Chatbots could enhance student-centered e-learning, which has shown to be a valuable tool for sustainability literacy (Diamond & Irwin, 2013). Nonetheless, existing research does not yet provide sufficient evidence on what learning outcomes (e.g., knowledge acquisition) can be achieved with this AI-based approach to learning. Therefore, it is crucial for us to determine whether and how they can be effectively utilized for this purpose.

In this study, we examine the impact of AI-based Chatbots on learning outcomes in the context of sustainable digitalization, in comparison to conventional digital learning methods. We conduct a field experiment with a pre- and post-test assessing the respective level of knowledge and sustainability-related competencies among participants. The participants of the study (N=269) engage with different types of supported learning activities related to sustainable development. Participants are randomly assigned to one of four advanced learning technologies: a) AI-assisted personal tutoring (Chatbot), b) non-AI-based conversational learning and c) interactive video with embedded activities. Variations in learning outcomes depending on design characteristics of the learning activity will be measured using the Self-Perceived Action Competence for Sustainability Questionnaire (SPACS-Q) (Olsson et al., 2020) as well as as well as a set of questions to assess knowledge retention.

Results indicate that AI-based chatbots may be a viable method to enhance knowledge about practices in sustainable digitalization. However, sustainability action competencies, such as confidence in one's own influence on shaping a more sustainable future and the willingness to undertake concrete actions, which may require higher-order learning processes, are not positively affected by short learning activities with our AI-based chatbot. We found evidence that non-AI-based learning activities yield similar increases in building knowledge on sustainable digitalization but also significantly enhance sustainability action competencies related to potential behavioral changes.

What does learner-centered pedagogy look like in reimagining the digital classroom of the future?

Assuming that our results are generalizable to other learning topics, the evidence found in this study suggests that AI-based chatbots can contribute to addressing our most significant transformational challenges, all characterized by a rapidly evolving knowledge base. Further research is particularly needed with respect to the preferable design characteristics of digital learning activities (both AI-based and non-AI-based) to achieve optimal outcomes in building sustainability competencies.

Keywords: Generative AI-based Chatbots, Sustainable Digitalization, Learning Outcomes, Knowledge Acquisition, Digital Learning Methods, Field Experiment

---

References

Al-Abdullatif, A. M. (2023). Modeling students' perceptions of chatbots in learning: integrating technology acceptance with the value-based adoption model. *Education Sciences, 13*(11), 1151. :10.3390/educsci13111151

Diamond, S., & Irwin, B. (2013). Using e-learning for student sustainability literacy: framework and review. *International Journal of Sustainability in Higher Education*, *14*(4), 338-348. :10.1108/ijshe-09-2011-0060

Olsson, D., Gericke, N., Sass, W., & Pauw, J. B.-D. (2020). Self-perceived action competence for sustainability: the theoretical grounding and empirical validation of a novel research instrument. *Environmental Education Research, 26*(5), 742-760. :10.1080/13504622.2020.1736991

A Generative AI Scenario-Based Learning Intervention in Pre-Service Teacher Education

John Meegan[1], Keith Young[2]

[1]The Froebel Department of Primary and Early Childhood Education, Maynooth University, Ireland; john.meegan@mu.ie
[2] The Education Department, Maynooth University, Ireland; keith.young@mu.ie

Correspondence: John Meegan: john.meegan@mu.ie

Abstract:

Our research aims to design and evaluate the impact of a Generative AI scenario-based learning intervention on pre-service teachers' self-efficacy and AI literacy. This cross-departmental research aims to explore the impact on both primary and post-primary student teachers in Ireland. In essence this project seeks to determine if Generative AI can be used to generate appropriate Scenario Based Learning (SBL) vignettes and assist students in productively exploring them from multiple perspectives. Proactively engaging with the technology will also afford opportunities to explore how they work and limitations associated with them which could potentially simultaneously improve learners AI Literacy.

Research questions:

- How can a scenario-based learning generative AI chat intervention be designed to enhance the self-efficacy and AI literacy of pre-service teachers in an initial teacher education program?
- Does a Generative AI scenario-based learning intervention impact pre-service teachers' sense of self-efficacy?
- Does a Generative AI scenario-based learning intervention impact pre-service teachers' AI Literacy?

Methodology:

This project will adopt an explanatory sequential mixed methods approach (Cohen et al. 2017). This approach is characterized by two distinct phases of data collection with the first informing or interacting with the second (Cresswell & Plano Clark 2011). This will form part of a broader three phase approach to the project. In the context of this study the purpose of the explanatory sequential model is to provide participants with an opportunity to reflect on their experiences participating in the workshop while affording the researchers an opportunity to explore in greater detail the factors which may influence teachers' self-efficacy and AI Literacy.

In phase 1 (Mar 24) a workshop-based intervention will be developed that aims to engage participants in SBL augmented with the use of generative AI (Generative AI) to enhance self-efficacy. The design of this workshop will be informed by an examination of the literature in order to ensure that it encapsulates key elements relating to self-efficacy, SBL, and development of AI Literacy among participants.

Phase 2 (Mar – May 24) will involve the recruitment of participants, the implementation of the intervention alongside the first phase of data collection which will be quantitative in nature, involving pre-post surveys for participants. These will include both the shortened Teacher Self-Efficacy Scale (Klassen et al. 2009) and AI Literacy Scale (Wang et al. 2022).

Phase 3 (May – June 24) will be the qualitative phase of data collection wherein focus groups will be conducted with two groups of participants to help understand the impact of the intervention and offer some explanatory data to the impact measured by each the Teacher Self-Efficacy Scale and AI Literacy Scale in Phase 2. The development of Phase 3 research instruments will in part be informed by the findings from phase 2.

Keywords: Generative AI, AI literacy, Scenario-based learning, Self-efficacy, Initial teacher education

References

Cohen, L., Manion, L., & Morrison, K. (2017). Mixed Methods Research. In Cohen, L., Manion, L., & Morrison, K. (eds), *Research Methods in Education* (pp. 31-50). London, Routledge. https://doi.org/10.4324/9781315456539

Creswell, J. W., & Clark, V. L. P. (2017). *Designing and conducting mixed methods research*. Sage publications.

Klassen, R. M., Bong, M., Usher, E. L., Chong, W. H., Huan, V. S., Wong, I. Y., & Georgiou, T. (2009). Exploring the validity of a teachers' self-efficacy scale in five countries. In *Contemporary Educational Psychology*, 34(1), 67-76. https://doi.org/10.1016/j.cedpsych.2008.08.001

Wang, B., Rau, P. L. P., & Yuan, T. (2023). Measuring user competence in using artificial intelligence: validity and reliability of artificial intelligence literacy scale. In *Behaviour & Information Technology*, 42(9), 1324-1337. https://doi.org/10.1080/0144929X.2022.2072768

Accelerating the Professionalization of Delft University of Technology as a Lifelong Learning Provider: How Can AI Play a Role?

Sofia Dopper[1], Beatriz de los Arcos[2], Willem van Valkenburg[3]

[1 2 3] Extension School for Continuing Education, Delft University of Technology, The Netherlands
[1] s.m.dopper@tudelft.nl
[2] b.delosarcos@tudelft.nl
[3] W.F.vanValkenburg@tudelft.nl

Correspondence: Sofia Dopper: s.m.dopper@tudelft.nl

Abstract:

The Extension School for Continuous Education (ES) at Delft University of Technology celebrated its 10th anniversary in April 2024. Over the years, a portfolio of more than 250 open and online courses for professionals and lifelong learners has been built up. In 2023 the Executive Board established a Lifelong Learning strategy for the university (Taskforce Lifelong Learning, 2023). To implement this strategy, the Extension School for Continuous Education (ES) was successful in applying for funds from the Dutch government (LLO-Katalysator) towards the further professionalization of Delft University of Technology as a Lifelong Learning (LLL) provider.

Already recognized as a front-runner and thought-leader in online engineering education (Graham, 2018), this new remit will see the ES strive towards four main goals: embedding LLL in the primary tasks and processes of the university; strengthening demand-driven education for professionals with a greater alignment of our portfolio with societal challenges and the needs of lifelong learners; guaranteeing the quality of education through external accreditation; and streamlining the support and delivery of our services both to faculties and learners outside the university.

With the surge of interest in generative AI, it is mainly in the latter that we have envisaged a role for this type of tool. In this brief presentation we will share our plans and experiences to date in three pilot projects:

- The potential of AI to translate content into multiple languages, thus lowering communication barriers and improving accessibility
- The use of AI to refine course development processes, without compromising meaningful learner interaction and authentic learning experiences
- Implementing an AI-chatbot for the helpdesk with the aim of personalizing and professionalizing the customer experience of internal as well as external users.

Keywords: lifelong learning, AI, professionalization

What does learner-centered pedagogy look like in reimagining the digital classroom of the future?

References

Graham, R. (2018). *The Global State of the Art in Engineering Education*. School of Engineering, Massachusetts Institute of Technology (MIT). https://www.rhgraham.org/resources/Global-state-of-the-art-in-engineering-education---March-2018.pdf

Taskforce Lifelong Learning (2023). *Lifelong Learning Strategy TU Delft*. Internal report: unpublished.

Developing Multilingual Competence through Educational Technologies in Museums: Methodology of a Semi-Experimental study with Italian Secondary School Students

Maria Tolaini[1]

[1] Languages and Cultures Department, University of Genova, Italy; maria.tolaini@edu.unige.it

Correspondence: Maria Tolaini: maria.tolaini@edu.unige.it

Abstract:

To ensure the active participation of all citizens in society, the European Council identified eight key competences that every individual (European Council, 2018), regardless of their socio-economic status or physical or mental disabilities (European Council Conclusions, 2021), should be able to develop during the course of their lifetime. One of them is the multilingual competence, that ca be defined as "the ability to use different languages appropriately and effectively for communication" (European Council, 2018). Learning languages in an efficient and inclusive way is particularly crucial for final-year high school students, as the acquisition of this competence can significantly improve their future prospects, both in continuing their studies and entering the job market. However, a survey conducted on a European level highlighted that only 42% of secondary school students reach an intermediate level (B1-B2) in their first foreign language, typically English (European Commission: Europeans and their Language, 2012). One possible strategy to improve this condition is to explore the effectiveness of informal learning environments, such as museums, and integrate digital learning tools, as suggested by the European Commission (European Council, 2021; European Council, 2019). This paper presents the methodology used in a semi-experimental research to design an educational experience aimed at developing multilingual competence through educational technology tools in a museum context. The design was based on systematic reviews, analysis of case studies and on the results of the precedent pilot study. The participants were 131 Italian high school and technical institute students with an A2-B2 English level and 27 teachers. They were divided into a control group and three experimental groups: one experimental group visited the museum with the support of educational technology (TEG), another visited the museum without the support of educational technology (TMEG), and one group used educational technology without visiting the museum (MEG). The 26-week experience comprised 62 sessions. Four groups participated in the initial encounter, during which the project was introduced and pre-tests were administered. The TMEG and MEG groups attended four museum visits, differing only in that TMEG used technological devices for grammar exercises. Both groups then participated in four post-visit workshops, where students collaborated to create a virtual museum room, described it in a text, and presented it to the class. Meanwhile, the TEG group attended only the workshops. Following the final encounter, during which post-tests were conducted, a follow-up test was held. Additionally, some students conducted a museum visit for another class. The evaluation tools include pre and post essays, a grammar test, a profiling questionnaire, a self-assessment learning questionnaire, and an evaluation questionnaire for teachers.

Keywords: language learning, educational technologies, museum education, semi-experimental research

What does learner-centered pedagogy look like in reimagining the digital classroom of the future?

References

European Council. (2018). Recommendation on key competences for lifelong learning 2018/C 189/01. Publications Office, Luxembourg.

European Council. (2021). Council conclusions on equity and inclusion in education and training in order to promote educational success for all 2021/C 221/02.Publications Office, Luxembourg.

European Commission. (2012). First European Survey on Language Competences. Final Report. Publications Office, Luxembourg.

European Council. (2019). Recommendation on a comprehensive approach to the teaching and learning of languages 2019/C 189/03, Publications Office, Luxembourg.Mayer, R. E. (2005). Cognitive theory of multimedia learning. In R. E. Mayer (Ed.), *The Cambridge handbook of multimedia learning* (pp. 31–48). Cambridge University Press.

Learning by Doing: The Case for Experiential Pedagogy in the Age of GenAI

Raphaël Zaffran[1], Jue Wang Szilas[2]

[1]Centre for Continuing and Distance Education, University of Geneva, Switzerland; raphael.zaffran@unige.ch
[2]Centre for Continuing and Distance Education, University of Geneva, Switzerland; jue.wangszilas@unige.ch

Correspondence: Raphaël Zaffran : raphael.zaffran@unige.ch

Abstract:

The recent developments in generative AI, including the release of ChatGPT by OpenAI in 2022, have generated significant discussion around the implications of conversational and other generative AIs for education. ChatGPT and other generative AIs demonstrate how AI can engage students to explore complex topics, ask follow-up questions, and provide explanations tailored to an individual's understanding. This shows how AI assistants have the potential to act as learning coaches that scaffold understanding through prompting and conversation.

Rather than replacing educators, these systems can free up instructor time and attention to focus on higher-order tasks like designing rich learning experiences, providing personalized feedback, and developing smarter evaluations and exams that more effectively assess learning outcomes and address real-world skills gaps. While the capabilities of generative AIs have generated fears among some teachers and higher education institutions about risks of plagiarism and cheating if these systems were to replace human instructors, they present new opportunities for experiential learning in higher education.

Experiential pedagogy is a teaching method based on practical experience and the application of knowledge in real-life contexts. It is increasingly used to meet the needs of students seeking to develop practical skills and gain relevant work experience. For example, the Centre for Continuing and Distance Education has shown using podcasts in learning designs and assessments offers many perspectives for a more experiential pedagogy offering flexibility, accessibility and engagement. In fact, integrating podcasts in learning designs can thus not only promote learning, but also help develop communication and collaboration skills, as well as reinforce the student's reflective abilities.

We present ways in which institutions may leverage generative AIs to enhance experiential learning and drive the design of improved assessments. AIs could guide virtual simulations, support collaborative project-based learning, and provide practice exams through interactive questioning. This will contribute to advancing the development of advanced competency-based evaluations. Overall, we argue that generative AI has the potential to transform higher education by allowing institutions and educators to design more immersive, customized experiential learning opportunities at scale as well as smarter evaluations that better fulfil societal and market needs. Properly implemented, AI can support innovative approaches to hands-on, applied and collaborative learning that develop complex skills for the future of work.

In response to challenges and opportunities posed by generative artificial intelligence, the Centre for Continuing and Distance Education has taken proactive measures to empower its teaching and coordinating staff, by encouraging the experiential learning. The proactive strategy focuses on raising awareness, fostering preparedness, and staying updated on AI developments in education. The Center actively encourages staff to explore and experiment with innovative tools and ideas through various channels, including workshops, podcasts, informal seminars, etc., as detailed in the following table.

Focus	Measures
Raising awareness	• Podcast • Workshops • Interviews

What does learner-centered pedagogy look like in reimagining the digital classroom of the future?

Fostering preparedness	• Internal training • Workshops
Keeping updated on AI developments in education	• Encouraging participation in different conferences and seminars • Interactive content that reassembles the latest AI tools and their applications

We hope that this forward-thinking approach positions our Centre at the forefront of embracing the potential of generative AI, ensuring that our teaching and coordination staff are not only well-informed but also adept at leveraging these technologies for the enhancement of lifelong learning experiences.

Keywords: experiential learning, continuing education, lifelong learning, proactive strategy

References

Barnett, T. (2023). The Role Of Professional AI Prompters In Ensuring Successful AI Implementations.

Breunig, M. (2017). Experientially learning and teaching in a student-directed classroom. *Journal of Experiential Education.*

Brassard, N. (2012). Pourquoi varier les approches pédagogiques? *Le Tableau, 1*(1).

Frost, G., & Connolly, M. (2015). The road less travelled? Pathways from passivity to agency in student learning. *Collected Essays on Learning & Teaching*, , 8, 47-54.

Gardner, H. E. (2011). Frames of Mind: The Theory of Multiple Intelligences. Basic books.

Hutchison, D. (2018). Scaffolding project management best practices through experiential learning in a large enrollment online course. *Transformative Dialogues: Teaching & Learning Journal,* 11(1).

Peltier, C. (2016). Usage des podcasts en milieu universitaire: une revue de la littérature. *Revue internationale des technologies en pédagogie universitaire / International Journal of Technologies in Higher Education, 13*(2-3), 17–35.

Temperman, G., & De Lièvre, B. (2009). Développement et usage intégré des podcasts pour l'apprentissage. *Distances et savoirs, 7*, 179-190. Retrieved from https://www.cairn.info/revue--2009-2-page-179.htm

Zaffran, R. (2023). ChatGPT: An ongoing and unprecedented disruption for education and training? *NewsSpecial, April 2023,* 28-31.

Zaffran, R. (2023a). Se concentrer à l'ère de l'économie de l'attention et des IA génératives: la super-compétence du 21e siècle? *L'apprentissage à l'heure de l'intelligence artificielle (blog).* Retrieved from https://www.unige.ch/formcont/promotions/ia/concentration

Zaffran, R. (2023b). Le podcast: un levier pour l'apprentissage expérientiel à contre-courant de ChatGPT. *L'apprentissage à l'heure de l'intelligence artificielle.* Retrieved from https://www.unige.ch/formcont/promotions/ia/podcast-chatgpt

Teaching in the Age of Technology: Towards a Teaching Framework for Digital Work-Based Learning

Laura Eigbrecht[1], Ulf-Daniel Ehlers[2]

[1] NextEducation Research Group, Baden-Wuerttemberg Cooperative State University Karlsruhe, Germany, laura.eigbrecht@dhbw-karlsruhe.de
[2] NextEducation Research Group, Baden-Wuerttemberg Cooperative State University Karlsruhe, Germany, ulf-daniel.ehlers@dhbw-karlsruhe.de

Correspondence: Laura Eigbrecht : laura.eigbrecht@dhbw-karlsruhe.de

Abstract:

The growing sophistication and use of Artificial intelligence and large language models have disrupted the debate on higher education – and address the questions that have imposed themselves increasingly within the last years: how can we rethink (higher) education in an age of digital transformation of all domains of working, living and learning together? How can we prepare learners to not only cope with, but thrive in digitally permeated contexts? How can we enrich and deepen learning experiences related to practical and work-based learning contexts? How can we, as teachers and educators, take the advantages of digital technology for creating rich digital learning experiences while productively dealing with the risks and challenges – and which ones are the competences we need for these purposes?

These are the questions at the core of an international research and practice initiative that involved educators, instructional designers and digital learning experts in the field of vocational teaching and learning, teaching and learning innovation and Future Skills (Ehlers, 2020) in an interdisciplinary community of practice. The aim was for participants to motivate and inspire each other to try out and experiment with digitally enhanced learning experiences while reflecting on the competences needed in order to design, realize and reflect on rich and practice-related learning environments.

The initiative realized 19 workshops with eight partners from five European countries and developed, in a qualitative and iterative research design, a competence framework for future educators in practice-related teaching and learning contexts. It is specific to the domain of work-integrated or work-based learning (Yorke & Knight, 2004; Peach & Matthews, 2011) but can serve as an orientation within other teaching and learning contexts. The framework promotes an empowering vision in which educators and trainers go beyond merely replacing their existing teaching methods. They are encouraged to reassess and rethink their approaches in light of emerging possibilities and developments – and thus develop a future vision of learning together with learners. It aims to encourage educators to support learners in developing learner agency (OECD, 2022), preparing them to successfully navigate in emergent (Stephan, 2016) teaching and learning contexts.

Future Skills and a Future Work-Based Learning Teaching mindset serve as the foundation and background for the six Core Competences of the framework:

- Collaborative Learning Design and Implementation
- Resource Creation and Curation
- Workplace Teaching
- Collaboration and Networking
- Technology, Tools and Resources

What does learner-centered pedagogy look like in reimagining the digital classroom of the future?

- Teaching and Learning Reflection (including Social and Sustainability Reflection)

The aim of the Competence Framework is to support teachers, trainers and organizations in reflecting on their future teaching competences and in creating suitable training opportunities. The framework is specific in its focus on Digital Work-Based Learning, but also in emphasizing the importance of peer support and learning when creating and managing educational experiences. Moreover, it takes a critical approach in prominently including the reflection on social, societal, inclusion and sustainable aspects, moving beyond the narrow focus on digital skills to a broader consideration of how these competencies are applied in real-world contexts.

Keywords: work-based learning; practice-based learning, new pedagogy, Future Skills, teaching competences

References

Ehlers, U.-D. (2020). *Future Skills. The Future of Learning and Higher Education.* https://nextskills.org/wp-content/uploads/2020/03/Future-Skills-The-Future-of-learning-and-higher-education.pdf

OECD (2022). *Education Policy Outlook 2022: Transforming Pathways for Lifelong Learners.* https://doi.org/10.1787/c77c7a97-en

Peach, D. & Matthews, J. (2011). Work integrated learning for life: Encouraging agentic engagement. In K.L. Krause, C. Grimmer, M. Buckridge & S. Purbrick-Illek (Eds.), *Research and Development in Higher Education: Higher Education on the Edge, Volume 34: Refereed papers from the 34th HERDSA Annual International Conference* (pp. 227-237).

Stephan, A. (2016). *Emergenz: Von der Unvorhersagbarkeit zur Selbstorganisation*. Mentis.

Yorke, M., & Knight, P. (2004). *Learning, curriculum and employability in higher education*. Routledge Falmer.

How Is Artificial Intelligence Transforming Teacher Education? Presentation and Discussion of an Explorative Research Concept on Trends and Developments

Katharina Maitz[1], Thomas Leitgeb[2], Marlies Matischek-Jauk[3], Corinna Mößlacher[4], Marie Knaus[3]

[1] Private Pädagogische Hochschule Augustinum, Austria; Katharina.maitz@pph-augustinum.at
[2] Private Pädagogische Hochschule Burgenland, Austria; Thomas.leitgeb@ph-burgenland.at
[3] Pädagogische Hochschule Steiermark, Austria; marlies.matischek@phst.at; marie.knaus@phst.at
[4] Pädagogische Hochschule Kärnten, Austria; corinna.moesslacher@ph-kaernten.ac.at

Correspondence: Katharina Maitz: katharina.maitz@pph-augustinum.at

Abstract:

Developments in the field of artificial intelligence (AI) demonstrate the disruptive power of artificial intelligence (AI) in many areas of our lives, including the education system (Kasneci et al., 2023). The area of teacher training is particularly affected here, as the aim is to prepare prospective teachers to teach in an educational world transformed by AI and to further provide students from primary school level onwards with basic understanding of AI and the ability to use and critically evaluate AI tools (Southworth et al., 2023). These skills are often referred to as AI literacy (Long & Magerko, 2020; Ng et al., 2021).

To effectively prepare teacher students within teacher education and training programs at higher education institutions, it is imperative to develop and implement concepts that enhance their AI literacy. Establishing a baseline to assess the current state of AI literacy is essential in this context; it allows for the tailoring of study programmes to effectively foster this crucial competency. The integration of AI tools in teaching and learning processes at the university level demands not only specific skills but also the development of specialized teaching and learning concepts. The significance of teaching with AI extends beyond teacher educators to include students aspiring to become school teachers, necessitating an initial assessment of teacher students' current AI literacy levels to ensure the effectiveness of these educational interventions.

There is an urgent need for systematic research that addresses the implementation and consequences of AI tools in teacher education from two perspectives – the perspective of the teacher students and the perspective of the teacher educators – and through different scientific lenses, namely a learning sciences lens and a sociological and pedagogical lens. We present the concept of a research project that aims to comprehensively analyse transformations in teacher education over the course of four years. This explorative project applies a mixed-methods approach to answer research questions regarding trends and developments in teacher students' and teacher educators' AI literacy and their AI usage behaviour (replicative cross-sectional surveys), and aims at the development and implementation of a multi-level model that captures changes in the usage behaviour of teacher students and teacher educators. Recommendations for content and didactic approaches for targeted support and intervention measures are to be developed on the basis of this model.

Keywords: teacher training, higher education development, AI usage behaviour, trends, mixed-methods approach, teaching concepts, explorative research

What does learner-centered pedagogy look like in reimagining the digital classroom of the future?

References

Long, D., & Magerko, B. (2020). What is AI literacy? Competencies and design considerations. *Proceedings of the 2020 CHI Conference on Human Factors in Computing Systems*, 1-16. Association for Computing Machinery. https://doi.org/10.1145/3313831.3376727

Kasneci, E., Seßler, K., Küchemann, S., et al. (2023). ChatGPT for good? On opportunities and challenges of large language models for education. *Learning and Individual Differences*. https://www.edu.sot.tum.de/fileadmin/w00bed/hctl/_my_direct_uploads/ChatGPT_for_Good_.pdf

Ng, D., Leung, J., Chu, S., & Qiao, M. (2021). Conceptualizing AI literacy: An exploratory review. *Computers and Education: Artificial Intelligence, 2*, 1-11.

Southworth, J., Migliaccio, K., Glover, J., et al. (2023). Developing a model for AI across the curriculum: transforming the higher education landscape via innovation in AI literacy. *Computers & Education: Artificial Intelligence, 4*(100127). https://doi.org/10.1016/j.caeai.2023.100127

Teaching for the Learning Process in an Age of AI

Bruce Lenthall[1]

[1] Center for Excellence in Teaching, Learning and Innovation, University of Pennsylvania, USA; lenthall@upenn.edu

Correspondence: Bruce Lenthall: lenthall@upenn.edu

Many of us, considering whether and how to use Artificial Intelligence in our teaching are tempted to focus on all students can do with AI. As educators, though, we are concerned not with what AI makes possible, but with how we help our students learn. Consequently, we should consider four principles:

Focus on the learning process, not how experts complete tasks:

We need to ask ourselves not how experts do a task, but how novices learn to do that task. This means thinking about what students need to learn and how we scaffold that learning. Does AI have a role to play in those steps?

For example, many AI advocates assert that because students will use AI in their writing in future jobs, students should routinely write with AI. But some of us write effectively with AI because we developed writing skills through other means. As teachers we care not about how to exercise expertise, but how to develop it.

There are places for AI in the learning process, though. One professor finds that by having students define narrow pieces of the coding process and ask AI for help there, they better learn the relevant steps.

Value slow thinking, not speed:

This focus on the learning process encourages us to resist AI's emphasis on efficiency. Teaching students to think slowly – to consider nuance, to reflect on alternatives, to ask why – is often central to the learning we seek.

Thinking about AI in our teaching, we should ask whether we can use AI to make our students' thinking more deliberate. One professor, using what he calls "slow AI," has students share their work with AI not for revision, but to foster a conversation in which students test their ideas.

Teach judgment:

The development of expertise remains relevant even when AI can complete many tasks that call on those skills. To engage effectively with AI, we need the expertise to assess that AI. Our teaching must equip students to make such judgments.

If, as some claim, the future of writing amounts to selecting among AI-generated sentences, we need to cultivate the skills to independently make such choices. In the content realm, for all AI excels at assembling information, it also makes mistakes. Only with independent knowledge and a tendency to question can we hold AI accountable here. The more AI is part of our lives, the more we need to teach students the judgment to weigh what they are given.

How might AI itself help us do so?

Cultivate interaction:

All of this suggests AI's deepest potential for teaching may lie in interaction. Confronting AI's capacities to synthesize, we should remember the importance of conversation for education. Interaction – challenging others' positions, checking your own, developing new ideas through this – facilitates learning. AI can make possible these back-and-forths. It can ask questions of us. We can argue back with it. It can individualize learning.

Such exchanges are vital for the learning process. They also raise a final question: how much do they need to take place with other humans?

Keywords: Learning process, slow thinking, judgment, interaction

The RODEO Hackathon – Empowering Students to Become Road Safety Champions

Anca Colibaba[1], Irina Gheorghiu[2], Ioan Juncu[3], Lucretia Pascariu[4], Adrian Dinu[5]

[1] EuroEd Foundation Iasi, Romania; anca_colibaba@yahoo.com
[2] Albert-Ludwigs University Freiburg, Germany; irina_gheorghiu16@yahoo.com
[3] EuroEd School Iasi, Romania; ioan.juncu@euroed.ro
[4] EuroEd School Iasi, Romania; lucretia.pascariu@euroed.ro
[5] Al.I.Cuza University Iasi, Romania; pradriandinu@yahoo.com

Correspondence: Anca Colibaba: anca_colibaba@yahoo.com

Abstract:

The concise paper is a study on the Rodeo project funded by the European Commission under the Erasmus+ and implemented by the EuroED Foundation, Iasi, Romania, in a partnership of universities, schools, and NGOs from Italy, Denmark, Turkey and Romania.

The project seeks to increase student awareness on the importance of road safety education, develop new digital technologies to support secondary school teachers in training and testing road safety education, and promote active and inclusive student participation. The paper specifically focuses on the hackathon as the project's innovative teaching strategy. A hackathon brings together computer experts to create a new software programme. In the RODEO project, students were asked to collaborate within a team to solve a traffic problem using the hackathon method. The paper highlights the benefits and challenges of the hackathon strategy as experienced by the students.

The Rodeo Hackathon was organized to raise awareness among students about the importance of road safety education. It aimed to help students identify the challenges they face on the road and find solutions to them. The hackathon proposed three challenges: organizing a social publicity campaign on road safety, finding solutions to a problematic traffic issue in their town, and creating a safe environment for people with disabilities. To participate, the students had to register on the Rodeo platform and work in teams on a single challenge. Each challenge was accompanied by tutorials to help students create a digital version of the solution. The students had to set clear objectives, do field research, initiate solutions, use visual resources, and be creative when presenting their results. Thirteen schools and a total of 317 students registered for the event. They worked both online and offline and presented their solutions to their peers in an online meeting.

All final products started from real traffic cases and focused on problematic traffic issues near their schools. Low visibility, few pedestrian crossings, drivers' high speed or students not paying attention when crossing the street were among the main problems. The solutions were realistic including roundabouts, traffic lights, elevated pedestrian bridges, and safe road education. Some students chose the third challenge supporting people with disabilities and came up with creative ideas such as using sounds in pedestrian crossings, Braille, dogs, parking spaces, sidewalk ramps, and car-assisted technology. Regarding the students' choice of presentation for their project, most of the teams chose to create videos, suggestive drawings, or a combination of images, text, and drawings.

A questionnaire conducted on the students revealed that the Rodeo hackathon was popular among them. They appreciated the experience and signaled its benefits (innovative, collaborative, relaxing, offering a sense of self-achievement, useful and enjoyable) and challenges (competitive, limited time, fast-paced, etc).

The findings of the *Rodeo project (2021-1-IT02-KA220-SCH-000030039)* suggest that Hackathons are innovative and pedagogically engaging ways to educate students. They:

What does learner-centered pedagogy look like in reimagining the digital classroom of the future?

- can apply to other fields
- must be designed with clearly defined learning outcomes
- must be accompanied by judging criteria and a hackathon jury
- must engage students and participants in conclusions

Keywords: *road safety education, students, traffic, risks, inclusion, hackathon*

References

Correia, N. N. (2021). *Co-organising hackathons with students: opportunities and best practices.* Compass Journal. Retrieved from https://doi.org/10.21100/compass.v14i2.1216

Lyons, R., Brown, M., & Donlon, E. (2021). *Moving the hackathon online: Reimagining pedagogy for the digital age.* Distance Education in China, 7. Retrieved from https://www.academia.edu/92562502/Moving_the_Hackathon_Online_Reimagining_Pedagogy_for_the_Digital_Age

Moshirpour, M. (2022). *Hackathon as an Effective Learning and Assessment Tool: An Analysis of Student Proficiency against Bloom's Taxonomy.* In Proceedings 2022 Canadian Engineering Education Association (CEEA-ACEG22) Conference. Retrieved from https://www.academia.edu/104089588/Hackathon_as_an_Effective_Learning_and_Assessment_Tool_An_Analysis_of_Student_Proficiency_against_Blooms_Taxonomy

Oyetade, K. (2022). *Educational benefits of hackathon: A systematic literature review.* World Journal on Educational Technology. Retrieved from, https://www.academia.edu/100574468/Educational_benefits_of_hackathon_A_systematic_literature_review

Surredan, et al. (2023). *The use of extracurricular hackathons to promote and enhance students' academic and employability skills.* International Journal of Educational Research Open, *5.* Retrieved from https://doi.org/10.1016/j.ijedro.2023.100307, https://www.sciencedirect.com/science/article/pii/S2666374023000821

AI-Powered Degree Optimisation for Improved Student Retention

Sarah Eden[1]

[1] Product Innovation and Academic Engagement, University of London, UK; sarah.eden@london.ac.uk

Correspondence: Sarah Eden: sarah.eden@london.ac.uk

Abstract:

While the rise of online education has widened access to education, low online student retention rates suggests that access is only truly widened when educators focus on improving persistence and attainment (Woodley and Simpson, 2014). Recent focus on research in teaching and learning in online education has centred on learner characteristics and online engagement (Martin, Sun, and Westine, 2020). While personalised interventions have their place in improving retention, so too do opportunities in improving overall course content and design (Harackiewicz and Priniski, 2018).

The value of delivering regular enhancements to modules – for currency, improved alignment to subject benchmarks, and/or accuracy – is universally appreciated. However, the time and cost required to deliver module optimisations so often limits our ability to regularly do so (Hai-Jew, 2010). With this pilot, we focussed on delivering academic content optimisations with an aim to support student success and retention. We used virtual learning environment (VLE) data and genAI to enhance and augment study materials – all with a 72%[2] reduction in the implementation timeline.

We targeted two compulsory modules on our BSc Computer Science programme that all first-year students must take (average cohort size = 700-1,000 students). Using four years of VLE data from these modules, we pinpointed areas where students struggled – and opportunities for us to intervene. Learning designers used this data and genAI to create optimised academic materials, focussing on:

- scaffolding materials around key assessment points; and
- additional, engaging material around weeks we saw student engagement drop.

Academics reviewed these materials, made revisions where necessary, and then published the content. Most suggestions were accepted, with some corrections needed.

At the conclusion of this pilot, we will assess the impact on student session-on-session retention as well as end-of-module attainment. Interim results appear promising[3], including 11.7% increase in on-time completion of assignments, a 55% decrease in students withdrawing from the module, and a 2.8% increase in average grade achieved on summative assessments

Attendees can expect to see a real-time example of using genAI to optimise academic materials. They will have an opportunity to ask questions about the pilot and hear about the lessons being learned during this ongoing project.

[2] The historical average time required to implement content enhancements on internally is 213 days. This work took 60 days to complete (time here is measured in elapsed time from the start of the enhancement work to the finish, not active time required to implement).

[3] Compared with the October 2022 and April 2023 study sessions at the same point in time.

What does learner-centered pedagogy look like in reimagining the digital classroom of the future?

Keywords: genAI, educational AI, retention, persistence, online learning, higher education, innovation

References

Hai-Jew, S. An instructional design approach to updating an online course curriculum. *EDUCAUSE Quarterly Magazine, 33.* https://er.educause.edu/articles/2010/12/an-instructional-design-approach-to-updating-an-online-course-curriculum#ART

Harackiewicz, J. M. & Priniski, S. J. Improving student outcomes in higher education: The science of targeted intervention. *Annual Review of Psychology, 69,* 409-35. https://doi.org/10.1146/annurev-psych-122216-011725

Martin, F., Sun, T. & Westine, C. D. (2020). A systematic review of research on online teaching and learning from 2009 to 2018, *Computers & Education, 159,* 1-17. https://doi.org/10.1016/j.compedu.2020.104009

Woodley, Alan & Simpson, Ormond. (2014). *Online distance education – Toward a research agenda.* AU Press Athabasca University.

Collaboration in Action: Learning and Utilizing AI for Effective Research Projects

Muesser Nat[1]

[1]Management Information Systems, Cyprus International University, Turkey, mnat@ciu.edu.tr

Correspondence: Muesser Nat: mnat@ciu.edu.tr

Abstract:

Artificial intelligence (AI) presents a transformative opportunity for higher education, potentially reshaping pedagogical approaches and empowering students. Moving beyond rote memorization, AI could personalize learning experiences, unlocking students' full potential and fostering essential skills (Crompton & Burke, 2023). Applications in Higher Education (HE) include student profiling and performance prediction, automated assessment with feedback, and personalized learning paths catering to individual needs (Zawacki-Richter et al., 2019; Chen et al., 2020; Singh & Hiran, 2022). However, despite growing interest, robust evidence regarding the pedagogical effectiveness of AI in HE remains limited. While ethical considerations around data bias, transparency, and student privacy deserve careful attention, the focus should shift from automation toward utilizing AI to enhance learning and empower educators (Crompton & Burke, 2023). This paper proposes a method for integrating AI into postgraduate courses, specifically aiming to cultivate a collaborative learning environment while empowering students to leverage AI as a learning tool. This method's successful implementation has the potential to enhance student engagement, collaborative learning, and foster a deeper understanding of AI within the postgraduate curriculum.

The initial stage of this ongoing study involved a brief online module in prompt engineering during the first week of the course. This introductory module consisted of four concise video lectures, encompassing the fundamental principles of prompt engineering, its practical applications, ethical considerations, and key factors for constructing effective prompts. Following successful completion of the online module, students were assigned research topics requiring them to leverage various AI tools. This research culminated in two mandatory presentations and a report submission.

The first presentation focused on the AI tools employed and the practical application of prompt engineering in initiating the research process. Students demonstrated their understanding by providing detailed explanations of the prompts constructed to achieve desired results. This fostered collaborative learning by encouraging students to share their experiences and successes, optimizing the exploration of AI capabilities. The second presentation aimed at communicating and disseminating research findings. Students elaborated on the process of crafting a comprehensive research report that effectively communicated the results of their AI-driven investigation. This included a detailed explanation of key findings, their significance within the broader research context, and any potential limitations of the study.

This combined approach equips students with the necessary knowledge and skills to leverage AI responsibly and collaboratively, preparing them for future success in an increasingly AI-driven world. As Popenici & Kerr (2017) suggest, the true potential of technology in HE lies in extending human capabilities and possibilities when used effectively. The collaborative learning environment fosters knowledge sharing through student exchange of personal experiences with various AI tools. By leveraging collective intelligence, students learn from each other's successes and challenges, optimizing their exploration of AI capabilities. This not only reduces the need for individual exploration but also creates a valuable platform for ethical considerations. During student presentations, the instructor can identify and address potential ethical issues related to AI use through open discussions and critical analysis. This proactive approach equips students with not only the technical knowledge of AI tools but also the necessary ethical awareness to ensure responsible AI application. This method offers a promising approach to integrate AI into postgraduate courses, fostering collaborative learning and responsible AI application. Further research is needed to explore the long-term impact on student learning outcomes and to identify additional methods for effectively integrating AI into the HE curriculum.

Keywords: AI in Higher Education, Collaborative Learning, Prompt Engineering

References

Crompton, H., & Burke, D. (2023). Artificial intelligence in higher education: The state of the field. International Journal of Educational Technology in Higher Education, 20(22). https://doi.org/10.1186/s41239-023-00392

L. Chen, P. Chen and Z. Lin, "Artificial Intelligence in Education: A Review," in IEEE Access, vol. 8, pp. 75264-75278, 2020, doi: 10.1109/ACCESS.2020.2988510

Popenici, S. A., & Kerr, S. (2017). Exploring the impact of artificial intelligence on teaching and learning in higher education. Research and Practice in Technology Enhanced Learning, 12(1), 1-13. https://doi.org/10.1186/s41039-017-0062-8

Singh, S. V., & Hiran, K. K. (2022). The impact of AI on teaching and learning in higher education technology. Journal of Higher Education Theory and Practice, 22(13)

Zawacki-Richter, O., Marín, V. I., Bond, M., & Gouverneur, F. (2019). Systematic review of research on artificial intelligence applications in higher education – where are the educators? International Journal of Educational Technology in Higher Education, 16(39). https://doi.org/10.1186/s41239-019-0171-0

Technology-Driven Solutions to the Challenges of Authentic Assessment

Elva Casey [1], Mary Kelly [2]

[1] Hibernia College, Ireland, ecasey@hiberniacollege.net
[2] Hibernia College, Ireland, ecasey@hiberniacollege.net

Correspondence: Elva Casey, ecasey@hibernicollege.net

Abstract:

This paper, based on a Quality and Qualifications Ireland (QQI) funded project carried out by Hibernia College, reports on the development and testing of an integrated, authentic virtual scenario-based learning (VSBL) environment designed to support student mentoring and formative and authentic assessment. The project is a response to the perceived need in higher education for purposeful, supportive and sustainable formative assessment. More broadly, it seeks to promote and support self-efficacy of student teachers (STs) through the provision of virtual mastery experiences, mirroring professional scenarios. Work integrated learning (WIL) is an important aspect of many professional qualifications at higher level. However, it is an area which causes students disproportionate anxiety. This project is therefore a response to the need for opportunities for aspiring professionals and students to experiment in replicas of 'real life' professional experiences without the pressures of summative assessment. The project seeks to use technological solutions to formatively evaluate the learning outcomes of students on professional programmes of education.

The project addresses the research question, 'What are the characteristics of a VSBL authentic assessment environment to improve pre-service teachers' self-efficacy and assess programme learning outcomes which will best support pre-service teachers before their first school-based experience on a Professional Master of Education (PME) programme?'

A multi-ontological framework was developed to inform the VSBL prototype (Hall & Flanagan, 2017).

The STAR framework:

Scenario-based to improve professional sense of self-efficacy

Technology-enhanced to improve engagement, authenticity/lifelikeness, and making it easy to access, use and scale.

Authentic assessment of programme learning outcomes.

Reflective practice to support teacher/professional identity

Errington (2005) describes scenario-based learning (SBL) as involving intentional use of scenarios for very specific learning intentions. It can consequently provide opportunities for students to apply subject knowledge and problem-solving skills which are usually tested in WIL within a simulated context. SBL can supplement authentic experiences through WIL or, as proposed in this project, provide a preparation phase to bridge the gap between theory and the real experience. The primary advantage of this is that students can make mistakes, learn from those mistakes and adapt their practices. Studies exploring the application of SBL in schools show positive impact on academic achievement (Aslan, 2019). Sorin's (2013) work identified that the applications of scenario-based learning acts like a bridge between theory and practice in teacher education.

What does learner-centered pedagogy look like in reimagining the digital classroom of the future?

Teaching presents a multitude of challenges in ever increasingly complex contexts to learners with a variety of needs and interests. Preparing for these challenges and contexts can be difficult in isolation. Shulman (1986) speaks to the challenges, for example, of developing knowledge for teaching and learning. Knowledge, in itself, comes in a variety of shapes and sizes with Shulman identifying content knowledge, pedagogical content knowledge and curricular knowledge amongst others. Alongside this, teachers are expected to improve and develop a collection of skills and dispositions which will enable them to effectively address this multitude of challenges. The question this poses is: how can teachers develop such skills, knowledge, and dispositions in isolation from a clear context? VSBL has the potential to provide the solution by giving a mallable and safe context withing which to experiment, make choices and flourish.

In Hibernia College, Focus Groups were conducted with STs prior to, during and after the development of the scenarios. This was in order to ensure that they could provide meaningful, enriching experiences. It was important that these experiences met the needs of students on professional courses of study rather than adding an additional element to already busy programmes. The design of the VSBL simulation focused on encouraging active participation in teaching activities, such as delivering lessons, leading pupil discussions, or facilitating group activities that simulate SP settings (Bandura, 1977). The setting mirrored a school and class environment where the student was tasked with making a series of pedagogical, classroom management and UDL- informed decisions.

There is potential for the pilot VSBL simulations developed for this project in the context of teaching to be adapted within different professional contexts and for more nuanced and multi-layered scenarios to be developed. Potential uses in medical and legal professions are also evident.

Keywords: Virtual scenario-based learning, authentic assessment, formative assessment, work integrated learning

---

References

Aslan, S. (2019). The impact of argumentation-based teaching and scenario-based learning method on the students' academic achievement. Journal of Baltic Science Education, 18, 10.

Bandura, A. (1977). Self-efficacy: Toward a unifying theory of behavioral change. Psychological Review, 84(2), 191–215

Errington, E. (2005). Creating Learning Scenarios: A Planning Guide for Adult Educators. Palmerston North, New Zealand: Cool Books.

Flanagan, E;Hall, T (2017) 'Digital Ensemble: The ENaCT design-based research framework for technology-enhanced embodied assessment in English education'. *English in Education,* 51 :76-99

Shulman, L. (1986). Those who Understand: Knowledge Growth in Teaching. Educational Researcher, 15 (2), 4-14

Sorin, R. (2013). Scenario-based learning: Transforming tertiary teaching and learning

Leveraging AI to Embrace Open Education: A Workshop

Francesca Crudele[1], Beatrice Doria[2], Laura Carlotta Foschi[3], Valentina Grion[4], Graziano Cecchinato[5], Juliana Elisa Raffaghelli[6]

[123456] FISPPA Department of Philosophy, Sociology, Pedagogy and Applied Psychology, University of Padova, Italy
[1] francesca.crudele@phd.unipd.it
[2] beatrice.doria@phd.unipd.it
[3] lauracarlotta.foschi@unipd.it
[4] valentina.grion@unipd.it
[5] graziano.cecchinato@unipd.it
[6] juliana.raffaghelli@unipd.it

Correspondence: Francesca Crudele: francesca.crudele@phd.unipd.it

Abstract:

Over the past decade, governments and policies have taken a great deal of interest in spreading awareness about the needs and requirements of educational institutions to adapt to the many changes we are experiencing. The EU has emphasized the need to promote "innovative teaching and learning through new technologies and open educational resources" as a strategy for lifelong learning, further integrated into the EU Development Goals and Flagship Initiatives for 2020 (EU2020).

Recent times have seen a dramatic increase in the number of open educational resources (OER) available in learning object repositories. Teachers can use this wealth of information to focus on tasks including personalizing interactions with students and continuing to meet the demands of a changing curriculum and technology landscape. However, the transition from OERs to open educational practices (OEPs) is a complex process that requires multiple reflections (Ossianilsson, 2020).

Especially now that generative artificial intelligence (GenAI) has dramatically shifted priorities on educational changes to respond to, posing a significant challenge to educators' professionalism and skills (Tlili et al., 2023). The ease of access to and use of such systems and new strategies requires skills and a critical attitude to the use of technology.

In this context, we will present data from two workshops, respectively carried out by 22 and 18 participants, in which an AI tool based on an EU project was explored. We refer to ENCORE, a platform for HE lecturers and teaching assistants, teachers, VET trainers/providers, eLearning/staff development units, and undergraduates designed to embrace open education. This tool combines AI to retrieve relevant OERs and also integrate them into teachers' learning design.

Moreover, the tool organizes OER according to the DGE (Digital, Entrepreneurial, and Green) frameworks developed by the European Commission. It provides relevant interactions based on a Revised Bloom's taxonomy to plan learning goals and align the learning activities and assessment activities. Therefore, it also supports teachers aimed at developing skills required for contemporary challenges such as digitization, climate change, and post-COVID economic recovery. To complete the training system, ENCORE offers pedagogical scenarios created by other educators, available to the participants to get inspired and move from exploration to creativity (Raffaghelli et al., 2023).

Our research questions investigated two objectives:

- to improve participants' awareness relating to OERs in connection to the DGEs;
- to explore approaches to scenario design for learning by adopting some of the features of the ENCORE system.

Our preliminary analysis revealed a focus on the platform's main potential, both in terms of design and usability. ENCORE emerged as a medium and resource not only for exploring and inquiring about OERs themselves but also as a valuable tool for exploring useful resources for one's purposes and especially for enriching one's own and shared knowledge.

What does learner-centered pedagogy look like in reimagining the digital classroom of the future?

Keywords: Open Educational Resources, DGE, AI tool, learning scenario, ENCORE

References

European Council (2020). Council conclusions on "European teachers and trainers for the future". Official Journal of the European Union. https://eur-lex.europa.eu/legalcontent/EN/TXT/HTML/?uri=CELEX:52020XG0609(02)&rid=5

Ossiannilsson, E., Zhang, X., Wetzler, J., Gusmão, C., Aydin, C. H., Jhangiani, R., Glapa-Grossklag, J., Makoe, M., & Harichandan, D. (2020). From Open Educational Resources to Open Educational Practices. Distances et médiations des savoirs. Distance and Mediation of Knowledge, 31, Article 31. https://doi.org/10.4000/dms.5393

Raffaghelli, J. E., Foschi, L. C., Crudele, F., Doria, B., Grion, V., & Cecchinato, G. (2023). The ENCORE Approach. Pedagogy of an AI-driven system to integrate OER in Higher Education & VET (https://hdl.handle.net/11577/3502320; DLV 5.1; ENCORE Project Report Series, pp. 1–94). University of Padova; Padova Research Archives. https://www.research.unipd.it/handle/11577/3502320

Tlili, A., Shehata, B., Adarkwah, M. A., Bozkurt, A., Hickey, D. T., Huang, R., & Agyemang, B. (2023). What if the devil is my guardian angel: ChatGPT as a case study of using chatbots in education. Smart Learning Environments, 10(1), 15. https://doi.org/10.1186/s40561-023-00237-x

Trying for Thriving - Pedagogical Use of AI for Understanding Scientific Articles

Teresa Santos-Silva[1], João Couvaneiro[2]

[1]Centro Interuniversitário de História das Ciências e da Tecnologia, Universidade NOVA de Lisboa, Portugal; tsss@fct.unl.pt
[2]Centro Interuniversitário de História das Ciências e da Tecnologia, Universidade NOVA de Lisboa, Portugal; jcouvaneiro@egasmoniz.edu.pt

Correspondence: Teresa Santos-Silva: tsss@fct.unl.pt

Abstract:

Although artificial intelligence (AI) is already widely known among teachers and students, its pedagogical integration, as well as its careful and efficient application in the knowledge construction processes, is limited. The opportunities to improve learning experiences through the use of AI are vast and can be explored by teachers and students as an integral part of the activities planned within a curricular unit (CU).

It is common to expect that, in the last years of the first cycle of higher education, students have already developed the skills to analyze and interpret scientific articles within their field of study. However, they rarely receive adequate training for this, which negatively impacts the learning process and affects their relationship with knowledge, potentially leading to feelings of frustration (McBride, 2019). Our proposal aims to explore whether AI can serve as a supportive tool in this context, aiding in the analysis of content, pinpointing of key ideas, connecting concepts, while fostering critical thinking and deeper understanding of the subject matter (Hosseini, 2023).

To achieve this goal, we designed a 4-hour class specifically for third-year Biochemistry students at NOVA FCT, Portugal. During this session, students engaged in various methodologies to analyze and comprehend two Biochemistry-related spectroscopy articles. The assignment required collaborative effort, as students worked in groups and utilized artificial intelligence (AI), engaged in peer reviews, and created mind maps.

Initially, each group selected a research paper relevant to their course unit (CU) topics, from which they read and analyzed the content. They then synthesized their understanding into a mind map and a concise abstract. Subsequently, they employed AI tools to refine these outputs.

In the next phase, each group received a research article chosen by a different group. With this new article, they were tasked to create an abstract and a mind map, this time incorporating AI analysis from the beginning of their review process.

Finally, in the concluding phase, students exchanged their essays for peer evaluation, highlighting the strengths and weaknesses of the diverse approaches undertaken. This structure aimed to deepen their understanding and critique of scientific literature, leveraging AI as a pedagogical tool (Väyrynen, 2023; Wongvorachan, 2022).

At the end of the activity, students acknowledged the value of the methodologies used, underscored the significance of critical analysis, and noted the relevance of clear instructions to optimize their engagement with the AI tools. They also highlighted that while AI can generate content on a specific subject , this does not translate into learning; active participation in the process is essential for genuine knowledge acquisition.

Keywords: Artificial Intelligence, Mind Maps, Critical Thinking, Peer Feedback

What does learner-centered pedagogy look like in reimagining the digital classroom of the future?

References

McBride, M., & Sweeney, M. A. (2019). Frustration and Hope. *Journal of Basic Writing*, 38(2), 38-63.

Hosseini M, Gao CA, Liebovitz DM, Carvalho AM, Ahmad FS, Luo Y, et al. (2023) An exploratory survey about using ChatGPT in education, healthcare, and research. *PLoS ONE* 18(10).

Väyrynen, K., Lutovac, S., & Kaasila, R. (2023). Reflection on peer reviewing as a pedagogical tool in higher education. *Active Learning in Higher Education*, 24(3), 291-303.

Wongvorachan, T., Lai, K. W., Bulut, O., Tsai, Y.-S., & Chen, G. (2022). Artificial Intelligence: Transforming the Future of Feedback in Education. *Journal of Applied Testing Technology*, 23(Special Issue 1), 95-116.

Developing Writing Skills in the Age of AI: Students' Perceptions of AI, Peer, and Instructor Feedback in EFL

Jennifer Lucas [1], Irina Otmanine[2]

[1] SKILS departement, SKEMA Business School, France ; jennifer.lucas@skema.edu
[2] DILE, SKEMA Business School, France; irina.otmanine@skema.edu

Correspondence: Irina Otmanine: irina.otmanine@skema.edu

Abstract:

The question of effective and ethical use of AI-based tools for language learning has been raised after the release of ChatGPT in November 2022 and is still ongoing. As underlined in recent studies, educators face an increasing responsibility, as they must carefully deliberate and make well-informed choices regarding the utilization of generative AI tools to support the enhancement of students' writing abilities (Escalante et al.,2023). These decisions significantly impact the effectiveness of teaching and contribute to the overall learning experience. While students declare using AI based tools to support their learning in everyday life (data from student's survey at SKEMA Business School), they still need guidance and support to integrate this type of practices for the sustainable and qualitative learning results.

The importance of feedback for developing writing skills no longer needs to be proven. In the wake of constructivist and socio-constructivist currents, the relevance of the feedback given by peers as well as self-reflection and self-evaluation modalities has grown (Roy et Michaud, 2018). Students are called upon to take a more active role in developing their competence, thereby fostering their autonomy (Leroux, 2014). At the higher education level, the use of these assessment modalities should be encouraged, as they can continue to support students in their professional lives (Leroux, 2014; Lison and St-Laurent, 2015).

Our study investigates various types of feedback provided to students learning English as a foreign language: peer feedback, instructor feedback, and AI-generated feedback. Over the period from January to April 2024, a cohort of 670 undergraduate students (enrolled in the French "Programme Grande Ecole") was engaged in a writing repertoire series of assignments. These assignments involved regular submissions of written work with peer feedback, instructor feedback, and AI-generated feedback. Self-evaluation activities complemented the task. For research purposes, we collected and analyzed data from initial, mid-way, and final self-evaluations to gain insights into students' perceptions of these feedback types and their perceived utility for learning.

Throughout the course, students' overall perceptions of the utility of AI tools feedback improved. However, the study revealed the importance of students receiving feedback from not only AI tools but also from peers and instructors. Most students viewed these three types of feedback as complementary. This finding underscores the need for a balanced approach to feedback in language learning.

Keywords: feedback, AI, peer evaluation, self-assessment, blended learning

What does learner-centered pedagogy look like in reimagining the digital classroom of the future?

References

Escalante, J., Pack, A., & Barrett, A. (2023). AI-generated feedback on writing: insights into efficacy and ENL student preference. *International Journal of Educational Technology in Higher Education* 20(1), 57. https://doi.org/10.1186/s41239-023-00425-2

Leroux, J. L. (2014). Évaluer pour faire apprendre. In L. Ménard et L. St-Pierre (dir.), *Enseigner pour faire apprendre au collégial et à l'université* (p. 330-353). Montréal, QC : Chenelière Éducation/Association québécoise de pédagogie collégiale.

Lison, C. et St-Laurent, C. (2015). Développer la pratique réflexive des étudiants pour soutenir leur autoévaluation. In J. L. Leroux (dir.), *Évaluer les compétences au collégial et à l'université : un guide pratique.* Montréal, QC : Chenelière Éducation/Association québécoise de pédagogie collégiale.

Meyer, J., Jansen, T., Schiller, R., Liebenow, L. W., Steinbach, M., Horbach, A., & Fleckenstein, J. (2024). Using LLMs to bring evidence-based feedback into the classroom: AI-generated feedback increases secondary students' text revision, motivation, and positive emotions. *Computers and Education: Artificial Intelligence*, 6, 100199. https://doi.org/10.1016/j.caeai.2023.100199

Roy, M., & Michaud, N. (2018). L'autoévaluation et l'évaluation par les pairs en enseignement supérieur : promesses et défis. *Formation et Profession*, 26(2), 54. https://doi.org/10.18162/fp.2018.458

Digital Internship Model – Valuable Tool for Online and Hybrid Internships

Līga Roķe-Reimate[1], Jana Roze[2], Jānis Supe[3], Signe Vaičulena[4]

[1234] College of Business Administration, Latvia
[1] liga.roke@bvk.lv
[2] jana.roze@bvk.lv
[3] janis.supe@bvk.lv
[4] signe.vaiculena@bvk.lv

Correspondence: Firstname Lastname: email address

Abstract:

Developments of technology, including high-speed Internet connections, the low cost of portable devices, as well as the global proliferation of Covid-19 have made the virtual workplace a reality. Several research papers (e.g. Kniffin et.al, 2020; O'Mahony & Jeske, 2019) show that remote work has several advantages, and its volume tends to increase in the future. These changes in the labor market call for a reorientation of higher profession education, which would not only prepare young professionals for future virtual jobs, but also make higher education more accessible to different social groups, despite financial, geographical and time constraints, and help to overcome Covid-19 consequences. Research (Ruggiero & Boehmat, 2016) notes the importance of virtual internships in 1) preparing young professionals for future jobs not only in the local but also in the global labor market, 2) ensuring access to education, and 3) improving the quality of professional education. Studies (e.g. Jaske, 2019) confirm that the positive aspects of virtual programs are clearly visible: they facilitate access to education, reduce barriers (financial / time / geographical) common for physical mobility and are more inclusive. In addition, as the authors point out, they are creating a generation of graduates with digital thinking, ready for the digital workplace of the future. Despite the positive aspects of online and hybrid internships, there is still a lack of materials how to organise the internship process in this format.

The authors provide a new solution for organising online and hybrid internships – Digital Internship Model, which consists of several documents, guidelines, templates which can help all stakeholders to implement online and hybrid internships in a more effective and organised way. The new model provides separate set of materials for three main stakeholders – higher education institutions, students, and internship companies. The Model helps all involved parties to understand the internship process better, as in the model it is divided in three stages – before, during and after the internship, and all responsibilities of each stakeholder are described in detail in the model. The authors are analysing a case study - how this model has been used at the College of Business Administration.

Keywords: digital internships, online internships, hybrid internships

References

Kniffin et.al. (2020). COVID-19 and the Workplace: Implications, Issues, and Insights for Future Research and Action. The American psychologist. 76. 10.1037/amp0000716. Bannan-Ritland, B. (2003). The role of design in research: The integrative learning design framework. *Educational Researcher, 32*(1), 21-24. :10.3102/0013189X032001021

O'Mahony, Megan & Jeske, Debora. (2019). Study-Work-Life Balance of International Students in the Context of Temporal Boundaries. 7. 63-79. 10.32674/jise.v7i2.269.

What does learner-centered pedagogy look like in reimagining the digital classroom of the future?

Ruggiero, Dana & Boehm, Jeffrey D. (2016). Design and Development of a Learning Design Virtual Internship Program. The International Review of Research in Open and Distributed Learning. 17. 10.19173/irrodl.v17i4.2385.

Sustainable Meta-Class Model in Higher Education

Nukhet Hotar[1], Bahar Baran[2], Ayca Tokuc[3], Sirin Nur Yacı[4], L. Ozge Guney[5], Seda Nur Apdik[6]

[1] Union for the Mediterranean (UfM); Spain; nhotar@gmail.com
[2] Department of Computer Education and Instructional Technology; Dokuz Eylul University; Turkey; bahar.baran@deu.edu.tr
[3] Department of Building Information; Dokuz Eylul University; Turkey; ayca.tokuc@deu.edu.tr
[4] Distance Education Application and Research Center; Dokuz Eylul University; Turkey; sirinnur.kaptanoglu@deu.edu.tr
[5] Distance Education Application and Research Center; Dokuz Eylul University; Turkey; lozge.oral@deu.edu.tr
[6] Faculty of Architecture; Dokuz Eylul University; Turkey; sedanur.apdik@ogr.deu.edu.tr

Correspondence: Bahar Baran, bahar.baran@deu.edu.tr

Abstract:

The pandemic and natural disasters in the world have proven that it is imperative to develop more flexible and sustainable learning spaces for all students and instructors. Hybrid or blended learning spaces take importance in higher education, providing flexible participation options for students. Considering the challenges to continue education during the pandemic and the big earthquake in Turkiye, we proposed a research project in higher education. The main objective is to design a sustainable hybrid meta-classroom that uses sustainable architectural design techniques and educational technology including analyzing, designing, developing, implementing, and evaluating processes of learning environments to facilitate the learning process. To carry out the research objectives, educators, architects, and civil engineers have been studied collaboratively. The project is currently in progress, and it started with the selection of a lab class to convert to a hybrid class. Afterward, the architectural design was carried out and started to transform the class. While designing the physical space and furniture in the class, attention has been paid to the creation of flexible learning spaces suitable for disadvantaged students. Moreover, certified sustainable (eco) materials are preferred. In the meta class, it will be possible to provide online synchronous, online asynchronous, or face-to-face teaching (course delivery modes) considering the students' need. Students can select their course participation modes before the teaching process. This research can serve to improve Sustainable Development Goal 4 (Quality Education) and 11 (Sustainable cities and communities). In addition, this endeavor contributes to a broader shift towards at the Dokuz Eylul University (DEU) sustainability, hybrid learning methods, and codesign of classrooms with the potential to inspire other institutions and sectors to adopt similar practices.

Keywords: learning spaces, hybrid teaching, quality education, inclusive education, higher education

Acknowledgements

This study is one of the outputs of the project entitled "Sustainable Meta-Class Model in Active Education Processes" supported by Dokuz Eylul University Department of Scientific Research Project with the number SBA-2023-3045. The website of the project: http://metasinif.deu.edu.tr/.

Designing Hybrid and Flexible Learning Spaces in Higher Education: A Need Analysis

Nukhet Hotar[1], Bahar Baran[2], Sirin Nur Yacı[3], Deniz Eraslan[4], Ferit Serkan Akdogan[5], Aylin Dizdaroglu[6]

[1] Union for the Mediterranean (UfM); Spain; nhotar@gmail.com
[2] Department of Computer Education and Instructional Technology; Dokuz Eylul University; Turkey; bahar.baran@deu.edu.tr
[3] Distance Education Application and Research Center; Dokuz Eylul University; Turkey; sirinnur.kaptanoglu@deu.edu.tr
[4] Distance Education Application and Research Center; Dokuz Eylul University; Turkey; deniz.eraslan@deu.edu.tr
[5] Distance Education Application and Research Center; Dokuz Eylul University; Turkey; ferit.akdogan@deu.edu.tr
[6] Distance Education Application and Research Center; Dokuz Eylul University; Turkey; aylin.dizdaroglu@deu.edu.tr

Correspondence: Bahar Baran, bahar.baran@deu.edu.tr

Abstract:

Emergency distance education, including the big Maras earthquake in Turkiye in 2023 and the Covid-19 pandemic, indicated that communication technologies played a key role in continuing education. Teachers and students gained significant experience in teaching/learning at a distance during emergency distance education. However, after this period, the delivery methods of course content (on-site or online) in higher education remained ambiguous. The signs indicated to stakeholders that on-site learning would continue, and an online campus, including micro-credentials or elective courses, would be needed to support the lifelong learning needs of disadvantaged students who have difficulty accessing the learning process due to health, work, etc. In the 2023 Spring term, we decided to work on an innovative hybrid classroom model for higher education that prioritizes the needs of students and faculty members. This paper aims to present the results of a needs analysis on how to develop a hybrid and flexible learning space. Then, these results formed the Meta Class Model(http://metasinif.deu.edu.tr/), which is a hybrid and flexible learning space that incorporates sustainability issues and new technologies. In more detail, this study investigated 1) the views and expectations of an innovative learning space in higher education and 2) the importance of comfort and design elements in a learning space that affect learning. By using the qualitative research method, an open-ended questionnaire including 6 questions was directed to 215 students and 83 faculty members from various departments. The data were analyzed using qualitative data analysis software and reported using a content analysis method. Our research results highlighted common concerns about overcrowded classrooms and technical shortcomings in higher education. The participants advocated for instructors to integrate technology effectively and preferred blended learning. Furthermore, they emphasized the importance of comfort and design elements such as color, classroom size, climate and temperature, lighting, classroom layout, and sound. Overall, this study offers valuable insights into the user requirements for designing learning environments, including inclusiveness, adaptability, and sustainability.

Keywords: learning spaces, hybrid education, technology-supported teaching, higher education

Acknowledgements

This study is one of the outputs of the project entitled "Sustainable Meta-Class Model in Active Education Processes" supported by Dokuz Eylul University Department of Scientific Research Project with the number SBA-2023-3045. The website of the project: http://metasinif.deu.edu.tr/.

Exploring the Impact of Virtual Reality on Flexible Learning Environments: A Pilot Study

Gizéh Rangel De Lázaro[1], Delsa Silva Amino Cufuna[2], Josep M Duart[3]

[1 2 3] Universitat Oberta de Catalunya, Spain
[1] grangel@uoc.edu
[2] scufuna@uoc.edu
[3] jduart@uoc.edu

Correspondence: Gizéh Rangel De Lázaro: grangel@uoc.edu

Abstract:

Flexible learning spaces have gained significant attention in education to improve the educational process. By creating learning environments that promote participation, connection, and involvement, academic institutions can better prepare students for the demands of professional teaching. There is a potential in pairing flexible learning methodologies and virtual reality (VR) to allow students to immerse themselves in immersive environments that can simulate real-life scenarios and experiences. It not only provides students with a more engaging and interactive learning experience, but it also allows for greater flexibility in time and space. Here, we present the results of a pilot experimental study focused on designing and organizing flexible learning spaces using immersive VR resources in a group of students doing a Degree in Primary Education from the Universitat Oberta de Catalunya. The participants doing the Design of Educational Spaces module were asked to design and interact with the 3D flexible learning space, using a VR scenario and Oculus Rift headsets to provide an immersive 360-degree view of the virtual classroom. The learning experience included a pre-test and a post-test assessment.

The following research objectives were proposed:

1. To investigate the effectiveness of flexible learning spaces with VR in student engagement and interactivity within educational environments.

2. To examine the impact of immersive VR scenarios on student learning outcomes, including knowledge retention, understanding of theoretical concepts, and ability to apply learned concepts in real-life scenarios.

3. To evaluate the potential of VR-enabled flexible learning environments to provide students with opportunities for experiential learning and exposure to diverse educational scenarios that may not be accessible physically.

Results suggest that VR helped to eliminate the physical constraints and enabled students to improve the learning process by providing students with the freedom to explore and visualize concepts in a more immersive and interactive manner. Furthermore, students could extrapolate theoretical concepts using objects and the scene in the VR scenario, thereby improving their understanding and retention of information. Additionally, using the chosen VR environments allows students to experience situations that may not be accessible physically.

Keywords: Flexible learning spaces; Virtual reality; Immersive learning environments; Student engagement Educational technology: Experiential learning

References

Asad, M. M., Naz, A., Churi, P., & Tahanzadeh, M. M. (2021). Virtual reality as pedagogical tool to enhance experiential learning: a systematic literature review. Education Research International, 2021, 1-17. https://doi.org/10.1155/2021/7061623

Bates, T., Cobo, C., Mariño, O., & Wheeler, S. (2020). Can artificial intelligence transform higher education? International Journal of Educational Technology in Higher Education, 17(1). https://doi.org/10.1186/s41239-020-00218-x

Hernandez-de-Menendez, M., Escobar Díaz, C., & Morales-Menendez, R. (2020). Technologies for the future of learning: state of the art. International Journal on Interactive Design and Manufacturing, 14(2), 683–695. https://doi.org/10.1007/s12008-019-00640-0

Jia, Y. and Qi, R. (2023). Influence of an immersive virtual environment on learning effect and learning experience. International Journal of Emerging Technologies in Learning (Ijet), 18(06), 83-95. https://doi.org/10.3991/ijet.v18i06.37815

Moro, C., Birt, J. R., Štromberga, Z., Phelps, C., Clark, J., Glasziou, P., ... & Scott, A. M. (2021). Virtual and augmented reality enhancements to medical and science student physiology and anatomy test performance: a systematic review and meta-analysis. Anatomical Sciences Education, 14(3), 368-376. https://doi.org/10.1002/ase.2049

Radianti, J., Majchrzak, T. A., Fromm, J., & Wohlgenannt, I. (2020). A systematic review of immersive virtual reality applications for higher education: Design elements, lessons learned, and research agenda. Computers and Education, 147, 103778. https://doi.org/10.1016/j.compedu.2019.103778

Academics Approaches to Generative AI in Teaching and Assessment on a Postgraduate Programme

Felix Kwihangana[1]

[1] Manchester Institute of Education, University of Manchester, UK

Correspondence: Felix Kwihangana: felix.kwihangana@manchester.ac.uk

Abstract:

Since the public launch of ChatGPT, a generative AI (GenAI) tool that generates content from prompts in human-like fashion (Su & Yang 2023), it has been noted that teachers are becoming more suspicious of their students for "using GenAI inappropriately or against organisational policy, including in assessed work" (UK Department for Education 2023, p.11). Yet, researchers have also shown that GenAI improves education by creating opportunities for inclusive, personalised and supportive learning for their students (Ruiz-Rojas, Acosta-Vargas et al. 2023, p.3). With the acknowledged current and potentially significant impact of GenAI on education, and the awareness that there is a lot we do not yet know about the use of GenAI in education (Chiu 2023), how educators approach GenAI at a local level (e.g. a postgraduate programme at a large UK university) can affect how staff and students leverage AI's "unlimited possibilities to education" (Zhang and Ashlam 2021).

This presentation reports on a small-scale qualitative study that explored how academics on a postgraduate digital technology-focused programme approached Generative AI in their course units in the wake of institutional policies and guidelines on Generative AI in teaching and assessment. The project sought to identify approaches undertaken by academics and how these approaches are reflected in their teaching, learning and assessment practices.

A thematic analysis of semi-structured interview data collected in the study indicated that academics adopted a wide range of approaches that fell into four main categories. Approaches in the first category emphasised the *pivotal and irrevocability of Generative AI* as an educational technology that is "here to stay" and therefore must be dealt with. This is seconded by *dissuasive approaches* that sought to dissuade students from mis/over/ab/using GenAI, by emphasizing the need for non-AI-aided originality in their ideas. The third category of approaches were *permissive approaches* to GenAI which consisted in encouraging students to use GenAI but in specifically defined and controllable ways. The last category consisted of *GenAI Literacy-focussed* approaches through which academics sought to "balance their concerns about the misuse of these systems with efforts to equip students to engage successfully with AI-enhanced systems in the workplace and community" (Ovarec 2023, p. 216). Of all the approaches, academics who adopted this approach were the ones most interested in ensuring that graduates are equipped with the right "hard" and "soft" GenAI skills and competencies needed for their future success (Menshikova, Beloborodov, et al. 2023).

The findings also underscored significant gaps among academics regarding their understanding of institutional policies and guidelines on generative AI. They highlighted differences in academics' familiarity and experience with generative AI tools, with those more suspicious of students' abuse of GenAI also having less experience using the technology themselves.

Thus, besides a general audience interested in the use of Generative AI for education, the presentation may be of particular interest to academics and institutional policymakers undertaking the deployment of Generative AI on their programmes as well as those seeking to develop AI literacy skills and competencies for academics.

What does learner-centered pedagogy look like in reimagining the digital classroom of the future?

Keywords: Approaches to Generative AI, Generative AI in Education, AI literacy for academics, postgraduate education

References

Chiu, T. K. (2023). The impact of Generative AI (GenAI) on practices, policies and research direction in education: A case of ChatGPT and Midjourney. Interactive Learning Environments, 1-17.

Department for education (2023) Generative AI in education Call for Evidence: summary of responses. https://assets.publishing.service.gov.uk/media/65609be50c7ec8000d95bddd/Generative_AI_call_for_evidence_summary_of_responses.pdf

Menshikova, I. P., Beloborodov, P. I., Primakova, I. N., Glazyrin, A. V., Teplov, D. V., & Shipareva, K. V. (2023). Approaches to Develop Digital Competences to Create a Portrait of the Graduate of the Future. European Journal of Education and Pedagogy, 4(1), 62-66.

Oravec, J. A (2023). Artificial Intelligence Implications for Academic Cheating: Expanding the Dimensions of Responsible Human-AI Collaboration with ChatGPT." Journal of Interactive Learning Research 34(2): 213-237.

Ruiz-Rojas, L. I., Acosta-Vargas, P., De-Moreta-Llovet, J., & Gonzalez-Rodriguez, M. (2023). Empowering education with generative artificial intelligence tools: Approach with an instructional design matrix. Sustainability, 15(15), 11524.

Su, J., & Yang, W. (2023). Unlocking the Power of ChatGPT: A Framework for Applying Generative AI in Education. ECNU Review of Education, 6(3), 355-366. https://doi.org/10.1177/20965311231168423

Zhang, K., & Aslan, A. B. (2021). AI technologies for education: Recent research & future directions. Computers and Education: Artificial Intelligence, 2, 100025.

Digital Transformation in Education: Leveraging Scenario-Based Learning and Digital Tools for Enhanced Learning and Assessment to Meet the Challenges of the AI Era

Yvonne Sarsfield[1], Mary Malone[2], Caroline Mullan[3], Fionnuala Farrell[4]

[1] Advance Centre, Atlantic Technological University, Ireland; yvonne.sarsfield@atu.ie
[2] Engineering Department, Atlantic Technological University, Ireland; mary.malone@atu.ie
[3] Engineering Department, Atlantic Technological University, Ireland; caroline.mullan@atu.ie
[4] Engineering Department, Atlantic Technological University, Ireland; fionnuala.farrell@atu.ie

Correspondence: Yvonne Sarsfield: yvonne.sarsfield@atu.ie

Abstract:

The instructional design strategy for this project is based on a commitment to spearhead digital transformation in education. The pedagogical philosophy centres on equipping learners with the adaptability and innovation skills necessary to thrive in today's rapidly evolving digital landscape. As Weller (2011) suggests, the integration of innovative technology by educators significantly influences student satisfaction, emphasising the importance of leveraging modern tools and methods in education. The swift evolution of technology has reshaped how students interact with educational content, creating a disparity between traditional instructional approaches and the expectations of contemporary learners. Considering this digital transformation in education, it becomes imperative to embrace innovative instructional design techniques that effectively address the evolving requirements of learners.

This project is dedicated to surmounting the challenge of applying problem-solving methodologies, notably Lean Six Sigma's '5 Whys' tool, within online education environments. While online learning offers advantages such as self-paced learning and accessibility, it often lacks the experiential dimension crucial for fostering practical skill development.

To bridge this gap, our project employs a strategic fusion of instructional design techniques, with a primary focus on Scenario-Based Learning (SBL). SBL immerses learners in interactive scenarios, offering them real-world contexts to apply problem-solving techniques. By seamlessly integrating the '5 Whys' methodology within SBL frameworks, learners actively engage in problem-solving processes, thereby deepening their comprehension and practical application skills.

Central to the instructional design approach is the utilisation of ThingLink. Thinglink is a web-based platform tool that enhances learner engagement and provides a dynamic learning environment. ThingLink allows educators to create interactive images and videos by adding clickable hotspots that contain additional information, multimedia resources, or links to external content. This interactive feature enables learners to explore scenarios, investigate problems, and access relevant resources as they progress through the learning experience.

What digital transformations are needed for learning and teaching in the future?

This SBL Thinglink activity holds significant potential to revolutionise assessment practices in online education. By incorporating SBL principles into assessment design, educators can develop authentic assessment tasks that mirror real-world challenges. This approach not only evaluates students' problem-solving abilities but also cultivates critical thinking skills essential for success in the digital age.

This project has the potential to serve as an open education resource, accessible to learners worldwide. By leveraging digital platforms and open educational practices, educators can share the instructional materials, scenarios, and assessments developed through this project with a broader audience. This not only enhances accessibility but also promotes collaborative learning and knowledge sharing among educators and learners globally.

Aligned with the theme of "Learning in the Age of AI: Towards Imaginative Futures," this project underscores the importance of embracing digital transformations in education. Through innovative instructional design techniques such as SBL and leveraging digital tools like ThingLink, we empower learners to navigate complex problems and thrive in an AI-driven world. Moreover, by transforming assessment practices and embracing open education principles, we contribute to creating a more inclusive and accessible learning environment for all.

While this project is still a work in progress, preliminary feedback from lecturers and students has indicated that this tool could help improve the student's proficiency in applying the 5 whys. They also recognised its alignment with real industrial applications and its potential to engage students in learning. A comprehensive study is planned to be carried out to gain further insight into this tool via an online survey. The survey will encompass immediate and post intervention assessment to gauge the impact on learning outcomes. Additionally, qualitative feedback will be gathered to elucidate the perceived effectiveness and value of the approach.

Keywords: Digital Transformation, Scenario-Based Learning, Digital Tools, Enhanced Learning, Assessment, AI Era

References

Weller, M. (2011). *The Digital Scholar: How Technology is Transforming Scholarly Practice*. United Kingdom: Bloomsbury Publishing.

GenAI Curriculum Redefined: Students' Perspective

Gila Kurtz[1], Oren Ben- Aharon [2]

[1]Faculty of Instructional Technologies, Holon Institute of Technology, Israel; Gilaku@hit.ac.il
[2]Faculty of Instructional Technologies, Holon Institute of Technology, Israel; orenba@hit.ac.il

Correspondence: Gila Kurtz: Gilaku@hit.ac.il

Abstract:

The breakthrough of Generative Artificial Intelligence (GenAI) platforms such as ChatGPT, Midjourney, and others are leading to far-reaching changes in the employment market, learning, and humanity in general. They pose unprecedented challenges to academic teaching and learning methods as we have known them so far. Some see the current technological development as an expression of disruptive innovation that threatens the traditional ecosystem of academic education - to the point of its possible suppression. On the other hand, this innovative development can represent a transformative catalyst allowing higher education systems to improve their relevance and sustainability. The Faculty of Instructional Technologies at Holon Institute of Technology (HIT) in Israel is a pioneer in its field, aiming to meet the growing demand for skilled professionals in developing and implementing advanced learning technologies. The faculty's unique pedagogical approach combines real-world challenges with teamwork and project-based learning in innovative ways of learning and teaching. Following the emergence of GenAI and in line with the pedagogical philosophy of the Instructional Technologies Faculty management (Kurtz et al., 2023), we invited a team of outstanding graduate students to develop based on their perspective and with the guidelines of faculty members, a GenAI-based educational layer that will be integrated into the existing undergraduate curriculum. The emphasis was on the informed and critical integration of GenAI while maintaining and fostering the values of creativity, ethics, and academic excellence. The group developed GenAI-powered learning scenarios in six core courses [see example in Figure 1].

Figure 1. Screenshot from UX/AI course: Building personas to create a UX characterization process using GenAI Tools

The rationale behind this project is to harness the potential of GenAI to enhance the student's learning experience while maintaining the relevance of the academy to the GenAI era. In our presentation, we will share examples of students' scenarios and offer recommendations for future projects of this type [Link to the project (Hebrew) - https://facultyprojects.telem-hit.net/specialprojects/].

What digital transformations are needed for learning and teaching in the future?

Keywords: Generative AI, Curriculum, Project-Based Learning, Higher Education

References

Kurtz, G., Amzalag, M., Barak-Medina, E., Gal, E., Kohen-Vacs, D., Shaked, N., Zailer, G., & Zaguri, Y. (2023). *Higher education and generative ai (genai) in israel: opportunities, challenges and recommendations*. https://facultyprojects.telem-hit.net/HigherEducationGenAI/En/

AI Optimizing a Dashboard in Technological Environments for Enhancing Learning (TEL) Studies

Hayley Weigelt-Marom[1], Omri Kahana[2], Dan Kohen-Vacs[3]

[1 2 3] Faculty of Instructional Technologies, Holon Institute of Technology (HIT), Israel
[1] hayleyw@hit.ac.il
[2] omrika@hit.ac.il
[3] mrkohen@hit.ac.il

Correspondence: Hayley Weigelt-Merom, hayleyw@hit.ac.il

Abstract:

Technological Environments for Enhancing Learning (TEL) encompass various interconnected facets, often encapsulated in the Technological, Pedagogical, and Content Knowledge (TPACK) framework (Shen, & Ho, 2020). These TPACK's aspects emphasize their interdependence and are crucial for forming a comprehensive TEL environment. TPACK also encompasses implicit considerations related to User Interface (UI) and User Experience (UX) design that are crucial for offering educational experiences that are effective user-friendly and appealing.

The paper focuses on the practices employed at the User Experience Lab affiliated with the Faculty of Instructional Technologies at the Holon Institute of Technology in Israel for developing a customized dashboard. The lab utilizes various sensors, including Galvanic Skin Response (GSR), pulse rate, and eye tracking sensors, to gather numeric data related to user emotions, physiological responses, eye movements, and visual attention. This data is then consolidated and presented on a customized dashboard "Xsenso". A dashboard designed and developed by staff members and students as part of a final project at the Faculty (Fig. 1). The dashboard serves to provide insights to UX/UI in educational studies, in the nature of the educational experience within the TEL environment.

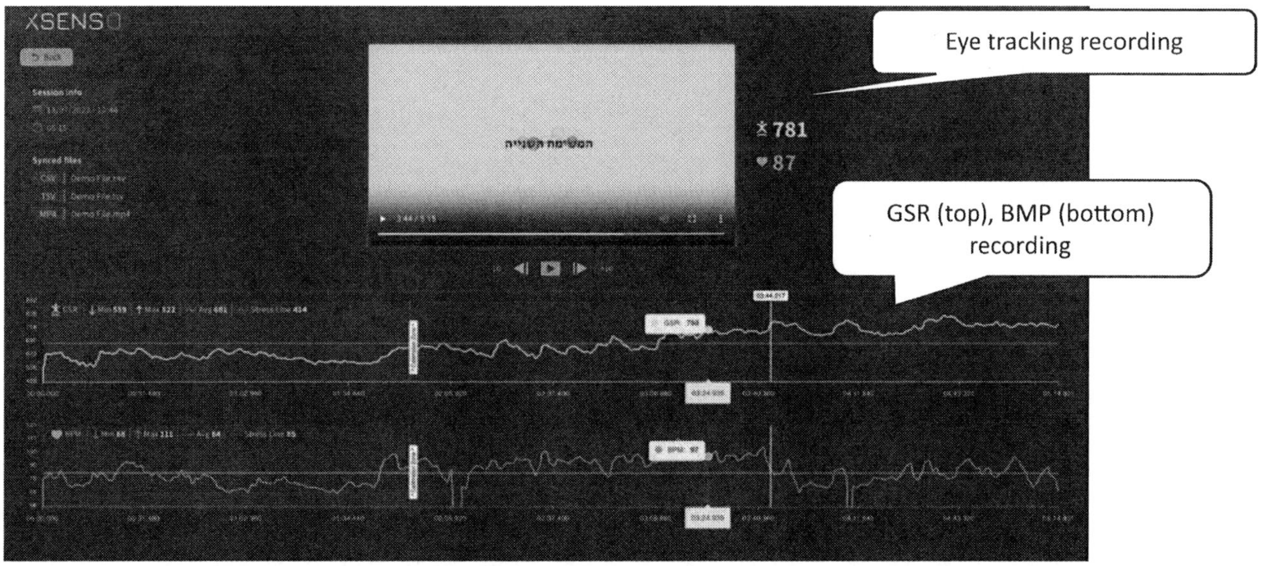

Figure 1. "Xsenso" dashboard

Following data collection, the information from different sensors is organized on the dashboard along a common timeline. The dataset is then analyzed and processed by artificial intelligence (AI) to generate a quick yet in-depth comprehensive overview of the results. This approach allows for a better understanding of study results and enables the refinement of the TEL environment. The AI analysis is particularly focused on detecting challenges related to UI and UX, aiming to enhance the overall user experience in TEL environments.

We believe that the preliminary examples presented at the conference will serve as a foundation for expanding the AI-enhanced dashboard with additional testing and study opportunities. This effort is undertaken as we envision a comprehensive architecture, including the dashboard, optimized for TEL communities seeking an effective approach to exploit data from users undergoing a learning process to improve educational artifacts and approaches. Furthermore, our ongoing efforts in the lab aim to provide a convenient approach capable of offering an effective and facilitated means to refine and enhance artifacts conceptualized, designed, and developed by communities of TEL practitioners. In our forthcoming endeavors, we intend to continue integrating more sensing capabilities and improving the AI-enhanced means to conduct data analysis, as well as to offer real-time recommendations for enhancing capabilities of TEL artifacts we examine in the lab.

Keywords: Technological Environments for Enhancing Learning and Training, AI for dashboard

References

Shen, C. W., & Ho, J. T. (2020). Technology-enhanced learning in higher education: A bibliometric analysis with latent semantic approach. *Computers in Human Behavior, 104*, 106177.

Xsenso (2023). *Faculty of Instructional Technologies at HIT , Israel.*

Empowering Learning Journeys with MyCareerPath.ie and a Micro Credential on Transversal Skills for Industry Supporting Regional Development from the Atlantic Technological University (ATU), Ireland

Carina Ginty[1], Bridie Killoran[2]

[1] Atlantic Technological University (ATU), Ireland; carina.ginty@atu.ie
[2] Atlantic Technological University (ATU), Ireland; bridie.killoran@atu.ie

Correspondence: Carina Ginty: carina.ginty@atu.ie

Abstract:

This paper session will provide an overview of My Career Path, a development of ATU's Higher Education 4.0 project and a new Micro Credential named Transversal Skills for Industry supported by the N-TUTORR Transforming Learning project. My Career Path is an online learning career development platform and embeds career guidance into the RPL process by helping prospective students identify appropriate courses that align to their career and professional goals. This is an external facing ATU service aimed at people in the workplace looking to upskill, re-skill or re-train.

Keywords: Transversal Skills, Micro Credential, Artificial Intelligence, Career Tools, Embedding Career Guidance, Workplace Development, Mentoring, Industry Engagement, Life Long Learning, Digital Transformation, Sustainable Employability, Higher Education.

Summary

This paper session will provide an overview of My Career Path, a development of ATU's Higher Education 4.0 project and a new Micro Credential named Transversal Skills for Industry supported by the N-TUTORR Transforming Learning project. My Career Path is an online learning career development platform and embeds career guidance into the RPL process by helping prospective students identify appropriate courses that align to their career and professional goals. This is an external facing ATU service aimed at people in the workplace looking to upskill, re-skill or re-train.

An important aspect of this initiative is leveraging partnerships with local employers, raising awareness and building confidence among employees in relation to their capabilities, competencies and transversal skills. This results in informed career and educational decisions, for example choosing the right course and the appropriate use of access routes, including recognised prior learning.

What digital transformations are needed for learning and teaching in the future?

The importance of transversal skills at all levels in the workplace has been accelerated by the double disruption of the pandemic and fourth industrial revolution. 'Transversal skills' are skills which are not confined to any one discipline, but rather can be applied across multiple areas. Examples of transversal skills include, but are not limited to, the following: communication skills, creativity, digital literacy, problem solving, critical thinking, innovation, ability to work in teams, and a growth mindset. Such skills are seen as increasingly important in the contemporary workplace.

Based on the in-demand transversal skills identified by Whiting (The World Economic Forum, 2020) this micro credential enables students to understand transversal skills and their relevance in the workplace. Students rate their associated level of professional competence across 12 identified skills (Figure 1), using an AI enhanced tool called Skills Pulse Checker. Students embark on a transformative journey, strategically utilising a range of skills as catalysts for success to enhance their careers and their employability. Career guidance supports include one-to-one mentoring sessions as well as access to a curated learning pathway that covers micro learning resources. The various reflective activities completed in the programme are amplified by the use of AI-powered tools within the innovative framework of My Career Path platform, such as the STARR Framework, CV Builder, CV 360, and Interview 360. This combined approach empowers students to adeptly navigate the intricate landscape of career advancement.

Figure 1: Transversal Skills identified and developed in the Micro Credential

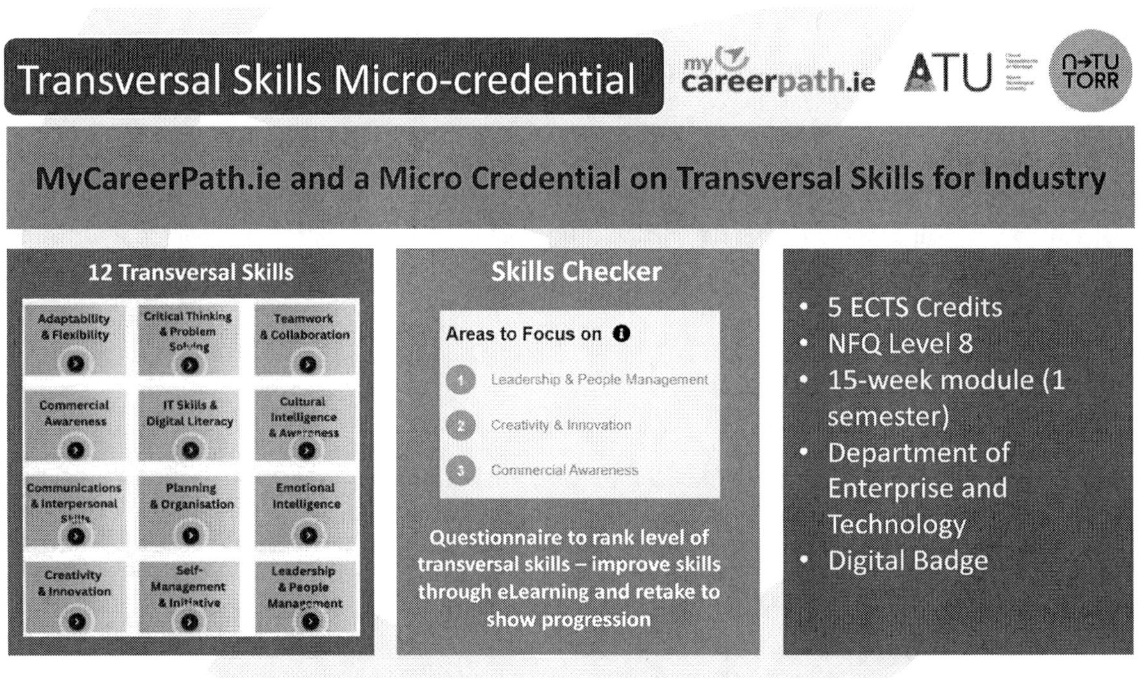

What digital transformations are needed for learning and teaching in the future?

This paper session will demonstrate the value of embedding career guidance supported by AI tools into the Transversal Skills Micro Credential and the various My Career Path service case studies including Medtronic and Merit Medical. Overall, My Career Path platform has digitally transformed and demystified the career guidance and skills development process and is supporting industry engagement with micro credentials.

The development of the Transversal Skills for Industry Micro Credential was supported by the ATU N-TUTORR Transforming Learning project. N-TUTORR is a national programme of work designed to enable and leverage digital transformations to achieve sustainable and long-lasting change in the higher education technological university sector (see ATU.ie/NTUTORR).

References

Whiting, K., (2020). These are the top 10 job skills of tomorrow–and how long it takes to learn them. In World Economic Forum (Vol. 21).

Voogt, J. and Roblin, N.P., (2010). 21st century skills. Discussienota. Zoetermeer: The Netherlands: Kennisnet, 23(03), p.2000.

Medium Naturalness and Social Presence: The Online Classroom of the Future

Ewout Buckens[1]

[1] Warwick Business School, University of Warwick, UK; Ewout.buckens@wbs.ac.uk

Correspondence: Ewout Buckens: Ewout.buckens@wbs.ac.uk

Abstract:

Since the COVID-19 pandemic, students and faculty alike have been exposed to numerous hours of online synchronous sessions in a variety of forms. A vast majority of sessions has stayed quite basic and traditional: an instructor runs their session from a laptop or computer, sharing presentations and other content from their office or from home (Pregowska et al., 1999). In fact, a JISC survey on teaching staff's digital experience, collecting responses from universities across the UK, said that "most (87%) teaching staff used a laptop for teaching, and two-thirds used a desktop (68%)". Only 3% used a virtual reality headset and no more than 5% made use of any alternative/virtual/extended reality (AR/VR/XR) technologies (Joint Information Systems Committee, 2023). Very few innovative leaps have been made in synchronous online teaching.

We realised that this set-up massively limits the student experience during synchronous session and stops us from creating a better learning environment and increasing instructional effectiveness. So we set out to address these challenges. Our solution was SmartStage.

Warwick Business School's SmartStage facility has provided a cutting-edge solution and has transformed these traditional online sessions into an immersive, augmented reality learning environment with highly interactive elements. It combines the benefits of a physical teaching space with augmented reality graphics, holograms, learning technology and the use of camera and live editing to provide a unique and optimal learning experience for online students. The stage is operated by a specialist team, allowing the presenter to entirely focus on their content and interaction with students.

The stage itself is part physical space, allowing presenters to walk around and interact with their content, and part augmented reality, making the environment look like a full classroom to online learners. This allows for a higher degree of medium naturalness, as the teaching environment has the appearance of a real classroom. This reduces the learner's cognitive load and ambiguity in messages conveyed and heightens psychological arousal, thus improving learning effectiveness (Kock, 2004). The ability to fully display the presenter, enabling them to interact with content and making learners an active part of the stage (by adding their video screens on a display panel on stage) also allows the instructor to have a stronger social presence (Garrison et al., 1999). It further enables clearer non-verbal immediacy behaviours such as gesturing, smiling, maintaining a relaxed body position, due to a more natural and user-friendly environment. This is a very important factor in increasing instructional effectiveness (Andersen, 1979; Andersen & Withrow, 1981).

During the presentation I will showcase the stage's use in practice with a range of examples from practitioners at the business school. I will also give an overview of the research done and students' reception of this new approach to synchronous online learning. I will finally elaborate on further developments, such as creating experimental and immersive teaching environments on stage, ranging from factory settings to different cities to even fully created fictional spaces.

Keywords: Innovation, online, transformative synchronous teaching spaces

What digital transformations are needed for learning and teaching in the future?

References

Andersen, J. F., & Withrow, J. G. (1981). The impact of lecturer nonverbal expressiveness on improving mediated instruction. *Communication Education*, 30(4), 342-353. https://doi.org/10.1080/03634528109378490

Andersen, J.F. (1979). Teacher immediacy as a predictor of teaching effectiveness. *Communication yearbook*, 3(1), 543-559. https://doi.org/10.1080/23808985.1979.11923782

Garrison, D. R., Anderson, T., & Archer, W. (1999). Critical inquiry in a text-based environment: computer conferencing in higher education. *The Internet and Higher Education* 2(2-3): 87–105. https://doi.org/10.1016/S1096-7516(00)00016-6

Joint Information Systems Committee (2023, October). *Teaching staff digital experience insights survey 2022/23: UK higher education (HE survey findings)*. JISC. https://repository.jisc.ac.uk/9282/1/DEI-2023-teaching-staff-he-report.pdf

Kock, N. (2004). The psychobiological model: towards a new theory of computer-mediated communication based on darwinian evolution. *Organization Science 15*(3), 327-348. https://doi.org/10.1287/orsc.1040.0071

Pregowska, A., Masztalerz, K., Garlińska, M., & Osial, M. (2021, March). A Worldwide Journey through Distance Education—From the Post Office to Virtual, Augmented and Mixed Realities, and Education during the COVID-19 Pandemic. *Education Sciences, 11*(3), 118. https://doi.org/10.3390/educsci11030118

Warwick Business School. (2023, December 15). *Your new immersive learning environment - coming soon!* [video]. YouTube. https://youtu.be/cMRnL7BsOms?feature=shared

Relationship Between Technological Literacy and Interdisciplinary Competence Development for VET Learners in Construction Sector

Ugne Supranaviciene [1], Genute Gedviliene[2], Lina Vaitkute[3]

[1 2 3] Education academy, Vytautas Magnus University, Lithuania
[1] ugne.supranaviciene@vdu.lt
[2] genute.gedviliene@vdu.lt
[3] lina.vaitkute@vdu.lt

Correspondence: Ugne Supranaviciene: ugne.supranaviciene@vdu.lt

Keywords: adult education; interdisciplinary competencies; sustainable development; technological literacy; VET.

Introduction

The development of interdisciplinary competencies through technological literacy is crucial for VET learners in the construction sector to stay competitive in the evolving landscape of the industry. As construction processes increasingly integrate advanced technologies, such as Building Information Modeling and automated construction equipment, VET learners need to possess a strong technological foundation to effectively understand, operate, and innovate within these new frameworks.

Technological literacy enables VET learners to comprehend and utilize digital tools and platforms, fostering a deeper understanding of the interdisciplinary nature of construction projects (Reddy et al., 2020). By merging proficiency in technology with their construction expertise, learners are better equipped to collaborate with professionals from various disciplines, such as architects, engineers, and project managers. This collaborative environment demands a high level of adaptability, problem-solving, and effective communication skills, all of which are nurtured through the development of technological literacy.

Additionally, as the construction sector becomes increasingly data-driven, the ability to make informed decisions based on digital information and data analytics is paramount. Technological literacy empowers VET learners to not only gather and interpret relevant data but also implement best practices and innovative solutions derived from this information (Moses, 2016). This enhances their interdisciplinary competencies, as they become adept at integrating technological insights into their decision-making processes, thereby optimizing project outcomes and contributing to the overall success of construction endeavors.

In conclusion, the cultivation of technological literacy within the VET education framework in the construction sector is integral to the development of interdisciplinary competencies. It equips learners with the necessary skills to effectively collaborate in interdisciplinary teams, adapt to technological advancements, and make informed decisions, thereby ensuring their readiness to meet the evolving demands of the construction industry (Luan et al., 2020).

Methodology. Quantative method applied. The research performed in compliance with the main principles of ethics: benevolence, insights and express their opinion; honesty. The research respondents were 260 managers and small construction organisation owners and their employees from different countries (Germany, Lithuania, Spain, The Netherlands, Finland, and Italy). The research based on the following methodological dispositions: transformative learning and experiential learning theory. Research was conducted in two stages: 1) research into required interdisciplinary competencies, identifying the importance of digital literacy and its relations with interdisciplinary competences development 2) research into the sustainable interdisciplinary competencies development.

What digital transformations are needed for learning and teaching in the future?

This paper will present what conditions are needed for a VET learner to develop interdisciplinary competencies in the construction sector and how it is related to the technological literacy? What prerequisites are needed to ensure sustainable interdisciplinary competencies development?
The aim of this paper is to reveal technological literacy importance in developing interdisciplinary competencies in the construction sector.

Results

In an initial study to find out what and whether interdisciplinary competences are needed, we interviewed 138 small business owners, team leaders or individuals working in the construction sector. Figure 1 shows the distribution of the survey participants across the different activities. 16 respondents (12%) of respondents indicated that their area of activity is 'other'. 64% of respondents are working in at least 2 areas and every fourth (34) - only in one area. Of those, the majority (18) - in electric installation.

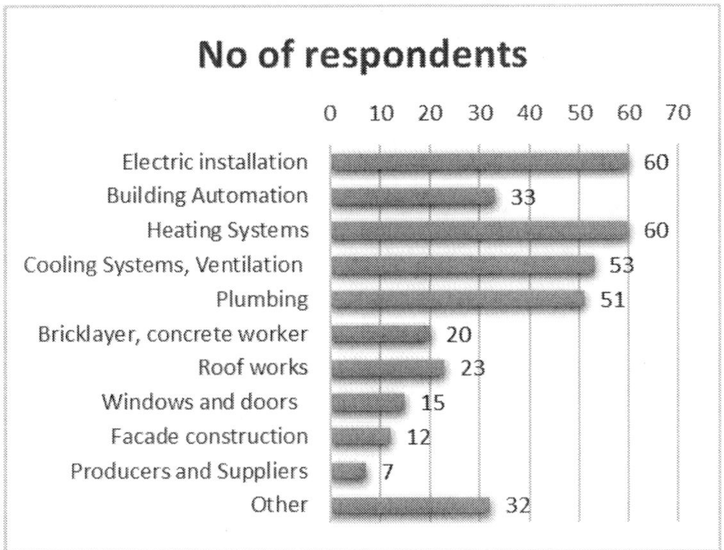

Figure 1. Survey respondents from different areas in Construction sector

We also asked: does your company, when providing construction services, establish contacts and collaborate with other professions on the construction site? We were first interested in the extent to which companies' network and cooperate on the construction site. The results are presented in Figure 2, where the findings suggest that collaboration with other professions seems to be the operating principle.

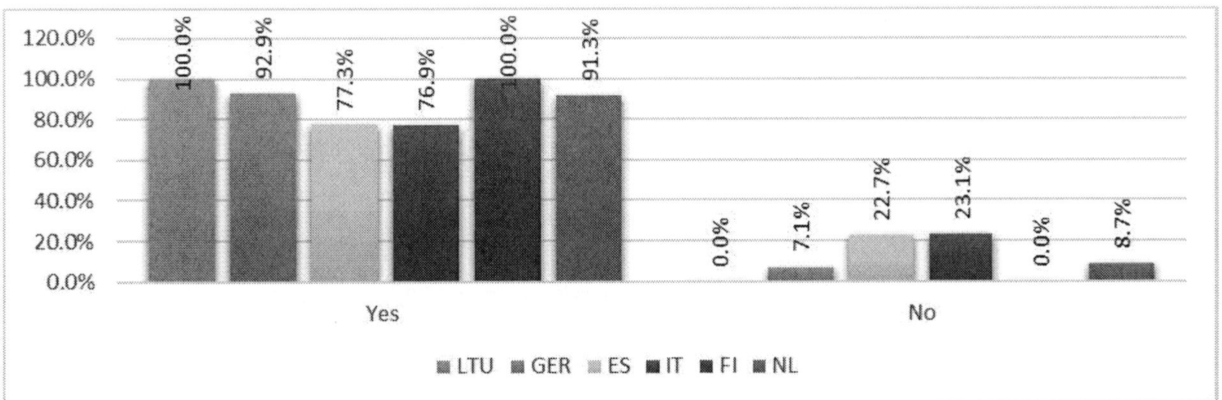

Figure 2. The need for collaboration with other professions

Figure 3 shows distribution of respondents' answers about the importance of interdisciplinary and cross-disciplinary competences. In green color are those which were assessed as the most relevant and in red – those which were assessed as less important.
A general conclusion is that our assumptions about the competences which are important for building engineering services were right. All our statements were assessed as relevant.

The most important competences are: the ability to solve problems systematically in complex systems; a basic knowledge on different technical systems in a building and their interconnection; the ability to communicate and collaborate with employees from other trades.
The least important competences (but certainly relevant) are: understanding multiple disciplines including engineering, computer science, electronics and control systems; the ability to integrate and automate various building systems; the ability to collect, analyze and interpret data from various sensors to optimize building performance.

Statement	No of respondents				
	Important	Neither important nor unimportant	Unimportant	Don't know	No answer
The ability to recognize and understand relationships between different Trades	107	22	2	3	4
The ability to solve problems systematically in complex systems	124	7	2	1	4
A basic knowledge on different technical systems in a building and their interconnection	113	14	3	2	6
Understanding multiple disciplines including engineering, computer science, electronics and control systems	77	46	7	3	5
Combining expertise in different trades to implement innovation	90	35	5	2	6
The ability to integrate and automate various building systems	80	40	8	4	6
The ability to identify, analyse and resolve complex technical tasks	103	25	4	2	4
The ability to collect, analyse and interpret data from various sensors to optimize building performance	83	36	7	6	6
The ability to communicate and collaborate with employees from other trades	117	13	1	2	5

Figure 3. The need for collaboration with other professions

The findings from this employer survey provide insights into the key competences that are prioritized and valued within building engineering services. Most Important Competences:
Systematic Problem-Solving in Complex Systems. This competency highlights the importance of being able to analyze and address issues within intricate building systems. Building engineers must possess the skills to identify, diagnose, and resolve problems efficiently and methodically.
Basic Knowledge of Technical Systems and Interconnections: *Understanding different technical systems within a building and how they interact* is fundamental. This knowledge enables effective planning, maintenance, and troubleshooting of building services.
Communication and Collaboration Across Trades: *Building engineering involves coordination with various professionals* from different disciplines. Effective communication and collaboration skills are essential for successful project management and implementation.
In conclusion, these findings highlight the essential competences required for success in building engineering services, emphasizing problem-solving, technical knowledge, and effective communication.

Conclusions

The survey confirmed that technical skills and operational knowledge in building engineering services is still relevant. Professionals need proficiency in such tasks as assembling, dismantling, servicing, maintaining, and operating building systems or their components to ensure their functionality and sustainability. Furthermore, survey confirmed the industry's shift towards automation, renewable energy integration, and advanced building technologies and strong demand for professionals with specialized knowledge and skills in these areas with strong focus on technological literacy. Building engineering services technicians need to be versatile and responsive to varied demands, requiring a broad skill set that encompasses not only technical expertise but also and foremost transversal skills, such as communication skills, foreign languages skills, adaptability, and problem-solving capabilities, which could be acquired with usage and enablement of certain technological tools (Figure 4).

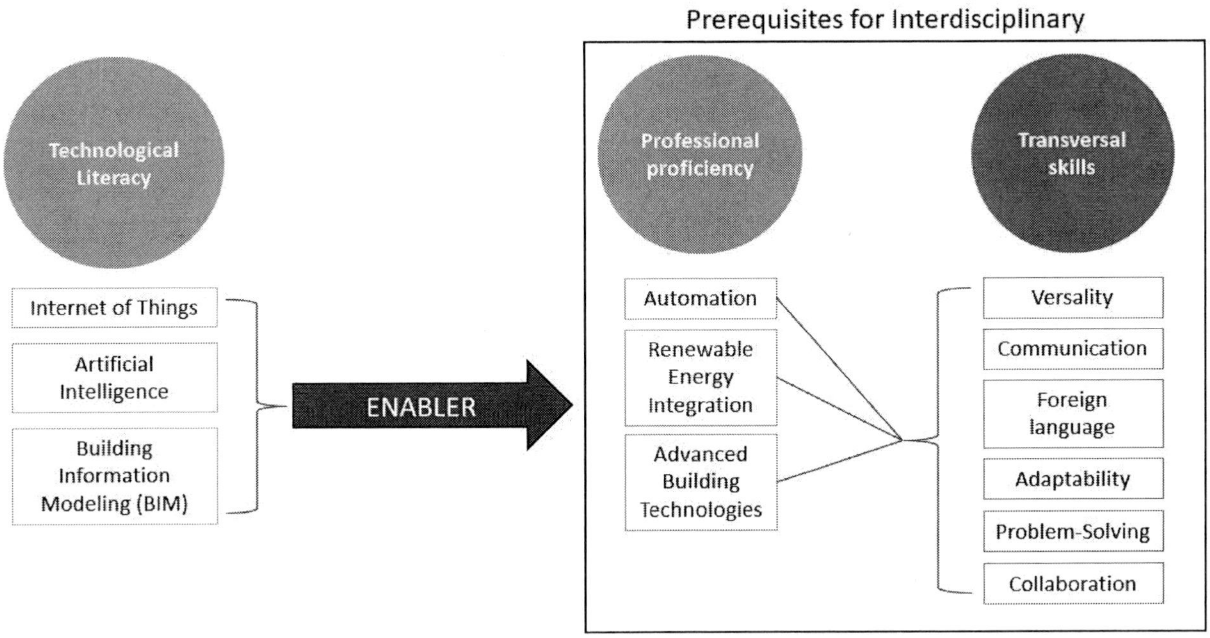

Figure 4. The Relationship between Technological Literacy and Interdisciplinary prerequisites

There is no clear consensus among survey participants regarding whether certain professional situations require collaboration across different professions or can be handled by a single profession with multidisciplinary knowledge, however training should incorporate cross section learning and interdisciplinary contexts. VET learners in construction sector need to have access to interdisciplinary training on sustainable construction and how to handle new technologies and building engineering services solutions, based on Internet of Things, Artificial Intelligence, building information modelling (BIM) through hybrid learning and high-quality work-based learning. This would help to tackle outdated perception and image of construction industry and to attract young persons and women into this occupation.

References

Luan, H., Géczy, P., Lai, H., Gobert, J D., Yang, S J H., Ogata, H., Baltes, J., Guerra, R D S., Li, P., & Tsai, C C. (2020, October 19). Challenges and Future Directions of Big Data and Artificial Intelligence in Education. https://doi.org/10.3389/fpsyg.2020.580820

Moses, K M. (2016, January 1). Improving the quality and competence of technical vocational education and training output through vocational school cooperation with industry: A case study of Uganda. https://doi.org/10.1063/1.4965794

Reddy, P., Sharma, B., & Chaudhary, K. (2020, July 1). Digital Literacy: A Review of Literature. https://www.igi-global.com/gateway/article/258971

What Can LMS Data Tell Us About University Teachers' Course Design Skills Development? Results of an Institution-Wide Intervention of Online Course Development

Krisztina Ildikó Lénárt[1], Helga Dorner[2], Szilvia Tóth-Mózer[3]

[1] Doctoral School of Education, Faculty of Education and Psychology, Eötvös Loránd University, Hungary; krisztina.lenart@oktig.elte.hu
[2] Faculty of Education and Psychology, Eötvös Loránd University, Hungary; helga.dorner@ppk.elte.hu
[3] Eötvös Loránd University, Hungary; toth-mozer.szilvia@oktig.elte.hu

Correspondence: Krisztina Ildikó Lénárt: krisztina.lenart@oktig.elte.hu

Abstract:

The literature which focuses on the digital competence of teachers in K12 settings is vast (Ala-Mutka, 2011; Amhag et al., 2019; UNESCO, 2018; Vuorikari et al.,2022). Nevertheless, there is a need for higher education institutions to know better how university teachers' digital competence should be developed by which instruments (Matarranz, & Otto, 2022). By digital competence in this context, we mean the ability to use digital technologies for creating digital resources to use in teaching and learning processes, enhancing assessment and inclusion and empowering learners using digital technologies. This paper thus discusses the results of a university-wide institutional intervention which aimed to engage university teachers in online course design by involving them in self-paced digital competence training. Volunteering instructors participated in three different self-paced courses — designed by the University's e-learning centre. Participation was incentivized also by offering a laptop for individual use.

This research focuses on instructors (n=40) who completed one particular online self-paced training and integrated skills and competences acquired in their online course design. Hence, we investigated how their courses changed after the intervention. We used a mixed-method research design, that is, collected data about the courses in the LMS before and after the intervention using the LMS database with anonymized data. We used quantitative analysis to compare the course content. It was difficult to define the criteria for the course interface, since the University has a broad spectrum of disciplines and forms of training. We also used the quality criteria of Quality Matters (https://qualitymatters.org/) and Vai and Sosulski's (2011) criteria, which have been synthesized and adapted to the specificities of the work at the University. To better understand participants' motivations and recognize the changes in their course design, semi-structured interviews were also recorded. We used qualitative content analysis, also including deductive codes based on the DigCompEdu (Punie & Redecker, 2017) to analyze those. Preliminary analyses have shown that the competence acquired by teachers is mainly reflected in the design of online activities on the online course interface, namely, in its complexity, collaborative approach and interactivity. Further results will help us to identify the elements of teachers' digital competence change, particularly, that of course design and its impact on their course content. In addition to subjective success criteria for the intervention, objective indicators will be identified.

Keywords: TDC (teachers' digital competence), self-paced course, competency framework, course design

References

Ala-Mutka, K. (2011). Mapping Digital Competence: Towards a Conceptual Understanding. (JRC Technical Notes No. JRC67075). IPTS. https://doi.org/10.13140/ RG.2.2.18046.00322

Matarranz, M., & Otto, A. (2022). Teachers' digital competencies in higher education: A systematic literature review. International Journal of Educational Technology in Higher Education, 19(1), 1-16. https://doi.org/10.1186/s41239-021-00312-8

Lisbeth Amhag, Lisa Hellström & Martin Stigmar (2019) Teacher Educators' Use of Digital Tools and Needs for Digital Competence in Higher Education, Journal of Digital Learning in Teacher Education, 35(4), 203-220, DOI: 10.1080/21532974.2019.1646169

Punie, Y., editor(s), Redecker, C., European Framework for the Digital Competence of Educators: DigCompEdu , EUR 28775 EN, Publications Office of the European Union, Luxembourg, 2017, ISBN 978-92-79-73718-3 (print),978-92-79-73494-6 (pdf), doi:10.2760/178382 (print),10.2760/159770 (online), JRC107466.

UNESCO Institute for Statistics (2018), A Global Framework of Reference on Digital Literacy Skills for Indicator 4.4.2. https://uis.unesco.org/sites/default/files/documents/ip51-global-framework-reference-digital-literacy-skills-2018-en.pdf

Vai, M., & Sosulski, K. (2011). Essentials of Online Course Design. Routledge.

Vuorikari, R., Kluzer, S. and Punie, Y., DigComp 2.2: The Digital Competence Framework for Citizens - With new examples of knowledge, skills and attitudes, EUR 31006 EN, Publications Office of the European Union, Luxembourg, 2022, ISBN 978-92-76-48883-5, doi:10.2760/490274, JRC128415.

https://qualitymatters.org/

Internationalization of Open and Distance Teaching Universities. A Comparative Case Study

Svenja Bedenlier[1]

[1] Friedrich-Alexander-Universität Erlangen-Nürnberg, Germany

Correspondence: Svenja Bedenlier, svenja.bedenlier@fau.de

Abstract:

The history of open and distance teaching universities is intertwined with the individual and societal quest for access to higher education for working adults, learners with care responsibility or disadvantaged groups – students who benefit from studying flexibly in time and space at a distance (Keegan, 1980, Stöter et al., 2014). The oftentimes implicit focus to cater to a primarily national student body continues to be characteristic of open and distance teaching universities.

However, the environment in which they operate has changed (Tait, 2018), with digitization and internationalization being two central drivers for change in higher education. Whilst on-site universities have long pursued internationalization as a transversal topic (e.g. Knight, 2003; Hudzik, 2011), for open and distance education it has yet to enter the mainstream of research and practice. Therefore, research is needed on how open and distance teaching universities conceive internationalization and how they incorporate it into their institutional strategies and practices.

To this end, a comparative case study design is developed (Yin, 2018), that investigates the institutional internationalization of three different European open and distance teaching universities. The concepts of virtual internationalization (Bruhn, 2020) and internationalization at a distance (Mittelmeier et al., 2020) are applied as analytical lenses, to address the overarching research questions: How do open and distance teaching universities perceive themselves in an international higher education environment? Which strategic approaches do they develop to internationalize teaching and learning at a distance?

As the research is ongoing, the presentation outlines the theoretical conception of the study, introduces the research design and reflects on the choice of cases.

Keywords: open and distance teaching universities, internationalization, strategy, case study

References

Bruhn (2020). *Virtual internationalization in higher education.* Gütersloh: wbv.

Hudzik, J. K. (2015). *Comprehensive internationalization: Institutional pathways to success*. Abingdon: Routledge.

Keegan, D. (1980). On defining distance education. *Distance Education*, *1*(1), 13–36.

Knight, J. (2003). Updated definition of internationalization. *International Higher Education*, *33*, 2–3.

Mittelmeier, J., Rienties, B., Gunter, A., & Raghuram, P. (2020). Conceptualizing internationalization at a distance: a "third category" of university internationalization. *Journal of Studies in International Education*, https://doi.org/10.1177/1028315320906176

Stöter, J., Bullen, M., Zawacki-Richter, O., & von Prümmer, C. (2014). From the back door into the mainstream: the characteristics of lifelong learners. In O. Zawacki-Richter & T. Anderson (eds.), *Online distance education: towards a research agenda* (pp. 421–457). Athabasca University Press.

Tait, A. (2018). Open Universities: the next phase. *Asian Association of Open Universities Journal, 13*(1), 13-23.

Yin, R. K. (2018). *Case study research: Design and methods* (6th ed). SAGE.

Agile Continuous Education (ACE): An End-to-End Model to Support Lifelong Learning for Employability

Mitchell Peters[1], Federico Christmann[2], Ulf-Daniel Ehlers[3]

[1] Universitat Oberta de Catalunya (UOC), Spain; mjosephp@uoc.edu
[2] Universitat Oberta de Catalunya (UOC), Spain; fchristmann@uoc.edu
[3] Baden-Wuerttemberg Cooperative State University (DHBW), Germany; ulf-daniel.ehlers@dhbw-karlsruhe.de

Correspondence: Mitchell Peters mjosephp@uoc.edu

Abstract

The evolution of the European workforce, reflected in the concept of Industry 5.0, emphasises collaboration between people and smart systems, maintaining a human-centered approach that aims to increase efficiency and productivity, while prioritising personalisation, sustainability, and the well-being of the workforce (European Commission 2020, 2021). Although the transition to Industry 5.0 represents a shift towards a more resilient approach for the European industry, achieving this transition poses various challenges for lifelong learning goals, particularly in the higher education sector.

The disruptive forces mentioned above are challenging higher education institutions (HEIs) to align continuous education and training with the emerging mix of transversal, managerial, and technical skills needed for professional and organisational growth in Industry 5.0 (Chiarello et al. 2021, Spada et al. 2023). The rise of a competency-based model has pushed education systems to rethink traditional learning practices and provide responsive programmes to adapt workers to a rapidly changing labour market environment (Ehlers 2020; Peters et al., 2023). However, HEIs face several obstacles in putting skills alignment into practice. Common barriers include the need for increased technical capacity, financial constraints, low interaction between working groups from different disciplines, limited consensus about the best practices, and dispersed responsibilities within and between institutions. For these reasons, higher education institutions have a weak track record in adapting programmes to skills needs through flexible and modular learning pathways.

In recognition of this, the Agile Continuous Education (ACE) model aims to contribute to developing a robust educational delivery model. ACE is defined as an approach to education that brings the principles of dynamic and continuous improvement to higher education. Firstly, it includes skills anticipation initiatives based on data science techniques to develop labour market intelligence (LMI) tools on current and future skills needs (Spada et al. 2023). Secondly, iterative skills alignment initiatives ensure this knowledge translates into updated or new educational offerings, where skills and knowledge can be applied to lifelong learners in short training cycles through micro-credentials. As a result, an ACE approach creates rapid responsiveness to feedback from industry and labour market stakeholders for novel curriculum development while providing a strategic institutional response through micro-credentialing (Brown et al., 2023).

Given the actual poor record of HEIs for adapting educational offerings to emerging skill needs, there is a critical need to promote the institutional capacity for delivering an ACE model. Recognizing this, our research aims to contribute to developing a robust ACE model by providing a conceptual framework for integrating these practices in support of lifelong learning for employability. The research offers an end-to-end ACE delivery model that requires organisational coordination and implementation across various actors, roles, and responsibilities. The key practices are highlighted in Figure 1 below:

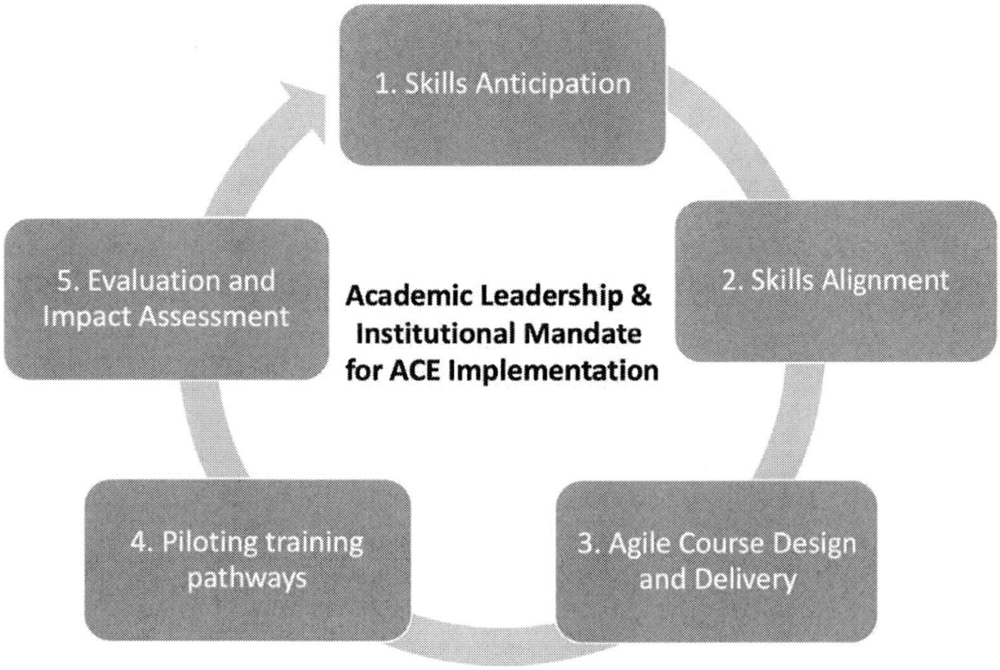

Figure 1: Agile Continuous Education End-to-End Model.

Despite the benefits of this approach, further challenges are related to the strategic academic leadership and institutional mission necessary for ACE delivery, as well as the pedagogical approaches to teach the emerging mix of skills needed for Industry 5.0. Online HEIs provide sufficient flexibility for lifelong learners who combine education with professional and personal commitments. However, teaching a mix of transversal, managerial, and technical skills requires learning from peers and extensive supervised practice, which has proven difficult to provide in online modalities. Therefore, novel and innovative pedagogical designs should be developed in the future.

Keywords: ACE model, Industry 5.0, Micro-credentialing, Reskilling, Skills Alignment, Skills Anticipation, Upskilling

References

Brown, M., McGreal, R., & Peters, M. (2023). A strategic institutional response to micro-credentials: Key questions for educational leaders. *Journal of Interactive Media in Education*, *2023*(1). https://doi.org/10.5334/jime.801

Chiarello, Filippo; Fantoni, Gualtiero; Hogarth, Terence; Giordano, Vito; Baltina, Liga; Spada, Irene (2021). Towards ESCO 4.0 – Is the European classification of skills in line with Industry 4.0? A text mining approach. Technological Forecasting and Social Change, Volume 173, 121177, ISSN 0040-1625, https://doi.org/10.1016/j.techfore.2021.121177

Ehlers, U.D. (2020). Future Skills: Future Learning and Future Higher Education. Karlsruhe

European Commission, Directorate-General for Research and Innovation (2021). Industry 5.0, a transformative vision for Europe – Governing systemic transformations towards a sustainable industry, Publications Office of the European Union. https://data.europa.eu/doi/10.2777/17322

European Commission, Directorate-General for Research and Innovation (2020). Industry 5.0: human-centric, sustainable and resilient. Publications Office of the European Union. https://data.europa.eu/doi/10.2777/073781

Peters, M., Aubert, C., Rochet, F. V., Pagés, C., & Bullini, F. Skills Alignment for Lifelong Learners in Higher Education: Smart Catalogues for Reskilling and Upskilling Pathways 2023 Ubiquity Proceedings, 3(1): 71-82. DOI: https://doi.org/10.5334/uproc.71

Spada, Irene; Giordano, Vito; Chiarello, Filippo; Abate, Marco; Dovetto, Francesca M.; and Fantoni, Gualtiero (2023). Tracing topic evolution in higher education: a text mining study on Italian universities. Studies in Higher Education, (0), (0), 1-19. https://doi.org/10.1080/03075079.2023.2284813

Instructional Designers' Integration of Generative AI in Curriculum Development

Swapna Kumar[1], Ariel Gunn[2], Rhiannon Pollard[3], Robert Rose[4], Margeaux Johnson[5], Albert Ritzhaupt[6]

[1] College of Education, University of Florida, USA; swapnak@ufl.edu
[2] College of Medicine, University of Florida, USA; Ariel.Gunn@medicine.ufl.edu
[3] UF Online, University of Florida, USA; rhiannon@ufonline.ufl.edu
[4] Center for Instruction Research and Technology, University of North Florida, USA; r.rose@unf.edu
[5] Center for Instructional Technology and Training, University of Florida, USA; margeaux@ufl.edu
[6] College of Education, University of Florida, USA; aritzhaupt@coe.ufl.edu

Correspondence: Swapna Kumar: swapnak@ufl.edu

Abstract:

Instructional designers (ID) play a crucial role in the development, implementation, and quality assessment of online and blended learning in higher education institutions in the USA. They collaborate with faculty members on curriculum development, improvement, and quality assurance; support faculty and students; and provide professional development for faculty (Pollard & Kumar, 2022). Generative AI (GenAI) technologies are increasingly being integrated into higher education teaching and learning processes, for instance in assessments, personalized learning, and feedback (Kilinc, 2023; Wang & Chen, 2023). Simultaneously, AI-generated content, AI-based assessment, and GenAI technologies use usher challenges related to privacy, ethics, and academic integrity (Crawford et al., 2023). As enablers in the digital transformation of teaching and learning processes, IDs are tasked with understanding and integrating GenAI in institutions of higher education.

The research question driving this research was "How do instructional designers integrate generative AI in curriculum development"? Using convenience sampling, a network of IDs (ca. 80) at one research university were invited to participate in semi-structured interviews in 2024. Fourteen Zoom interviews (30-45 minutes) were completed and the data was thematically analyzed (Braun & Clarke, 2006), resulting in two major themes related to curriculum development and curriculum guidance.

The IDs developed online and blended courses across disciplines in collaboration with instructors, and used various GenAI (e.g., ChatGPT, Adobe Firefly, Bing Image Creator) for different parts of the process. They created learning objectives, summaries, scenarios, quizzes, assessments, images, and also generated text for accessibility purposes during curriculum development. Nevertheless, all the IDs highlighted the importance of instructor verification of the content, appropriate level of assessments for students, and curriculum quality. They also provided guidance to instructors by showing them how to use GenAI for curriculum development and developing training, and resources related to GenAI. They also discussed with instructors their students' use of GenAI , the use of chatbots in their courses, and ethical and academic integrity issues. The results provide insights for educators and administrators into the potential of GenAI for curriculum development, but also the accompanying issues and concerns including copyright, ethics, data privacy, and academic integrity.

Keywords: generative AI, Instructional Design, online courses, blended courses, learning design, curriculum

What digital transformations are needed for learning and teaching in the future?

References

Braun, V., & Clarke, V. (2006). Using thematic analysis in psychology. *Qualitative research in psychology, 3*(2), 77-101.

Crawford, J., Cowling, M., & Allen, K. (2023). Leadership is needed for ethical ChatGPT: Character, assessment, and learning using artificial intelligence (AI). *Journal of University Teaching & Learning Practice, 20*(3). https://doi.org/10.53761/1.20.3.02

Kilinc, S. (2023). Embracing the future of distance science education: Opportunities and challenges of ChatGPT integration. *Asian Journal of Distance Education, 18*(1), 205-237. https://doi.org/10.5281/zenodo.7857396

Pollard, R., & Kumar, S. (2022). Instructional Designers in Higher Education: Roles, Challenges, and Supports. *Journal of Applied Instructional Design, 11*(1). https://doi.org/10.59668/354.5896

Wang, M., & Chen, Y. (2023). Research on the future vision of the Intelligent Integration of ChatGPT and Online Education. *Advances in Educational Technology and Psychology, 7*(2), 128–134. https://doi.org/10.23977/aetp.2023.070219

Human-Driven and AI-Driven Mediational Tool for Argumentative Reworking Skills: An Undergraduate Students Lab

Francesca Crudele[1], Juliana Elisa Raffaghelli[2]

[1] University of Padova, Italy - FISPPA Department of Philosophy, Sociology, Pedagogy and Applied Psychology; francesca.crudele@phd.unipd.it
[2] University of Padova, Italy - FISPPA Department of Philosophy, Sociology, Pedagogy and Applied Psychology; juliana.raffaghelli@unipd.it

Correspondence: Francesca Crudele: francesca.crudele@phd.unipd.it

Abstract:

The development of argumentative text and information comprehension (CoI) skills related to the critical reconstruction of meaning (critical thinking, CT) is important in undergraduate education. Argumentative skills are essential both personally and professionally (Colombo, 2018; Wambsganss et al., 2020; Alotto, 2021). Especially now in the era of social media and AI-mediated information (Raffaghelli & Stewart, 2020; Selwyn et al., 2021; Nguyen et al., 2022).

The use of generative AI (GenAI) seems to facilitate the information fruition process (OpenAI, 2022; Lund & Wang, 2023). However, unconscious use only increases the difficulty of navigating complex information (Roose, 2022; Bozkurt et al., 2023; Lund & Wang, 2023). In this regard, argument maps (AM), commonly used to analyze analog and static texts, could be a useful tool for visualizing, understanding, and reworking multimodal and dynamic arguments and information (Alotto, 2021; Harrell, 2022).

Our study used a design-based research approach with two groups to explore the role of AMs in supporting multimodal reworking. Prospective teachers were also exposed to interaction with ChatGPT, the most widely used GenAI technology, to investigate their first perception of "artificial collaboration". Parallel to the first method, we wanted to investigate the role of AI as an ally in understanding, reformulating, and rethinking argumentative perspectives.

Stemming from the Vygotskian idea, mediation involves learning within the zone of proximal development (ZDP) that does not lead to simple quantitative change but generates "qualitative transformation" (Raffaghelli, 2014). Mediation occurs by proposing "double stimulation" through "cultural artifacts" that both stimulate learners' response (or even better, activity), as well as reflection about the cultural system embedded in the artifact. In our case, the learners' response is argumentative reworking, and the double stimulation is produced by AMs and ChatGPT as a socio-technical artifact. To better understand the type of stimulation we investigated the different responses to the mediation in terms of understanding dynamic information (CoI) and hence developing CT. Therefore we set out to understand whether and which of the two methods offered effective moments of reformulation of one's conception of processes (reworkings) and products (written productions) (Raffaghelli, 2014). Our research questions investigated three objectives:

1. to investigate whether AMs support the enhancement of students' CoI and its critical reworking (CT);
2. whether communicative interaction with the ChatGPT artificial agent supports students in reworking information (connected to CoI) and using it for critical construction of assessment tools (connected to CT).
3. Whether there are differences in the way the two tools mediate learning within the ZPD (relating to the acquisition of skills - CoI and CT).

Our preliminary analysis showed that in both groups the AMs appear to have improved on average the CoI and CT proficiency levels of the elements of information after the workshop. The first look at the data collected on the interaction with the chatbot brought out a positive initial reflection of the students about the potential of ChatGPT. However, students encountered difficulties in properly collaborating with the AI. Further research could focus on constructing functional interaction prompts.

What digital transformations are needed for learning and teaching in the future?

Keywords: argument maps, argumentative skills, critical thinking, GenAI literacy, laboratory activity

References

Alotto, P. (2021). Laboratorio di argomentazione: Guida al critical thinking e all'argument thinking (Argumentation workshop: Guide to critical thinking and argument thinking). In A. Sani & A. Linguiti (Eds.), *Sinapsi. Storia della filosofia. Protagonisti, percorsi, connessioni.* La Scuola editrice.

Bozkurt, A., Xiao, F., Lambert, S., Pazurek, A., Crompton, H., Koseoglu, S., Farrow, R., Bond, M., Nerantzi, C., Honeychurch, S., Bali, M., Dron, J., Mir, K., Stewart, B., Stewart, B., Costello, E., Mason, J., Stracke, C., Romero-Hall, E., & Jandric, P. (2023). Speculative Futures on ChatGPT and Generative Artificial Intelligence (AI): A Collective Reflection from the Educational Landscape. *Asian Journal of Distance Education*, 18, 53–130 [Journal Article, Zenodo]. https://doi.org/10.5281/zenodo.7636568

Colombo, A. (2018). Il testo argomentativo: Presupposti pedagogici e modelli di analisi. (The argumentative text: Pedagogical assumptions and models of analysis.) In A. Colombo (Ed.), *Quaderni del Giscel: Vol. 11. I pro e i contro* (pp. 59–84). La Nuova Italia. https://giscel.it/wp-content/uploads/2018/04/Adriano-Colombo-Il-testo-argomentativo-Presupposti-pedagogici-e-modelli-di-analisi.pdf

Harrell, M. (2022). Representing the structure of a debate. *Argumentation*, 36, 595–610. https://doi.org/10.1007/s10503-022-09586-2 .

Lund, B., & Wang, T. (2023). Chatting about ChatGPT: How may AI and GPT impact academia and libraries? *Library Hi Tech News*, 40. https://doi.org/10.1108/LHTN-01-2023-0009

Nguyen, T. T., Nguyen, Q. V. H., Nguyen, D. T., Nguyen, D. T., Huynh-The, T., Nahavandi, S., Nguyen, T. T., Pham, Q.-V., & Nguyen, C. M. (2022). Deep learning for deepfakes creation and detection: A survey. *Computer Vision and Image Understanding,* 223. https://doi.org/10.1016/j.cviu.2022.103525

OpenAI. (2022, november 30th). Introducing ChatGPT [Blog]. Openai.Com. https://openai.com/blog/chatgpt

Raffaghelli, J. (2014). Keeping on doing what we do better or engaging in transformation? Achieving professional development through the usage of open educational resources. *Formazione & Insegnamento*, 9(3 Suppl.), 75–102. Retrieved from https://ojs.pensamultimedia.it/index.php/siref/article/view/906

Raffaghelli, J. E., & Stewart, B. (2020). Centering complexity in 'educators' data literacy' to support future practices in faculty development: A systematic review of the literature. *Teaching in Higher Education*, 25(4), 435–455. https://doi.org/10.1080/13562517.2019.1696301

Roose, K. (2022, december 5). The Brilliance and Weirdness of ChatGPT. The New York Times. https://www.nytimes.com/2022/12/05/technology/chatgpt-ai-twitter.html

Selwyn, N., Hillman, T., Bergviken Rensfeldt, A., & Perrotta, C. (2021). Digital technologies and the automation of education—Key questions and concerns. *Postdigital Science and Education*, 5, 15-24. https://doi.org/10.1007/s42438-021-00263-3

The Role of Telecommunication for Innovative Heritage Education Experiences: The Virtual Museum of RESTART Project

Maria Rosaria Re[1]

[1] Dept. History, Heritage, Education and Society, Tor Vergata University of Rome, Italy; maria.rosaria.re@uniroma2.it

Correspondence: Maria Rosaria Re: maria.rosaria.re@uniroma2.it

Abstract:

The research and development program RESTART "RESearch and innovation on future Telecommunications systems and networks, to make Italy more smart" has been funded by the European Union – NextGenerationEU. The program has the ambitious goal of contributing to shaping the evolution of Telecommunications in Italy, restarting a sector that possesses world-class expertise and experience. It focuses on the main topics of Telecommunications science and technology, including all types of related systems and networks for both human and non-human users.

Within the program, an innovative Virtual Museum of Tor Vergata University of Rome will be implemented. The Virtual Museum is intended to use the educational methodology of digital Object-Based Learning (OBL) as a tool for in-depth and active knowledge of the selected artistic and cultural heritage, for direct interaction with it, for the stimulation of transversal (in particular the 4Cs: Creativity, Communication, Collaboration and Critical Thinking) and digital skills, thus promoting community and participatory construction of interpretations of tangible and intangible heritage. The realisation of the Virtual Museum on the Tor Vergata University campus is part of a process of valorization, communication and education of the local urban heritage, with a view to social inclusion and the promotion of the well-being of students and university staff, but also, with reference to the third mission activities, to further categories of users, in particular users with cognitive or physical disabilities, children and the elderly who live in the areas close to the campus.

In the proposed virtual museum, a network of totems and immersive environments will be deployed to facilitate augmented reality experiences and digital OBL activities. These installations will be distributed across two distinct locations within the University of Tor Vergata. Connectivity between these sites will be achieved through a dedicated network, who will operate under 5G coverage, utilizing two distinct antennas strategically positioned.

The methodology and the technological solutions will be tested and validated through the realisation of pilot experiences, addressed to students, university staff and their families, with the aim of providing educational experiences on the cultural heritage of Tor Vergata urban area in an inclusive perspective, customized to the user's needs. Going beyond the acquisition of knowledge in a transmissive form, through learning methodologies centred on a real and deep experience, users become actors of a heritage experience in which technological and telecommunication solutions are built to support critical reflection, divergent and creative thinking, communication and sociality.

Keywords: Virtual Museum, VR, Heritage education, Telecommunication.

What digital transformations are needed for learning and teaching in the future?

References

Aiello, D., Fai, S., & Santagati, C. (2019). VIRTUAL MUSEUMS AS A MEANS FOR PROMOTION AND ENHANCEMENT OF CULTURAL HERITAGE. International Archives of the Photogrammetry, Remote Sensing and Spatial Information Sciences., XLII-2/W15, 33–40. https://doi.org/10.5194/isprs-archives-XLII-2-W15-33-2019

Antoniou, A., & Lepouras, G. (2010). Modeling visitors'profiles: Astudy to investigate adaptation aspects for museum learning technologies.Journal on Computing and Cultural Heritage,3(2), 71–89

Baloian, N., Biella, D., Luther, W., Pino, J., & Sacher, D. (2021). Designing, Realizing, Running, and Evaluating Virtual Museum - a Survey on Innovative Concepts and Technologies. *J.UCS (Annual Print and CD-ROM Archive Ed.)*, *27*(12), 1275–1299. https://doi.org/10.3897/jucs.77153

Ding, M. (2017). Augmented reality in museums. Museums & augmented reality–A collection of essays from the arts management and technology laboratory, 1-15.

Martinez, K. P., Untalan, M. Z. G., Burgos, D. F. M., Ramos, R. V., & Germentil, M. J. Q. (2019). CREATION OF A VIRTUAL REALITY ENVIRONMENT OF A UNIVERSITY MUSEUM USING 3D PHOTOGRAMMETRIC MODELS. International Archives of the Photogrammetry, Remote Sensing and Spatial Information Sciences., XLII-2/W13, 841–847. https://doi.org/10.5194/isprs-archives-XLII-2-W13-841-2019

Not, E., & Petrelli, D. (2018). Blending customisation, context-awareness and adaptivity for personalised tangible interaction in cultural heritage.International Journal of Human-Computer Studies,114, 3–19

Parry, R. (2010). Museums in a Digital Age. New York, NY: Routledge

Poce A., Re M. R., Amenduni F., De Medio C., Valente M. (2020). Using different learning methodologies and tools to exploit the educational impact of a University Art Collection: a pilot phase at Roma Tre University in *University Museum and Collection Journal (UMAC)* vol.12 n2 2020 ISSN 2071-7229

A Brand-New Field of Digital Maturity of Higher Education Institutions: Artificial Intelligence Readiness

Kristijan Zimmer[1], Dragana Kupres[2], Jasna Tingle[3]

[1 2 3] Sector for Artificial Intelligence, Croatian Academic and Research Network - CARNET, Croatia
[1] kristijan.zimmer@carnet.hr
[2] dragana.kupres@carnet.hr
[3] jasna.tingle@carnet.hr

Correspondence: Kristijan Zimmer: kristijan.zimmer@carnet.hr

Abstract:

The stakes for the digital transformation of higher education (HE) institutions are constantly being raised, and during the last year even more with the wider adoption of AI-based tools. How to assess the readiness of HE institutions in the ever-changing environment in which AI will play a currently unknown part, is a difficult task. An expert group within CARNET - public institution responsible for digital transformation of education in Croatia and AZVO - agency for science and higher education responsible for accreditations, envisioned the project targeting digital transformation of HE institutions as part of the national "e-Universities" project (CARNET, 2022). The project's digital maturity component named "DMaaS – Digital Maturity as a Service" has a goal of assuring a long-term measurement and guided development of digital maturity of HE institutions and is currently being developed and piloted with 24 selected Croatian HE institutions.

The basis for this model was previous developed in collaboration of OECD, European Commission, Ministry of science and education and CARNET, resulting in a study and report "Advancing Digital Maturity in Croatia's Higher Education System" (OECD, 2023). Another important source was the DIGI-HE's report "Developing a High-Performance Digital Education Ecosystem" (Volungevičienė et al., 2021) which provided an analysis of 20 digital maturity frameworks and tools for institutional self-assessment and recommending the "pick-and-mix" approach. Important lessons were previously learned while developing a framework for the digital maturity of all elementary and secondary schools in Croatia as part of the national "e-Schools" project (CARNET, 2018), used for self-evaluation and external evaluation.

As CARNET's institutional focus shifted largely toward the development and application of AI in the entire education system, the "DMaaS" model along with the 5 "conventional" fields: Leading the digital transformation, Digital infrastructure and support, Digital technologies in learning and teaching, Digital technologies in research and collaboration and Cyber security, witnessed the birth of a new, "unconventional" one – "AI readiness".

The scope of this field, its sub-fields, elements, their descriptions as well as the instrument (questions, answers, and their maturity levels) were created by the AI, as CARNET's experts prompt engineered OpenAI's ChatGPT v4 for that purpose. This was a complex process that required learning many new skills. The current list of elements that make up the "AI readiness" field is Development of AI competencies, Learning analytics, Research, Virtual learning assistant, Business intelligence, Data management, Academic librarianship, Online visibility, and Alumni community. The AI (ChatGPT) "forgot" all aspects of strategical guidance and regulation of itself as well as ethical standards, so they were later added by humans. The model is a "360-degree", with questionnaires for HE managers, teachers, IT professionals and students, and answers corresponding to 5 levels of digital maturity.

As piloting of the "AI readiness" field ended in early June 2024, the entire process including the first draft of the digital maturity model for AI readiness of HE institutions, including the instrument, will be presented.

What digital transformations are needed for learning and teaching in the future?

Keywords: Digital maturity Higher Education Artificial Intelligence

References

CARNET (2022), e-Universities project, https://www.carnet.hr/en/projekt/e-universities/

OECD (2023), Advancing digital maturity in Croatia's higher education system, *Higher Education, OECD Publishing, Paris,* https://doi.org/10.1787/c3c8d452-en

Volungevičienė, A., Brown, M., Greenspon, R., Gaebel, M. & Morrisroe, A. (2021). Developing a high-performance digital education system: institutional self-assessment instruments. *European University Association absl.,* https://eua.eu/resources/publications/953:developing-a-high-performance-digital-education-ecosystem.html

CARNET (2018), e-Schools - Development of the system of digitally mature schools (2nd phase), https://www.carnet.hr/en/projekt/e-schools-development-of-the-system-of-digitally-mature-schools-ii-phase/

KI-Campus.org – Open Microcredentials on AI, Designed with Recognition & Curriculum Integration in Mind, for Use in HE, VET & LLL

Jochen Ehrenreich[1], Mike Bernd[2], Florian Rampelt[3], Milena Stegner[4], Britta Lintfert[5], Regine Martschiske[6]

[1] Education Research, DHBW Cooperative State University Heilbronn, Germany; jochen.ehrenreich@heilbronn.dhbw.de
[2] Hochschulforum Digitalisierung, Stifterverband für die Deutsche Wissenschaft e.V., Germany; Mike.Bernd@stifterverband.de
[3] Hochschulforum Digitalisierung, Stifterverband für die Deutsche Wissenschaft e.V., Germany; Florian.Rampelt@stifterverband.de
[4] Education Research, DHBW Cooperative State University Heilbronn, Germany; milena.stegner@heilbronn.dhbw.de
[5] Education Research, DHBW Cooperative State University Heilbronn, Germany; britta.lintfert@heilbronn.dhbw.de
[6] Education Research, DHBW Cooperative State University Heilbronn, Germany; regine.martschiske@heilbronn.dhbw.de

Correspondence: Jochen Ehrenreich: jochen.ehrenreich@heilbronn.dhbw.de

Abstract:

About KI-Campus (engl.: AI Campus)

AI Campus is the learning platform for artificial intelligence, offering free online courses, videos and podcasts on various topics of AI and data literacy. While the focus of AI Campus is on offering content in German language, an increasing number of courses is also available in English. "AI Campus Originals" were produced specifically for the platform. We also appreciate and review educational online resources and publish those under the label "External" learning opportunities. All learning opportunities are available free of charge. In addition, AI Campus Originals are openly licensed (CC BY-SA 4.0).

Curriculum integration

To ensure wide usability of the learning resources, AI Campus is collaborating with HEIs and VET providers. AI Campus works closely with institutions and educators in the area of quality assurance to ensure that the content is well integrated into curricula at universities and/or in further education fields like Continuing Medical Education (CME). Through open licensing, high quality content and fellowship programs for the use of AI Campus content in digitally enhanced learning, AI Campus has been able to achieve an overarching impact regarding usage and recognition.

Example: AI_VET

The AI_VET program on AI Campus (https://ki-campus.org/microdegree/berufliche-bildung), developed by Universität Mannheim and Universität Stuttgart, consists of four online courses with 1 or 2 ECTS each. It covers several aspects of AI in vocational education: Learning and AI, Learning Analytics, AI as a topic in VET, and AI as a tool in VET. Each course offers a microcredential, and the microcredentials are stackable to form together a larger "Micro-Degree" with 5 ECTS, a standard module size easily to be integrated or recognized in university curricula.

Common Microcredential Framework (CMF)

The AI_Vet Micro-Degree fulfils the basic requirements of the Common Microcredential Framework, which AI Campus uses as a basis for its learning content development. Microcredentials are digital certificates that document a specific acquisition of competences through four central aspects: demonstration of a learning outcome/competence, transparent assessment, stand-alone value, and quality assurance.

European Digital Credentials for Learning (EDC)

To facilitate recognition and portability, AI Campus is preparing to issue digital credentials according to the EDC standard developed by European Commission.

Challenges

Recognition and portability of competences require transparent and secure assessment of learning outcomes. AI Campus is experimenting with several scenarios, such as on-site assessment, online assessment with proctoring, online assessment without ID verification, or issuing only certificates of participation, leaving the assessment to the recognizing institution.

The fast pace of development in the field requires courses, assessments and credentials to be regularly reviewed and updated.

To foster interdisciplinary collaboration and to develop a competence framework on AI, a research group is bringing together researchers with various backgrounds.

Funding

As an R&D project, the AI Campus is funded by the German Federal Ministry of Education and Research (BMBF). Stifterverband, Charité, German Research Center for Artificial Intelligence (DFKI), Baden-Wuerttemberg Cooperative State University (DHBW), FernUniversität in Hagen, Hasso Plattner Institute (HPI), Humboldt University of Berlin, mmb Institute and NEOCOSMO are developing the AI Campus together with numerous partners.

Keywords: AI, Artificial Intelligence, Micro-Credentials, OER, European Digital Credentials for Learning, KI-Campus

References

Flasdick, J., Mah, D.-K., Bernd, M., & Rampelt, F. (2023). *Micro-credentials and micro-degrees. Current developments and potentials for educational practice based on the example of the AI Campus.* https://doi.org/10.5281/ZENODO.7327638

Schleiss, J., Mah, D.-K., Böhme, K., Fischer, D., Mesenhöller, J., Paaßen, B., Schork, S., & Schrumpf, J. (2023). *Künstliche Intelligenz in der Bildung. Drei Zukunftsszenarien und fünf Handlungsfelder.* https://doi.org/10.5281/ZENODO.7702620

Professional Development and the Role of Technology in the Rescue Department

Filip Sever[1]

[1] University of Lapland / KAMK, Finland; filip.sever@kamk.fi

Correspondence: Filip Sever: filip.sever@kamk.fi

Abstract:

The modern workplace continuously evolves, driven by advancements in technology. Companies embrace various hardware and software solutions to boost workforce productivity and efficiency. However, integrating these technologies often necessitates adjustments in work processes and skill sets. To effectively utilize new technologies, employees must acquire new skills, competencies, and undergo retraining opportunities (Shahlaei & Lundh Snis, 2022). The concept of communities of practice (CoP) serves as the theoretical framework for analyzing workplace learning dynamics among firefighters (Lave & Wenger, 1991; Wenger, 1998). A CoP is understood as a social structure where individuals with shared expertise converge, fostering continuous learning and collaboration (Handley et al., 2006). Successful workplaces that promote learning typically exhibit common characteristics such as participation in multiple CoPs, access to learning opportunities, recognition of employees as learners, flexible work arrangements, clear role expectations, continuous support, and relationship-building facilitation. Technological advancements also enable the formation of virtual communities of practice (VCoP), where participants engage in the community with added flexibility in time and space (Shaw et al., 2022). In light of these considerations, understanding the dynamics of participatory learning practices within specific organizational contexts, such as the rescue department, becomes crucial for enhancing employee learning experiences. The research question is: What factors are beneficial for the workplace learning in the rescue department? Analysis reveals three main categories: 1) Peer support, 2) Learning methods, and 3) The role of technology. Peer support and learning methods underscore the social aspects of workplace learning, while technology serves as an integral component in connecting individuals and communities.

Keywords: workplace learning, communities of practice, technology, firefighters

References

Handley, K., Sturdy, A., Fincham, R., & Clark, T. (2006). Within and Beyond Communities of Practice: Making Sense of Learning Through Participation, Identity and Practice*. *Journal of Management Studies*, *43*(3), 641–653. https://doi.org/10.1111/j.1467-6486.2006.00605.x

Lave, J., & Wenger, E. (1991). *Situated learning: Legitimate peripheral participation* (p. 138). Cambridge University Press. https://doi.org/10.1017/CBO9780511815355

Shahlaei, C. A., & Lundh Snis, U. (2022). Conceptualizing industrial workplace learning: An information systems perspective. *Journal of Workplace Learning*, *35*(9), 1–21. https://doi.org/10.1108/JWL-04-2021-0048

Shaw, L., Jazayeri, D., Kiegaldie, D., & Morris, M. E. (2022). Implementation of Virtual Communities of Practice in Healthcare to Improve Capability and Capacity: A 10-Year Scoping Review. *International Journal of Environmental Research and Public Health*, *19*(13), 7994. https://doi.org/10.3390/ijerph19137994

What digital transformations are needed for learning and teaching in the future?

Wenger, E. (1998). *Communities of practice: Learning, meaning, and identity* (pp. xv, 318). Cambridge University Press. https://doi.org/10.1017/CBO9780511803932

Navigating Assessment in the Age of Generative AI

Orna Farrell[1], James Brunton[2], Sinead Lynch[3]

[1 2 3] Dublin City University, Ireland
[1] orna.farrell@dcu.ie
[2] james.brunton@dcu.ie
[3] sinead.lynch77@mail.dcu.ie

Correspondence: Orna Farrell: orna.farrell@dcu.ie

Abstract:

The emergence of generative Artificial Intelligence (AI) tools pose a challenge to the academic integrity of traditional higher education assessment approaches (Glesson, 2022). However, this challenge is also an opportunity to innovate and evolve higher education assessment to be more authentic, creative and inclusive. In response to this challenge, Higher Education Institutions (HEI) need to develop awareness and understanding of generative AI tools and how to design assessment which preserves academic integrity whilst harnessing the opportunities to innovate assessment and harness the potential of AI tools for educational good (QQI, 2023).

This paper will share insights from the recently funded DCU cross-faculty project: Artificial intelligence, Assessment and Academic Integrity. The aim of this cross-faculty collaborative and interdisciplinary project is to raise awareness and build capacity in the DCU community about the challenges and opportunities presented by generative AI tools in relation to assessment and academic integrity. Specifically, the project is researching, designing, developing and delivering digital resources and professional learning offerings to upskill DCU staff and students on how to design assessment and do assessment which takes account of these new technologies and the key principles of assessment design: validity, reliability and fairness. Emerging findings from the staff and student research will be presented.

Keywords: Assessment; Academic Integrity, Generative Artificial Intelligence; Authentic Assessment

References

AI, Assessment and Academic Integrity website https://sites.google.com/dcu.ie/aiandassessment/home

Concannon, F., Costello, E., Farrell, O., Farrelly, T., & Graves Wolf, L. (2023). Editorial: There's an AI for that: Rhetoric, reality, and reflections on EdTech in the dawn of GenAI. *Irish Journal of Technology Enhanced Learning*, 7(1). https://doi.org/10.22554/ijtel.v7i1.116

Eaton, S.J. (2023) 6 Tenets of Postplagiarism: Writing in the Age of Artificial Intelligence https://drsaraheaton.wordpress.com/2023/02/25/6-tenets-of-postplagiarism-writing-in-the-age-of-artificial-intelligence/

Southworth et al., (2023). Developing a model for AI Across the curriculum: Transforming the higher education landscape via innovation in AI literacy. *Computers in Education: Artificial Intelligence*, 4. https://doi.org/10.1016/j.caeai.2023.100127

Kaplan-Rakowski, R., Grotewold, K., Hartwick, P. & Papin, K. (2023). Generative AI and Teachers' Perspectives on Its Implementation in Education. *Journal of Interactive Learning Research*, 34(2), 313-338. Waynesville, NC:

Association for the Advancement of Computing in Education (AACE). Retrieved September 26, 2023 from https://www.learntechlib.org/primary/p/222363/.

Wolf, L., Farrelly, T., Farrell, O., & Concannon, F. (2023). Reflections on a Collective Creative Experiment with GenAI: Exploring the Boundaries of What is Possible . Irish Journal of Technology Enhanced Learning, 7(2), 1–7. https://doi.org/10.22554/ijtel.v7i2.155

Using AI to Improve Course Descriptions via Automated Multi-Lingual Skill Classification

Aljaz Leben[1], Kamarul Adha[2]

[1] Knowledge Innovation Centre, Malta; aljaz@knowledgeinnovation.eu
[2] Knowledge Innovation Centre, Malta; kamarul@knowledgeinnovation.eu

Correspondence: Aljaz Leben: aljaz@knowledgeinnovation.eu

Abstract:

Effective communication about skills and competencies is essential when aligning the needs of employers to the skills acquired through education and training. The European Skills, Competences, Qualifications and Occupations (ESCO) multilingual framework provides a standardized classification system of skills relevant to the needs of the EU labour market (https://esco.ec.europa.eu/), however, as discovered by the LCAMP project consortium (https://lcamp.eu/), employers often struggle to articulate their needs when posting job openings, while educational institutions grapple with aligning their curriculum with industry demands. To respond to the needs of the LCAMP consortium in skill-matching, we developed the Skill Finder tool (https://community.lcamp.eu/skill-finder/). In this paper, we introduce the development process behind Skill Finder, explore its key features, and discuss how it's poised to revolutionise the way employers and educational organizations communicate about skills. With a database of over 13,000 ESCO skills, our tool allows users to input titles or descriptions of learning outcomes, courses, or job profiles in the 27 supported languages and instantly receive related ESCO skill descriptions, resulting in accurate, efficient matching of skills across sectors and industries. The main issue we ran into when trying to translate national curriculum of institution to the ESCO framework is that searching their directory by keywords proved difficult and time-consuming while often not giving relevant results. By using text-embedding-3-large model by OpenAI we were able to convert skill titles, alternative labels and skill descriptions extracted from the ESCO database into vector embeddings, numerical representations of sentences that capture their meaning and relationships, allowing us to process textual data more effectively. To efficiently handle the extensive array of skills across all languages, we adopted a strategic approach of batching the data submission to OpenAI, significantly reducing processing time per language from 4-5 hours to approximately 3-4 minutes. We applied the same process of transforming text to embeddings when a user enters their skill, course, or job profile description into the search field of the tool. Vector searching is then used to search the ESCO database for semantic similarities between the input query and the skills in the database, displaying top 12 results as possible skill matches. To make sure that the results provided by the Skill Finder tool are accurate and relevant to the user, we also implemented a user feedback mechanism which allows user to vote on good and bad matches made by the tool. The user feedback data is currently being stored in a separate data table and will be used for Retrieval Augmented Generation (RAG), facilitating skill recommendation based on both artificial intelligence and human feedback. This will enable Skill Finder to return relevant results every time. Future research will consider implementation of skill extraction and skill type classification methods to increase the usability of the tool.

Keywords: Skill Finder, ESCO framework, artificial intelligence, vector embeddings, vector search, skill matching

What digital transformations are needed for learning and teaching in the future?

References

Amazon Web Services. (n.d.). Retrieval augmented generation. Retrieved from https://aws.amazon.com/what-is/retrieval-augmented-generation/

Chiarello, F., Fantoni, G., Hogarth, T., Giordano, V., Baltina, L., & Spada, I. (2021). Towards ESCO 4.0–Is the European classification of skills in line with Industry 4.0? A text mining approach. Technological Forecasting and Social Change, 173, 121177.

De Smedt, J., le Vrang, M., & Papantoniou, A. (2015, May). ESCO: Towards a Semantic Web for the European Labor Market. In Ldow@ www.

Gomez-Perez, J. M., Denaux, R., Garcia-Silva, A., Gomez-Perez, J. M., Denaux, R., & Garcia-Silva, A. (2020). Understanding word embeddings and language models. A Practical Guide to Hybrid Natural Language Processing: Combining Neural Models and Knowledge Graphs for NLP, 17-31.

Guru Rao, S. (2022). Ontology matching using domain-specific knowledge and semantic similarity (Master's thesis, University of Twente).

Elastic. (n.d.). What is vector search? Retrieved from https://www.elastic.co/what-is/vector-search

Rentzsch, R., & Staneva, M. (2020, September). Skills-Matching and Skills Intelligence through curated and data-driven ontologies. In Proceedings of the DELFI Workshops (pp. 46-58). Bonn: Gesellschaft für Informatik eVz.

Use of Collaborative Annotation Technology with Tutor AI in Computer Science Education

Mark Mccormack[1], John G. Keating[2]

[1]Maynooth University, Ireland; mark.mccormack@mu.ie
[2]Maynooth University, Ireland; john.keating@mu.ie

Correspondence: Mark Mccormack: mark.mccormack@mu.ie

Abstract:

Recent developments in the literature suggest that Large Language Model (LLM) systems, such as ChatGPT, are becoming increasingly more effective in the realm of computer science education (CSE)[1]. While most studies focus on their problem solving capabilities, new studies are emerging looking at how these and other Machine Learning (ML) models may be used in augmentation of students learning such as automated assessment[2], discussing assignments with students[3] and engaging in peer-programming exercises[4].

In this study, we look at how effective these Large Language Model systems can be in acting as tutors for students, and whether these tools help or hinder the students quality of learning. To do this, we provide this tool to a class of Higher Education Computer Science Masters' students. We divide the students into three groups. The control group will complete an assessment activity without the AI tutor, experiment group one will complete the activity with the AI tutor and experiment group two will complete the activity with the AI tutor who also has direct access to auxiliary resources relevant the assignment. The students using the AI tutor will use the LLaMa 7B model for this initial experiment. For the auxiliary resources, we select relevant materials from the Open Education Resources (OER) Commons webpage, as this information would be accessible and usable by every educator.

We look to analyse the students summative grade in the assignment, gather their opinions using the ASPECT questionnaire[5] and finally conduct a follow-up test some weeks later to assess if the knowledge was retained. From this, we can draw conclusions as to if this AI tutor improves students' quality of learning and if augmenting it with auxiliary relevant materials provides better feedback. Regarding future work, our study provides us preliminary results for several areas. Firstly, we can experiment with if different AI models (GPT-3, Mixtral, Claude etc.) are better or worse for particular assignments or activities. Also, should the students benefit from using AI with auxiliary resources, we can look to see what types of resources are the most relevant for the students.

Keywords: Education Technology, Large Language Models, ChatGPT, Computer Science Education, Intelligent Tutoring Systems

References

[1] Ouh, E. L., Gan, B. K. S., Jin Shim, K., & Wlodkowski, S. (2023, June). ChatGPT, Can You Generate Solutions for my Coding Exercises? An Evaluation on its Effectiveness in an undergraduate Java Programming Course. In *Proceedings of the 2023 Conference on Innovation and Technology in Computer Science Education V. 1* (pp. 54-60).

[2] Brun, Y., & Ernst, M. D. (2004, May). Finding latent code errors via machine learning over program executions. In *Proceedings. 26th International Conference on Software Engineering* (pp. 480-490). IEEE.

[3] Segedy, J., Kinnebrew, J., & Biswas, G. (2012). Supporting student learning using conversational agents in a teachable agent environment.

[4] Dos Santos, O. L., & Cury, D. (2023, October). Challenging the Confirmation Bias: Using ChatGPT as a Virtual Peer for Peer Instruction in Computer Programming Education. In *2023 IEEE Frontiers in Education Conference (FIE)* (pp. 1-7). IEEE.

[5] Wiggins, B. L., Eddy, S. L., Wener-Fligner, L., Freisem, K., Grunspan, D. Z., Theobald, E. J., ... & Crowe, A. J. (2017). ASPECT: A survey to assess student perspective of engagement in an active-learning classroom. CBE—Life Sciences Education, 16(2), ar32.

Empowering Teachers to Adapt Assessment Practices in the Generative AI Era

Jean-François (Jeff) Van de Poël [1]

[1] Centre de Soutien à l'Enseignement, University of Lausanne, Switzerland; jean-francois.vandepoel@unil.ch

Correspondence: Jean-François (Jeff) Van de Poël; jean-francois.vandepoel@unil.ch

Context

Although generative AI technologies have been around for more than 50 years, it wasn't until the end of 2022 and the availability of ChatGPT to the wider public that the university community and its teaching staff became concerned about this phenomenon and raised a number of questions, particularly in relation to the way academic work is produced and other existing assessment practices.

Indeed, the use of AI tools, particularly large language models (LLMs) such as ChatGPT or Claude or even Gemini, raises concerns about the risks of their use, particularly in relation to issues relating to academic integrity, as they can create original texts that may be difficult to detect.

Despite the relative novelty of the phenomenon, the use of AI in academic assessment is an area of growing interest, with the potential to revolutionise traditional methods. Many authors point to the potential of AI to improve assessment processes, emphasising the need for more flexible and student-centred approaches. But the presence of generative AI in teaching and assessment processes also raises many ethical questions, particularly in relation to the challenges and risks associated with algorithmic decision-making and algorithmic fairness, such as the accuracy and explicability of the answers given.

In order to help teachers at our institution address these issues, we are developing an interactive tool that will help teachers to position their assessment practices. This tool will enable them, firstly, to question their current practices with regard to the presence of generative AI and, secondly, to develop and implement appropriate assessment practices and materials by considering the most suitable pedagogical and ethical approaches to adopt.

Introducing AI-Contextual Assessment Positioning Interactive Guide (AICAPIG)

Our interactive guide will start by questioning whether the teacher authorizes the use of generative AI as part of his or her assessment using the AIAS scale (Perkins, M., Furze, L., Roe, J., MacVaugh, J, 2024), that propose 5 different levels.

The AIAS (AI Assistance in Assessment Scale) is designed to provide clear guidelines on the extent to which AI tools can be utilized in student assessments. This scale helps ensure transparency and fairness in the evaluation process while encouraging students to develop their skills and critical thinking abilities in conjunction with AI technology. The scale consists of five levels, each with specific criteria and conditions for AI usage.

What digital transformations are needed for learning and teaching in the future?

1	NO AI	The assessment is completed entirely without AI assistance. This level ensures that students rely solely on their knowledge, understanding, and skills. **AI must not be used at any point during the assessment.**
2	AI-ASSISTED IDEA GENERATION AND STRUCTURING	AI can be used in the assessment for brainstorming, creating structures, and generating ideas for improving work. **No AI content is allowed in the final submission.**
3	AI-ASSISTED EDITING	AI can be used to make improvements to the clarity or quality of student created work to improve the final output, but no new content can be created using AI. **AI can be used, but your original work with no AI content must be provided in an appendix.**
4	AI TASK COMPLETION, HUMAN EVALUATION	AI is used to complete certain elements of the task, with students providing discussion or commentary on the AI-generated content. This level requires critical engagement with AI generated content and evaluating its output. **You will use AI to complete specified tasks in your assessment. Any AI created content must be cited.**
5	FULL AI	AI should be used as a 'co-pilot' in order to meet the requirements of the assessment, allowing for a collaborative approach with AI and enhancing creativity. **You may use AI throughout your assessment to support your own work and do not have to specify which content is AI generated.**

Figure 2 : AIAS Scale : Perkins, M., Furze, L., Roe, J., MacVaugh, J. (2024)

The AIAS scale provides a structured framework that helps educators and students understand the appropriate use of AI in assessments, ensuring academic integrity and fostering a balanced integration of AI technology in education.

From this initial position, it will guide the teacher towards questions and resources that will enable him or her to make informed decisions on all aspect involved such as:

- AI competencies and level of mastery needing to be fostered.
- AI competencies framework he or she can reflect upon.
- Equitable access to technologies.
- Inclusion of new learning outcomes or the adaptation of learning outcomes associated to the presence and influence of AI in its teaching field.
- Adaptation of the assessment methods proposed as part of the course
- Adaptation of assessment grids for examinations and other course-related assignments.
- Proposal to provide more precise information about the rules governing ethics and citation.
- Examination procedures and process for carrying out course assessment work

We will present this interactive guide, which is an ongoing project, at this conference so that we can gather feedback and opinions from the colleagues present. The prototype of the guide will be presented on a Miro Board.

Link : https://miro.com/app/board/uXjVK87Ti_o=/?share_link_id=831095828891

Keywords: Higher Education, Generative AI, Assessment, Professional Development

What digital transformations are needed for learning and teaching in the future?

References

Baidoo-Anu, David and Owusu Ansah, Leticia, Education in the Era of Generative Artificial Intelligence (AI): Understanding the Potential Benefits of ChatGPT in Promoting Teaching and Learning (January 25, 2023). Available at SSRN: https://ssrn.com/abstract=4337484 or http://dx.doi.org/10.2139/ssrn.4337484

Burger, B., Kanbach, D.K., Kraus, S., Breier, M., & Corvello, V. (2023). On the use of AI-based tools like ChatGPT to support management research. *European Journal of Innovation Management*.

Chan, C.K., & Tsi, L.H. (2023). The AI Revolution in Education: Will AI Replace or Assist Teachers in Higher Education? *ArXiv, abs/2305.01185*.

Fütterer, T., Fischer, C., Alekseeva, A., Chen, X., Tate, T., Warschauer, M., & Gerjets, P. (2023). ChatGPT in education: global reactions to AI innovations. *Scientific reports*, *13*(1), 15310.

Hooda, M., Rana, C., Dahiya, O., Rizwan, A., & Hossain, M. (2022). Artificial Intelligence for Assessment and Feedback to Enhance Student Success in Higher Education. *Mathematical Problems in Engineering*.

Kilani, A., Hamida, A.B., & Hamam, H. (2019). Artificial Intelligence Review. *Advanced Methodologies and Technologies in Artificial Intelligence, Computer Simulation, and Human-Computer Interaction*.

Knoth, N., Decker, M., Laupichler, M., Pinski, M., Buchholtz, N., Bata, K., Schultz, B. (2024) Developing a holistic AI literacy assessment matrix – Bridging generic, domain-specific, and ethical competencies, Computers and Education Open, Volume 6, https://doi.org/10.1016/j.caeo.2024.100177.

Mao, J., Chen, B., & Liu, J. C. (2024). Generative Artificial Intelligence in Education and Its Implications for Assessment. *TechTrends*, *68*(1), 58-66.

Montenegro-Rueda, M., Fernández-Cerero, J., Fernández-Batanero, J. M., & López-Meneses, E. (2023). Impact of the implementation of ChatGPT in education: A systematic review. *Computers*, *12*(8), 153.

Moorhouse, B. L., Yeo, M. A., & Wan, Y. (2023). Generative AI tools and assessment: Guidelines of the world's top-ranking universities. *Computers and Education Open*, *5*, 100151.

Ng, D.T.K., Leung, J.K.L., Su, J. *et al.* (2023). Teachers' AI digital competencies and twenty-first century skills in the post-pandemic world. *Education Tech Research Dev* **71**, 137–161 https://doi.org/10.1007/s11423-023-10203-6

Perkins, M. (2023). Academic integrity considerations of AI Large Language Models in the post-pandemic era: ChatGPT and beyond. *Journal of University Teaching and Learning Practice*.

Perkins, M., Furze, L., Roe, J., MacVaugh, J. (2024). The Artificial Intelligence Assessment Scale (AIAS): A Framework for Ethical Integration of Generative AI in Educational Assessment. Journal of University Teaching and Learning Practice, 21(6).

F. J. Pinzolits, R. (2023). AI in academia: An overview of selected tools and their areas of application. *MAP Education and Humanities*.

Salas-Pilco, S.Z., Xiao, K., & Hu, X. (2022). Artificial Intelligence and Learning Analytics in Teacher Education: A Systematic Review. *Education Sciences*.

What digital transformations are needed for learning and teaching in the future?

Salinas-Navarro, D.E.; Vilalta-Perdomo, E.; Michel-Villarreal, R.; Montesinos, L. Using Generative Artificial Intelligence Tools to Explain and Enhance Experiential Learning for Authentic Assessment. Educ. Sci. 2024, 14, 83. https://doi.org/10.3390/educsci14010083

Xia, Q., Weng, X., Ouyang, F. *et al.* A scoping review on how generative artificial intelligence transforms assessment in higher education. *Int J Educ Technol High Educ* **21**, 40 (2024). https://doi.org/10.1186/s41239-024-00468-z

Wang, T., Lund, B.D., Marengo, A., Pagano, A., Mannuru, N.R., Teel, Z.(., & Pange, J. (2023). Exploring the Potential Impact of Artificial Intelligence (AI) on International Students in Higher Education: Generative AI, Chatbots, Analytics, and International Student Success. *Applied Sciences*.

Williams, P. (2023). AI, Analytics and a New Assessment Model for Universities. *Education Sciences*.

POSTER ABSTRACTS

AI Pioneers: Advancing AI in VET and Adult Education

Giedrė Tamoliūnė[1], Josep M. Duart[2], Denise Whitelock[3]

[1] EDEN Digital Learning Europe, Estonia; giedre.tamoliune@gmail.com
[2] Universitat Oberta de Catalunya, Spain; jduart@uoc.edu
[3] The Open University, UK; denise.whitelock@open.ac.uk

Correspondence: Giedrė Tamoliūnė, giedre.tamoliune@gmail.com

Abstract:

The AI Pioneers project, funded by the European Commission's Erasmus+ program, aims to integrate Artificial Intelligence (AI) into vocational education and training (VET) and adult education. This project enhances the DigCompEdu framework with essential AI competencies for educators, addressing ethical considerations while promoting responsible AI deployment. The project establishes a supportive network of AI pioneers through collaboration with stakeholders, policymakers, and vocational schools. Events like consultation seminars and the AI Pioneers Reference Network on Mastodon facilitate professional knowledge exchange and community building. The project aims to advance AI integration in education while fostering a safe and inclusive learning environment by analyzing best practices and AI technologies and emphasizing ethical AI use.

Keywords: artificial intelligence, vocational education and training, adult education, AI in education

Summary

The AI Pioneers project, under the ERASMUS+ Forward Looking Project, is a multifaceted initiative aiming to promote Artificial Intelligence (AI) in education, particularly in Adult Education and Vocational Education and Training (VET). The project focuses on building a network of pioneers from the education sector who are actively involved in the field of artificial intelligence (AI). This involves trainers, stakeholders, policymakers, and educational planners to promote the use of AI in VET and adult education. Involving relevant stakeholders such as companies and vocational schools is at the center of the project. The project focuses on policy recommendations, toolkits, and implementation guidelines for AI pioneers on the use of AI, and the identification, development, and piloting of AI use cases in education. Furthermore, a supplement to the Digital Competence Framework for Educators (DigCompEdu) has been developed. Finally, the development of guidelines (in line with existing EU policy) for the ethical and trustworthy use of AI in education is foreseen in the project.

Project objectives are: (1) develop a reference network of AI Pioneers (trainers, stakeholders, policy makers, and educational planners) for promoting the use and teaching of AI in Adult Education and VET; (2) produce recommendations, toolkits, and implementation guidelines for AI Pioneers at organisational and systemic levels and disseminate and exploit the use of AI in education and training; (3) develop a supplement to the DigCompEDU Framework describing the skills and competences of teachers and trainers related to AI in Education; and (4) develop guidelines (in line with existing EU policies) for ethical and trustworthy use of AI in education, to produce evaluation schema, and to pilot these in practice.

Some of the results achieved are:

- ➔ ***the Supplement to the DigCompEdu framework outlining the skills and competences of educators related to education***. This Supplement (Bekiaridis, 2023) enhances the DigCompEdu framework by integrating essential AI competencies for educators. It addresses AI's impact on teaching and learning, emphasizing responsible AI use. Key competencies include data literacy, computational thinking, and ethical AI use. Challenges like data privacy and unequal access are outlined, emphasizing the need for ethical integration. The Supplement offers strategies and activities for skill development, ensuring educators are prepared for AI's transformative role in education.

- ➔ ***AI Pioneers evaluation schema.*** Ethical considerations play a crucial role in the project's endeavors. Recognizing the potential risks associated with AI technologies, the project aims to develop guidelines for the ethical use of AI in education. This includes addressing data privacy, algorithmic bias, and equitable access to AI technology. By aligning with existing EU policies and promoting responsible AI deployment, the project endeavors to ensure that AI integration in educational settings upholds ethical standards and fosters a supportive learning environment.

- ➔ ***AI Pioneers Reference Network.*** Central to the project's agenda is establishing a network of pioneers in AI education. The project strives to create a supportive ecosystem for driving AI integration in vocational education and adult learning through collaboration with stakeholders, policymakers, and vocational schools. Events like consultation seminars and the AI Pioneers Reference Network on Mastodon serve as platforms for knowledge exchange, community building, and professional networking among AI professionals and educators.

- ➔ ***Project dissemination and exploitation.*** The project emphasizes the importance of social networks and widespread dissemination of its findings and initiatives through various channels, including conferences, webinars, workshops, and similar. These platforms facilitate sharing insights, fostering dialogue, and promoting best practices in AI integration within educational contexts.

In conclusion, the AI Pioneers project seeks to establish a supportive ecosystem for advancing AI integration in VET and adult education. It is dedicated to creating an environment fostering responsible AI deployment by enhancing educator skills, fostering collaboration and networking, addressing ethical concerns, and leveraging social networks to drive meaningful change in education.

Acknowledgments

The project "AI Pioneers – AI and the Future of Education" has been funded with the support of the European Commission within the framework of Erasmus+ programme call Partnerships for Innovation - Forward Looking Projects (ERASMUS-EDU-2022-PI-FORWARD). All mentioned project results are available at https://aipioneers.org/.

This publication reflects the views only of the authors, and the European Commission cannot be held responsible for any use that may be made of the information contained therein.

References

Bekiaridis, G. (2023). Supplement to the DigCompEdu Framework Outlining the Skills and Competences of Educators Related to AI in Education. Retrieved from https://aipioneers.org/supplement-to-the-digcompedu-framework/

Digi-Prof: Transparent Assessment for Online Learning by Digitally Competent Professors

Giedrė Tamoliūnė[1], Airina Volungevičienė[2], Estela Daukšienė[3], Elena Trepulė[4], Indrė Oleškevičienė[5], Rimantė Čepauskienė[6]

[1] Vytautas Magnus University, Lithuania; giedre.tamoliune@vdu.lt
[2] Vytautas Magnus University, Lithuania; airina.volungeviciene@vdu.lt
[3] Vytautas Magnus University, Lithuania; estela.dauksiene@vdu.lt
[4] Vytautas Magnus University, Lithuania; elena.trepule@vdu.lt
[5] Vytautas Magnus University, Lithuania; indre.oleskeviciene@vdu.lt
[6] EDEN Digital Learning Europe, Estonia; rimcepauskiene@gmail.com

Correspondence: Giedrė Tamoliūnė, giedre.tamoliune@vdu.lt

Abstract:
This paper aims to present results achieved during the implementation of the DIGIPROF project which aims to support HE teachers and HE institutions to design and implement transparent assessments for online learning and recognition of learning outcomes by proposing methodology, guidelines, practical tools, and training material to develop their digital competences. DIGI-PROF seeks to elevate teaching standards and digital proficiency in response to the Digital Education Action Plan (European Commission, 2020). By integrating DigCompOrg and DigCompEdu frameworks, it aims to enhance digital competencies among educators and institutions. Also, HE teachers and HE institutions will establish new scenarios for HE international collaboration designing new courses for the Bachelor study programs with transparent assessment, efficient student support, taught by digitally competent professors in virtual and blended study mode, and leading to micro-credentials.

Keywords: higher education, transparent assessment, digital micro-credentials, learning analytics, educators

Summary

The DIGIPROF project aims to support HE teachers and HE institutions to design and implement transparent assessments for online learning and recognition of learning outcomes by proposing methodology, guidelines, practical tools, and training material to develop their digital competences. This idea is based on the need to support teachers in HE by developing their competences, as well as to establish their good practice examples on how to successfully design transparent assessment for online learning in HE.

The aim of the project is reached through the following four objectives:

1) Prepare methodological guidelines, tools, and training material for HE teachers as references needed to: a) *design transparent assessment strategies for online learning in HE* (Moreiro et al., 2022), b) *monitor, support, and engage students based on the evidence generated by digital technologies* (Maina et al., 2022), c) *apply digital and micro-credentials in learning design leading to transparent assessment, validation and recognition of learning outcomes* (Goz and Čepauskienė, 2022). Methodological guidelines are translated into 6 languages (see Fig. 1).

What is required to help foster nestedness and integration in the complex digital learning ecosystem?

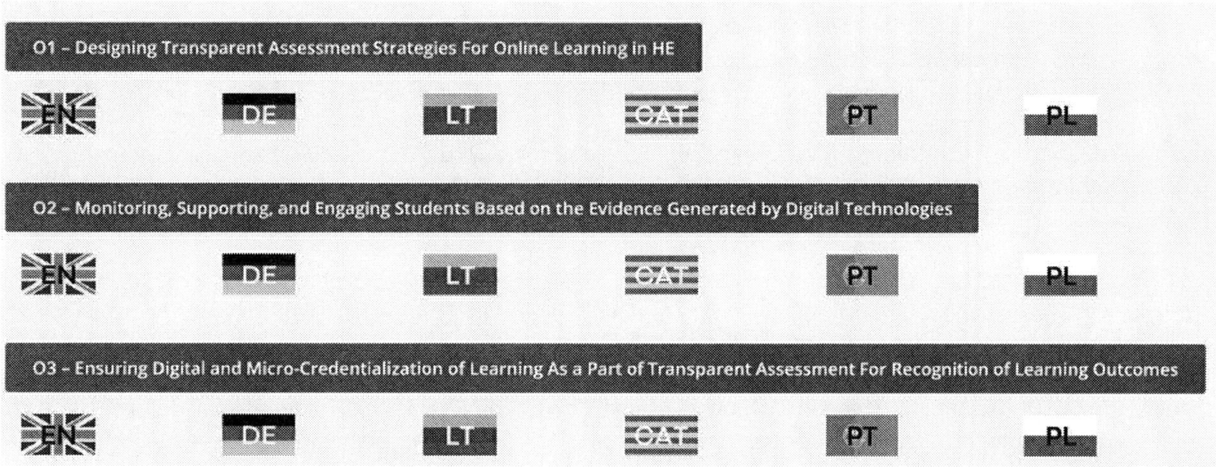

Fig. 1. The list of methodological guidelines developed within the DigiProf project framework.

2) Develop HE teacher digital assessment competences to enable them to: a) *design transparent assessment strategies for online learning*, b) *monitor, support and engage students based on the evidence generated by digital technologies*, c) *apply digital and micro-credentials in learning design leading to transparent assessment, validation and recognition of learning outcomes*.
3) Prepare the guidelines for HE institutions to implement transparent assessment of learning outcomes for online and blended learning, leading to digital and micro-credentials. The document aims to provide guidance for higher education institutions in planning and implementing transparent assessment of learning outcomes and issuing digital micro-credentials (Volungevičienė et al., 2023).
4) Design online and blended learning curricula for virtual and blended cooperation of consortium institutions embedding transparent assessment and mutual recognition of learning outcomes. As a result of this objective, international collaborative courses, embedding teacher and student collaborative activities following inter-institutional collaboration agreements for virtual and blended collaboration scenarios were created.

The overall results created during the project have a significant impact at multiple levels, starting with HE teachers, HE institutions, students, quality assurance agencies, policy and decision-makers, and, finally, stakeholders from other levels of education. This was achieved through extensive collaboration among DIGI-PROF project consortium members, representing HE institutions (DHBW, Germany; Vytautas Magnus University, Lithuania; University of Silesia in Katowice, Poland; University of Aveiro, Portugal; Open University of Catalonia, Spain) and a professional network of experts and academics (EDEN) covering Europe - wide membership and global partnerships, individual institutions and networks, reaching out more than 200 organizations at least in Europe.
All results mentioned and created are available on the project website https://eden-europe.eu/digi-prof/.

Acknowledgments

This research is being supported by the Erasmus+ Programme of the European Union (project "Transparent assessment for online learning by digitally competent professors", No. 2021-1-LT01-KA220-HED-000031154).

References

European Commission (2020). Digital Education Action Plan. Available online https://education.ec.europa.eu/sites/default/files/document-library-docs/digital-education-action-plan-factsheet.pdf

What is required to help foster nestedness and integration in the complex digital learning ecosystem?

Göz, U., Čepauskienė, R. (2022). *Ensuring digital and micro-credentialization of learning as a part of transparent assessment for recognition of learning outcomes.* DigiProf project training material https://teacamp.vdu.lt/course/index.php?categoryid=15

Maina, M.F., Guàrdia, L., Duart, J.M., Mancini, F., Malerba, M.L., Volungeviciene, A., Tamoliune, G. (2022). *Monitoring, supporting, and engaging students based on the evidence generated by digital technologies.* DigiProf project training material. https://teacamp.vdu.lt/course/index.php?categoryid=15

Moreira A., Balula A., Costa N., Vasconcelos S., Neto T., Volungeviciene A., Greenspon R. (2022). *Designing transparent assessment strategies for online learning in HE.* DigiProf project training *material. https://teacamp.vdu.lt/course/index.php?categoryid=15*

Volungevičienė, A., Daukšienė, E., Trepulė, E., Mamet-Michalkiewicz, M. (2023) The Guidelines for HE Institutions to Implement Transparent Assessment of Learning Outcomes for Online and Blended Learning Leading to Digital Micro-credentials. https://eden-europe.eu/wp-content/uploads/2023/10/The-MC-guidelines-for-HE.-Version-for-comments-from-HE-policy-makers-.pdf

FJORD Framework: Integrating Student Perspectives Through Holistic Course Design

Sigrun Lindaas Norhagen[1]

[1] Departement of Teacher Education, NLA University College, Norway

Correspondence: sigrun.norhagen@nla.no

Abstract:

The FJORD framework (Flexible, Journey-Oriented, Remote Design) emerges from Norway as a transformative approach to educational course design. It is derived from international methodologies and merged with local educational needs. This poster introduces the model, highlighting its adaptability, learner-centered approach, and digital integration, which are crucial for modern educational environments.

Keywords: FJORD, Learning Design, Norwegian Education, Constructive Alignment, Framework

Summary

The education landscape is continually evolving, necessitating innovative approaches to design learning experiences that accommodate changing needs and technologies.

The FJORD framework (Flexible, Journey-Oriented, Remote Design) emerges from Norway as an innovative framework in educational course design. It is derived from international methodologies (Fink, 2013; Salmon, n.d.) and merged with local educational needs.

This poster introduces the development project that led to the FJORD model, highlighting its adaptability, learner-centered approach, and digital integration, which are crucial for modern educational environments.

FJORD emphasizes Flexibility, supporting educators in creating courses that adapt to varied learning environments and student needs.

Its Journey-Oriented nature focuses on the progressive development of learners, ensuring a coherent and integrated educational pathway.

The Remote aspect reflects the increasing importance of online and distance learning Design, providing a robust structure for online-supported education.

The poster will showcase the FJORD framework and how its components interconnect to form a holistic learning design. Whether adapting a course to a more flexible design, adapting for cross-campus teaching, or going fully online, a FJORD workshop scaffolds and facilitates stakeholders' design for the course in question. Both a visual plan and an action plan are essential takeaways that support the continuous planning, development, and delivery of a course.

The FJORD framework workshop has profoundly impacted participants, fostering a collaborative environment and a shared vision among educators. Being asked about their experiences, participants praised team cohesion and a unified approach to student learning outcomes. The emphasis on student perspectives provided teachers with a clearer overview of their subjects and the crucial link between teaching activities and learning objectives. Participants highlighted the framework's utility in transforming abstract ideas into concrete teaching plans with a coherent structure in the LMS, focusing on student learning rather than teaching content. The surprising effectiveness of simple tools like color-coded Post-it notes in creating course structures was also noted. The workshop encouraged thorough contemplation of course content and coherence, enhancing awareness of the alignment between learning activities and assessments. Its influence extended beyond online courses, leading to changes in campus-based courses as well. The use of Post-it notes on office walls exemplifies the hands-on, reflective approach the workshop promotes, aiding educators in course development and design.

References

Fink, L. D. (2013). Creating significant learning experiences. John Wiley & Sons.

Salmon, G. (n.d.) Carpe Diem - a team-based approach to learning design. Gilly Salmon [online]. Available: http://www.gillysalmon.com/carpe-diem.html

What is required to help foster nestedness and integration in the complex digital learning ecosystem?

MICOO, Microcredentials Made Simple

Stefano Tirati[1]

[1] CEO, Learningdigital, Italy; st@learningdigital.eu

Correspondence: Stefano Tirati: st@learningdigital.eu

Abstract:

Based on the recommendations of the World Alliance for Microcredentials and its International Scientific Committee, composed by experts and organisation from all around the globe, we introduce you to MICOO, a digital platform to design microcredentials focused on skills, offering a mobile-first user experience to learners & earners, ensuring rigorous assessment processes based on evidences, and integrating the quality management frameworks and awarding bodies adopted by the organisations embarking on this journey.

Keywords: microcredentials, skills development, competence-based assessment, quality assurance, European Learning Model, AI, blockchain

Summary

We believe microcredentials have the potential to empower education professionals and career enthusiasts to shape unique learning pathways, increase flexibility and ensure better inclusiveness in their training offerings. We consider microcredentials as a powerful mechanism to effectively contribute to innovate the educational and training systems. Based on these opportunities, and related risks, we launched in 2023 an International Scientific Committee, headquartered in Europe together with experts from various countries across all continents, including Canada, US, New Zealand, Australia, where microcredentials have a legal base and the market recognises their values, to create a collaborative space, learn from each other, and reflect upon key and tricky questions, including ontology, assessment, quality assurance, interoperability with existing qualification frameworks.

The findings arising from the International Scientific Committee of the newly established World Alliance for Microcredentials have been supporting and guiding our work, in terms of conceptualising and shaping the technical specifications and requirements that characterises the workflow of MICOO, our solution to democratise and boost the adoption of microcredentials across formal, non-formal and informal education settings.

MICOO is a digital platform, powered by AI and Blockchain, that supports the design and management of microcredentials.

MICOO is an ecosystem of web apps, whose main goal (and challenge) is to enable a smooth and playful environment, while preserving compliance with and referencing to the European Learning Model and applicable qualification frameworks.

Our presentation delves into the following dimensions:

Designer App: playful design process of microcredentials focused on skills, powered by AI and Blockchain, Quality Assurance and international standards

What is required to help foster nestedness and integration in the complex digital learning ecosystem?

Earner App: mobile first challenge-based UX, enabling individualised learning and earning sharable, portable and stackable digital credentials

Assessor App: certified and accredited professionals implement structured evidence-based assessment, providing multidimensional feedback

Awarding App: institutions and organisations define requirements, monitor progress and audit implementation of microcredentials workflow

Trust and Reliability: MICOO leverages cutting-edge technologies such as AI and Blockchain, ensuring referencing and interoperability with international learning models, and occupational frameworks.

Business Benefits: our app ecosystem and customer success team are geared to ensure effective onboarding, adoption and deployment, for a smooth transition time and digital transformation.

Innovation in Education: microcredentials introduce change within multiple dimensions including pedagogical approaches, organisational settings, technical integration, business models.

World Alliance for Microcredentials (WAM): our International Scientific Committee has evolved into the WAM Foundation whose aim is to promote awareness and capacity building among training providers and industry, as well as advocacy towards public institutions responsible for integrating microcredentials within their education systems and practices. As a membership and multi-layered network, we welcome new organisations and experts interested to join forces.

References

Bigelow, A., Booth, C., Brockerhoff-Macdonald, B., Cormier, D., Dinsmore, C., Grey, S., ... & Zahedi, E. (2022). eCampusOntario's Micro-credential Toolkit. *https://openlibrary. ecampusontario. ca/item-details/#/3b7a4bed-0fa3-4b9d-bd02-4bcfdb919090.*

Brookhart, S. M. (2013). *How to create and use rubrics for formative assessment and grading*. Ascd.

Brown, D. (2019). *Research and educator micro-credentials*. Digital Promise.

Cook, E. (2021). Practice-based engineering: Mathematical competencies and micro-credentials. *International Journal of Research in Undergraduate Mathematics Education*, *7*(2), 284-305.

Cirlan, E., & Loukkola, T. (2020). Micro-credentials linked to the Bologna Key Commitments. *European University Association*.

Desmarchelier, R., & Cary, L. J. (2022). Toward just and equitable micro-credentials: an Australian perspective. *International Journal of Educational Technology in Higher Education*, *19*(1), 1-12.

Duklas, J. (2020). Micro-Credentials: Trends in Credit Transfer and Credentialing. *British Columbia Council on Admissions and Transfer*.

Duncan, O. J. (2020). Assessment of Digital Badges and Microcredentials on Student Learning Outcomes in the Introductory Public Speaking Course.

Gallardo, K. (2020). Competency-based assessment and the use of performance-based evaluation rubrics in higher education: Challenges towards the next decade. *Problems of Education in the 21st Century*, *78*(1), 61-79.

Jonsson, A. (2014). Rubrics as a way of providing transparency in assessment. *Assessment & Evaluation in Higher Education*, *39*(7), 840-852.

Jonsson, A., & Svingby, G. (2007). The use of scoring rubrics: Reliability, validity and educational consequences. *Educational research review*, *2*(2), 130-144.

Iniesto, F., Ferguson, R., Weller, M., Farrow, R., & Pitt, R. (2022). Introducing a reflective framework for the assessment and recognition of microcredentials. *Open Technology in Education, Society, and Scholarship Association (OTESSA) Journal*, in-press. DOI: https://doi.org/10.18357/otessaj.2022.2.2.37

Leesa Wheelahan & Gavin Moodie (2021) Analysing micro-credentials in higher education: a Bernsteinian analysis, Journal of Curriculum Studies, 53:2, 212-228, DOI:10.1080/00220272.2021.1887358

Leskes, A., & Wright, B. D. (2005). *The art & science of assessing general education outcomes: A practical guide*. Association of American Colleges and Universities.

Maina, M. F., Guàrdia Ortiz, L., Mancini, F., & Martinez Melo, M. (2022). A micro-credentialing methodology for improved recognition of HE employability skills. *International Journal of Educational Technology in Higher Education*, *19*(1), 1-22.

McGreal, R., & Olcott Jr, D. (2022). A strategic reset: micro-credentials for higher education leaders. *Smart Learning Environments*, *9*(1), 9.

Moskal, B. M. (2000). Scoring rubrics: What, when and how?. *Practical Assessment, Research, and Evaluation*, *7*(1), 3.

Reed, A. (2023). Micro-credentials and the role of evidence: increasing the potential for learner-centeredness, inclusivity and an expansive model of assessment and credentialing. *The International Journal of Information and Learning Technology*.

What is required to help foster nestedness and integration in the complex digital learning ecosystem?

Open Digital Competences Training for School Educators

Diana Andone[1], Sandra Kučina Softić[2], Demetrios Sampson[3], Sofia Mougiakou[4], Anna Krassa[5], Andrei Ternauciuc[6]

[1] Politehnica University Timisoara, Romania; diana.andone@upt.ro
[2] University of Zagreb University Computing Centre, Croatia; sskucina@srce.hr
[3] University of Piraeus, Greece; sampson@unipi.gr
[4] University of Piraeus, Greece; mougiakou@gmail.com
[5] Moodle, Spain; anna@moodle.com
[6] Politehnica University Timisoara, Romania; andrei.ternauciuc@upt.ro

Correspondence: Diana Andone: diana.andone@upt.ro

Abstract:

The OpenDigCompEdu Erasmus+ project accelerates the digital competences of educators in school education from Spain, Romania, Croatia, Greece and Norway towards the sustainable adoption of more online and blended approaches in education through the use of open educational technologies and open education principles. To validate this the partners have developed 5 courses using the framework of the Moodle ABCtoLD method and implemented in national languages.

Keywords: Open Digital Competences, Moodle, school education, microcertificate

Summary

The concept of Digital Competences for Educators is very important within European educational policies. Recent definitions of DigCompEdu are provided in a scientifically sound framework describing what it means for educators to be digitally competent DigCompEdu: European Framework for the Digital Competence of Educators (Carretero Gomez et al., 2017) and in the EU DEAP (Digital Education Action Plan 2021-2027 Resetting Education and Training for the Digital Age, 2020) defined in Sep 2020. This poster presents the results of the OpenDigCompEdu Erasmus+ project as to accelerate the digital competences of educators in school education from Spain, Romania, Croatia, Greece and Norway towards the sustainable adoption of more online and blended approaches in education through the use of open educational technologies and open education principles. To validate this the partners have developed 5 courses using the framework of the Moodle ABCtoLD method (Andone, et. al, 2020). The courses of: Open Digital Education ecosystem, Learn Moodle Basics, Teaching with Open Digital Tools, New Assessment models, OpenEdTech for Sustainability, Diversity & Inclusion and Climate Change in Education are small, online, multimedia rich courses developed with study cases from all partners, interactive online activities and using existing OERs – figure 1. The courses are integrated in Moodle Academy and they are created following the European microcredential principles, as to be independent, stackable and certifies and validate the school educators digital competences.

What is required to help foster nestedness and integration in the complex digital learning ecosystem?

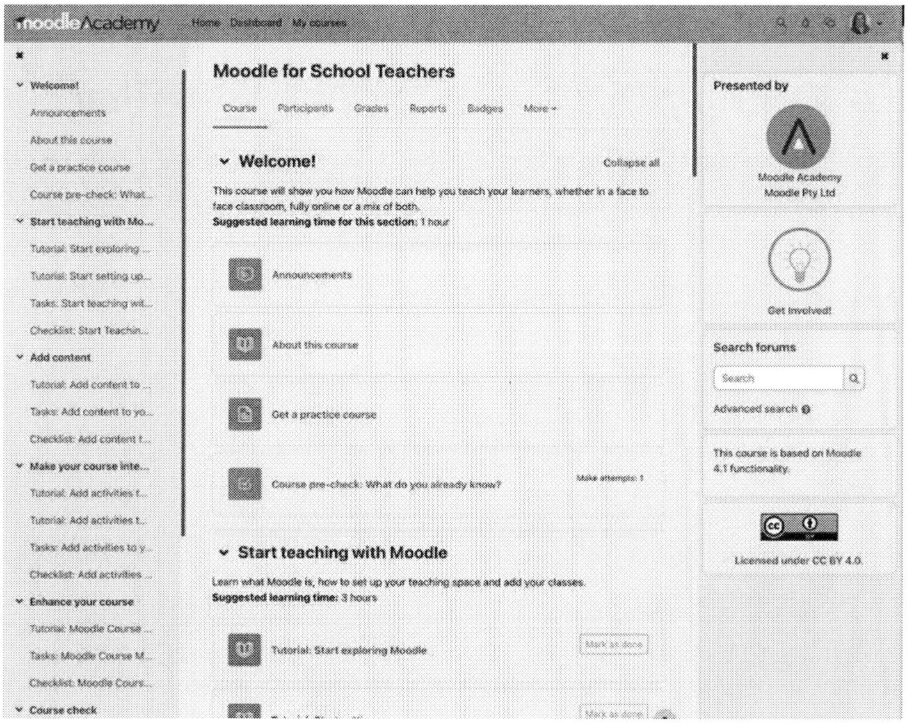

Figure 1: Caption from Moodle Academy of the Moodle for School Teachers course

References

Andone, D., Mihaescu, V., & Vasiu, R. (2020). ABCTOVLE - ABC-LD Course Design Experiences for Blended and Online Education. 3, 142–149. https://doi.org/10.12753/2066-026X-20-188

Carretero Gomez, S., Vuorikari, R., & Punie, Y. (2017). DigComp 2.1: The Digital Competence Framework for Citizens with eight proficiency levels and examples of use (JRC106281) [EUR - Scientific and Technical Research Reports]. Publications Office of the European Union. https://doi.org/10.2760/38842 (online)

Digital Education Action Plan 2021-2027 Resetting education and training for the digital age, (2020) (testimony of European Commission). https://eur-lex.europa.eu/legal-content/EN/TXT/?uri=CELEX:52020DC0624

Rako, S., & Softic, S. K. (2020). DEVELOPMENT AND USAGE OF OPEN EDUCATIONAL RESOURCES AMONG TEACHERS. EDULEARN20 Proceedings, 3849–3854. https://doi.org/10.21125/edulearn.2020.1053

Development of 21st-Century Digital Competencies in Teacher Training: Innovation with Augmented Reality for Undergraduate Students in Education

Delsa Silva Amino Cufuna[1], Josep M Duart[2], Gizéh Rangel De Lázaro[3]

[1 2 3] Universitat Oberta de Catalunya, Spain
[1] scufuna@uoc.edu
[2] jduart@uoc.edu
[3] grangel@uoc.edu

Correspondence: Delsa Silva Amino Cufuna: scufuna@uoc.edu

Abstract:

The integration of technologies in educational practice represents a growing concern among educators of different levels and areas, marked by the constant advance of technological presence. In this context, augmented reality (AR) proposes a disruptive approach in the framework of a new learning culture adapted to the educational demands of the 21st century. Here, we present a participatory action research design using focus groups to understand the impact of AR on developing digital competencies in university students pursuing a degree in Education. First, a systematic literature review will be conducted to analyze the state of the question. Following a mixed-method approach, combining quantitative (through questionnaires) and qualitative (through focus groups) data will be used to understand the phenomenon comprehensively. Units of analysis include the impact of AR, AR-related digital competencies, impacts of AR assessment, and practical applications of AR. Methodologically, focus groups will facilitate discussion on how AR influences teaching and learning, while questionnaires assess the perceived impact of AR on learning effectiveness and satisfaction. Participants will be carefully selected to ensure a diverse representation of experiences and opinions, including those directly involved in AR and those with relevant educational and technological perspectives. The study hypothesizes that integrating AR into teacher education significantly enhances pedagogical practice and academic innovation. It postulates that students exposed to AR-enriched curricula develop advanced digital competencies, enhancing their ability to create and customize digital content. The results will help to improve concrete practices and contribute to decision-making in the pedagogical structures of trainee teacher education programs. In conclusion, it explores the specific digital competencies acquired by students, the facilitation of digital content creation and editing, the educational advantages and challenges of AR integration, and the pedagogical strategies used to foster the use of AR and develop digital competencies.

Keywords: augmented reality (AR), digital competencies, pedagogical innovation, focus groups, participant observation, educational technologies.

Summary

Context: Study on Augmented Reality (AR) to improve the training of undergraduate education students in digital competencies.
Research objectives: To identify digital competencies acquired through AR, its role in creating digital content, and related pedagogical strategies.
Methodology: Mixed approach with qualitative and quantitative methods to collect and analyze data.
Results: RA in teacher education is expected to improve pedagogical practices and prepare educators for the digital future.

What does learner-centered pedagogy look like in reimagining the digital classroom of the future?

Implications: Potential contributions to educational innovation and understanding of digital education.
Conclusions: AR is expected to significantly contribute to pedagogy and address challenges such as the digital divide and teacher training.

References

Cabero, J., & Barroso, J. (2020). El valor educativo de la Realidad Aumentada. *Revista Latinoamericana de Tecnología Educativa, 19*(1), 131-146. https://doi.org/10.17398/1695-288X.19.1.131

Garzón, J., Pavón, I., & Baldiris, S. (2020). Systematic review and meta-analysis of augmented reality in educational settings. *Virtual Reality, 24*, 447-470. https://doi.org/10.1007/s10055-019-00419-8

Lakkala, M., Ilomäki, L. & Kantosalo, A. (2011). Which areas of digital competence are important for a teacher? *European Schoolnet*, 1-8.

Prendes, M. P., Castañeda, L. & Gutiérrez, I. (2010). Competencias para el uso de TIC de los futuros maestros. *Comunicar, 18*(35), 175-182.

Veletsianos, G. (2010). A definition of emerging technologies for education. En G. Veletsianos (ed.). *Emerging technologies in distance education*, 3-22.

Being a Wizard: Insights from a Teaching Intervention in a Virtual Makerspace

Melanie Gürentz[1], Olena Beskorsa[2], Iris Mendel[3], Kathrin Otrel-Cass[4], Michael Reicho[5]

[12345] Institute for teacher education and education research, University of Graz, Austria
[1] melanie.guerentz@uni-graz.at
[2] lolena.beskorsa@uni-graz.at
[3] iris.mendel@uni-graz.at
[4] kathrin.otrel-cass@uni-graz.at
[5] michael.reicho@uni-graz.at

Correspondence: Melanie Gürentz: melanie.guerentz@uni-graz.at

Abstract:

Moving educational interactions into a virtual space dramatically changes the nature of human-technology interactions. Virtual environments change the embodied ways of being together (Vindenes & Wasson, 2021). We are presenting three cartoons that share insights about the nature of participation in a virtual world we identified as a virtual makerspace, since various education interested groups came together to 'make' an educational product as a team. The cartoons reflect on the experiences of the team who organized and set up the virtual world and dreamed up the educational intervention that formed part of the "Hacking Innovative Pedagogies" project (https://hip-project.uni-graz.at/de/) activities. Being in the virtual world meant for people to present themselves as a character or play a role that either closely mirrors their actual identities or embodies alternative virtual selves (Turkle, 1994). The reflections of our interactions echo also how we perceived this environment as teachers and researchers who sometimes "spy" on others. The poster shows three comic strips, each with a QR code that allows a reader to finish each story. Using comics for communication was a deliberate choice of methodology, allowing us to use visual vocabulary (Eisner, 1985) and visual grammar (McCloud, 1993). The semantics of the visual language in comics allowed us to share subtle shades of how it "feels" to have an educational experience in a virtual makerspace.

Keywords: Human-Technology Interaction, Makerspace, Learning Environments

References

Bayne, S., Evans, P., Ewins, R., Knox, J., & Lamb, J. (2020). The manifesto for teaching online. MIT Press.

Eisner, W. (2008). Comics and sequential art: principles and practices from the legendary cartoonist. New York, NY: W. W. Norton & Company.

Foucault, M. (1977, French 1975). Discipline and Punish. The Birth of the Prison. New York: Vintage books.

Freud, S. (1926, German 1923). The Ego and the Id. Retrieved from https://archive.org/details/in.ernet.dli.2015.221832/mode/2up.

McCloud, S. (1993). Understanding comics: The invisible art. New York, NY: HarperCollins Publishers

Nardi, B. (2010). My life as a night elf priest: An anthropological account of World of Warcraft. University of Michigan Press.

What does learner-centered pedagogy look like in reimagining the digital classroom of the future?

Petkova, D., & Lehtonen, J. (2005). Cultural identity in an intercultural context. University of Jyväskylä.

Przybylski, A. K., Weinstein, N., Murayama, K., Lynch, M. F., & Ryan, R. M. (2012). The Ideal Self at Play: The Appeal of Video Games That Let You Be All You Can Be. *Psychological Science*, 23(1), 69-76. https://doi.org/10.1177/0956797611418676

Turkle, S. (1994). Constructions and reconstructions of self in virtual reality: Playing in the MUDs. *Mind, Culture, and Activity*, 1(3), 158-167. https://doi.org/10.1080/10749039409524667

Vindenes, J., & Wasson, B. (2021). A postphenomenological framework for studying user experience of immersive virtual reality. *Frontiers in Virtual Reality*, 2, 656423.

Zuboff, S. (2019). The Age of Surveillance Capitalism. The Fight for a Human Future at the New Frontier of Power. New York: Public Affairs.

Application for Self-Evaluation of Online Courses

Domagoj Horvatović[1], Tona Radobolja[2], Zvonko Martinović[3], Sandra Kučina Softić[4], Mirna Granatir[5]

[12345]University of Zagreb University Computing Centre, Croatia
[1] domagoj.horvatovic@srce.hr
[2] tona.radobolja@srce.hr
[3] zvonko.martinovic@srce.hr
[4] sskucina@srce.hr
[5] mirna.granatir@srce.hr

Correspondence: Sandra Kučina Softić, sskucina@srce.hr

Abstract:

How to meet the challenges of teaching in a virtual environment and create a good online course? How to ensure that you are doing good work while having such a course? The E-learning Centre at the University of Zagreb University Computing Centre SRCE, in collaboration with teachers from the University of Zagreb, experts in the field of digital education, designed an application for self-assessment of online courses as one more possibility that could be helpful to them in the preparation and design of courses in an online environment. The application is connected to the e-learning platform Merlin and is available to teachers directly within their e-course (in the Administration block) in the platform.
Teachers, who already have experience in online courses, using this application, can check how well they designed their e-course. For teachers who are just getting involved in the adventure of teaching in an online environment and designing an online course, this application can offer good ideas and clarify possible doubts about the use of different digital tools and teaching methods.

In this paper (poster) we will present the application for self-evaluation of online courses, how it can benefit teachers working in online environments and its applicability in similar environments.

Keywords: self-evaluation, online course, course design, digital education

Summary

The University of Zagreb University Computing Centre SRCE (https://www.srce.unizg.hr/en) is the national e-infrastructure institution for the academic and research community in the area of application of information and communication technologies (ICT) in Croatia. Furthermore, SRCE is the competence centre for information and communication technologies as well as the centre for education and support in the area of ICT application. The E-learning Centre at SRCE (ELC) (https://www.srce.unizg.hr/en/elc) is the national centre for the implementation of e-learning in higher education in Croatia. The E-learning Centre provides support to higher education in e-learning, primarily to teachers, for 16 years. The E-learning Centre is maintaining Merlin - the e-learning platform for higher education institutions in Croatia based on the open-source software Moodle and provides technical support in its use and use of other digital tools and technologies the ELC is providing. Along with technical support, the ELC provides support to teachers in the design and preparation of their online courses and through educational activities trains them to get digital skills and to be able to perform high-quality teaching in an online environment.

Digital technologies have become part of our lives, work and education; therefore, they are used in the educational process as well in higher education in Croatia. Although e-learning has been present in higher education since the

90's of the 20th century, the digital age has increased its use for the preparation of teaching, in addition to classroom teaching and learning and has replaced face-to-face teaching and learning in a smaller percentage (about 20%). Nevertheless, the majority of courses in higher education in Croatia have their online version, especially after the pandemic. In the use of digital tools and technologies, higher education teachers rely mostly on the E-learning Centre at SRCE, therefore high-quality and easily reachable support is crucial.

The design of the application for self-evaluation of online courses (https://moodle.srce.hr/procjena-epredmeta/app/) offers teachers the possibility of evaluating their e-courses according to four groups of criteria and a graphical representation of the obtained results. Criteria groups are Course Design, Course Materials, Assessment and Learning Outcomes and Communication. Each criterion is described to provide information on how it could be used at some basic level or to its full potential. Within descriptions of criteria person can find as well recommendations and examples of good practices in the creation of some parts of the e-course or the e-course as a whole. Of course, there are always e-courses, and perhaps entire fields, to which some criteria are not applicable.

The application is available to everyone and is available at https://www.srce.unizg.hr/ceu/aplikacija-samoprocjene-e-predmeta or through the e-course in the e-learning platform Merlin. Saving the results within the user profile enables the comparison of the same e-course over several years, and the teacher can compare two or more of his/her online courses.

In addition, teachers can ask for the evaluation of their online course from the experts at the E-learning Centre at SRCE. To apply for the evaluation of the ELC, teachers need to do a self-evaluation of their course first. Received feedback from teachers is very positive and they find such a possibility very useful. This application enables them to monitor the design and development of their online courses and to have feedback from the experts at the ELC, when they want, where they can discuss the results and with their support work on the improvement of their online courses.

References

Kučina Softić, S., Odak, M., Lasić Lazić, J. (2021). *Digitalna transformacija: Novi pristupi i izazovi u obrazovanju.* Sveučilište Sjever, Koprivnica.

Kučina Softić, S., Čičko, T., Radobolja, T. (2023) Open online courses and MOOCs for students' extended learning experience, ICERI2023 Proceedings, pp. 3209-3215. doi: 10.21125/iceri.2023.0841

Kučina Softić, S.; Radobolja, T. (2022). How did we support education in the pandemic - the role of the E-learning Centre. *EDEN Conference Proceedings: Shaping the Digital Transformation of the Education Ecosystem in Europe* (str. 37-42). Tallinn: EDEN Digital Learning Europe. Available: https://urn.nsk.hr/urn:nbn:hr:102:240424

Workshops to Test Peer Assessment Through a Digital Platform. Comparing Two Pilot Experiences

Mara Valente[1]

[1] Department of Education, Roma Tre University, Italy; mara.valente@uniroma3.it

Correspondence: Mara Valente: mara.valente@uniroma3.it

Abstract:

The poster aims to describe the outcomes of two pilot activities carrying out in a university context to investigate peer assessment practices among student using an online platform. The objective is to assess how this process aids students in enhancing their soft and digital skills and to evaluate the advantages of peer feedback in fostering self-reflection and self-assessment of completed tasks. The reported pilot experiences compare activities with and without the use of exemplum used in the peer review process. In particular, the poster describes the educational activities, learning tools, assessment methods, and the online platform utilized for reviewing and exchanging feedback, and a brief overview of the results.

Keywords: Self-assessment; peer review; transversal skills; digital skills; peer evaluation.

Summary

The new teaching styles suggest an increasing focus on placing the student at the center of the teaching/learning process, aiming for strategies and methodologies that promote their engagement and active participation, also using technology, thus creating new learning environments. In this regard, Peer Assessment is recognized as one of the most effective strategies. This type of assessment is meant to support students in planning their learning, identifying their strengths and weaknesses, finding areas for corrective interventions, and developing metacognitive and other transferable skills on a personal and professional level (Boud, 1990; Brown et al., 1994; Topping 1998). Giving students the opportunity to take an active part in their assessment alters the balance between teacher and learner and encourages appropriate control over their learning, as stated by Vickerman (2009). Peer interaction engages students in developing their learning, not only from an academic perspective but also from a cognitive and emotional one (Vickerman, 2009). Falchikov (1986) underlines the importance of adopting peer assessment strategies in stimulating transversal skills. Additionally, through the use of new technologies, this methodology solicits digital competence, as mandated by guidelines from the European Commission, as one of the eight skills that European citizens should master by the end of compulsory schooling from a lifelong learning perspective[4]. The acquisition of digital skills does not only result from the ability to use digital tools; digital technologies evolve and change rapidly, so mastering digital skills means, above all, being able to approach the use of new digital tools in a flexible way (Poce, 2015). Considering these premises, the intention of the poster is to illustrate the results obtained during two pilot experiences carried out in a university context with the objective of involving students in peer review processes using a digital platform and testing the level of implementation of transversal and digital competences due to participation in these experiences. In particular, the impact in terms of performance and improved skills will be

[4] https://data.europa.eu/doi/10.2760/115376

highlighted regarding the use (or lack thereof) of exemplum to be employ as a reference in the evaluation processes. The results obtained show, in fact, that this support encourages the implementation of skills such as Critical Thinking, Communication, and Collaboration and opens up further research possibilities in this specific area.

References

Bloxham, S., & Boyd, P. (2007). *Developing Effective Assessment in Higher Education: A practical guide*. Open University Press.

Boud D., Molloy E. (2013). *Feedback in Higher and Professional Education. Understanding it and doing it well.* Routledge.

Brown, S., Rust, C. & Gibbs, G., (1994). *Strategies for Diversifying Assessment in Higher Education*. Oxford Centre for Staff Development.

Falchikov, N. (1986). Product comparisons and process benefits of collaborative peer group and self assessments. *Assessment & Evaluation in Higher Education*, 11:2, 146-166, DOI: 10.1080/0260293860110206

Poce, A. (2015). *Tecnologia critica, Creatività e Didattica della Scienza*. Franco Angeli.

Topping, K.J. (1998). Peer Assessment between Students in Colleges and Universities. *Review of Educational Research*, 68(3), 249-276.

Vickerman, P. (2009). Student perspectives on formative peer assessment: an attempt to deepen learning? *Assessment & Evaluation in Higher Education*, 34(2), 221-230.

Project UnimSTEM: School and University Integration of STEAM and Digital Competences

Raül Peinado Alamillo [1], Victoria I. Marín[2], David Aguilar[3]

[1 2 3] Departament of Education Sciences, Universitat de Lleida, Spain
[1] raul.peinado@udl.cat
[2] victoria.marin@udl.cat
[3] david.aguilar@udl.cat

Correspondence: Raül Peinado Alamillo: raul.peinado@udl.cat

Abstract:

The UnimSTEM project aims to promote digital competences for teachers and STE(A)M during the primary education level. In this project, the minor in STEM offered in the Degree in Primary Education of the Faculty of Education, Psychology and Social Work of the University of Lleida (UdL, Catalonia, Spain) is extended to a group of active primary school teachers from different schools in Lleida province. The collaboration between the university and the schools through the project has resulted in a network of collaboration between the different participants, where teaching resources and methodologies have been designed and implemented to promote digital competences linked to the STEAM fields.

Keywords: STEAM, digital competences for teachers, primary education, university, teacher professional development

Summary:

The transformation and digitalization of schools requires improving the digital competence of their teachers in order to ensure that it leads to a true transformation of the teaching-learning processes in primary education classrooms. For example, the SAMR model of educational innovation aims at transformation through innovative digital practices, which cannot take place without the digital competence of the teachers involved in the design and implementation of these practices. Likewise, models such as TPACK emphasize the need to consider technological, pedagogical and content knowledge in teacher training. In this sense, digital competences for teachers necessarily need to be connected with pedagogical and content aspects that give them significance in educational practices. In this project, it is understood that STEAM fields, and their methodologies, can provide this significance and have a relevant link with the digital transformative possibility of educational practices (Arabit & Prendes, 2020; Ghome & Redecker, 2019).

From September 2023 to June 2024 (10 months), 32 in-service teachers from 7 primary schools in Lleida that had not participated in training programmes on digital competences and STEAM yet, and 5 pre-service teachers in the minor in STEM from UdL participated in the UnimSTEM project. Participation in the project has meant attendance at blended training sessions, financial resources for the acquisition of teaching equipment, guidance on the training use of the equipment acquired and personalized supervision. This relationship between the schools and the university has contributed to the implementation of STEAM teaching innovation projects in the participating primary education schools, the creation of eportfolios where the designed projects have been documented, as well as the revitalization of physical spaces in the schools to promote digital competences and STEAM fields. All the teaching experiences implemented and the training programs designed have been shared among all the participating schools to enrich community learning.

Acknowledgements

Funding: UnimSTEM project (grant EDU128/23/00016)

Finançat per la Unió Europea NextGenerationEU · Gobierno de España · Plan de Recuperación, Transformación y Resiliencia · Next Generation Catalunya · Generalitat de Catalunya

References

Arabit, J., & Prendes, M. P. (2020). Metodologías y Tecnologías para enseñar STEM en Educación Primaria: análisis de necesidades. *Pixel-Bit: Revista de Medios y Educación, 57,* 107-128. https://doi.org/10.12795/pixelbit.2020.i57.04

Ghomi, M., & Redecker, C. (2019). Digital Competence of Educators (DigCompEdu): Development and Evaluation of a Self-assessment Instrument for Teachers' Digital Competence. In *Proceedings of the 11th International Conference on Computer Supported Education - Volume 1: CSEDU* (pp. 541-548). http://dx.doi.org/10.5220/0007679005410548

Learning Designers as Change Agents: Pioneering AI Integration in Higher Education

Sasha Stubbs[1]

[1] Learning Design, RMIT Vietnam, Vietnam; sasha.stubbs2@rmit.edu.vn

Correspondence: Sasha Stubbs: sasha.stubbs2@rmit.edu.vn

Abstract:

Amidst the double disruption of post-COVID rapid blended learning adoption at our institution (Stubbs & Nguyen, 2023) and the emergence of AI in education (Carvalho et al., 2022), learning designers have emerged as crucial change agents, uniquely positioned to drive the university's AI adoption. As third-space professionals bridging academic and professional domains (Whitchurch, 2008), and building on the existing effectiveness of academic-designer partnerships in fostering technology-enhanced learning (Huber & Jacka, 2022), learning designers have leveraged their relationships with academics to prompt consideration of how AI is used professionally within their discipline and to create meaningful AI informed learning experiences.

Early experimentation with AI has allowed our learning designers to develop a fluency, enabling them to incorporate AI into various aspects of the learning design process. They use AI to analyze learning outcomes, create engaging explanations, analogies, activities, create alternative text, brainstorm ideas, write copy and scripts, and generate insights from LMS data. This familiarity, combined with the co-design approach employed, emphasising equal partnership among actors, with shared values such as trust, respect, reciprocity, responsibility, and openness (Huber & Jacka, 2022), positions learning designers as ideal catalysts for AI integration. The nature of the codesign relationship provides an opening for learning designers to act as change agents, harnessing academic relationships to integrate AI into authentic disciplinary learning activities, empowering students with crucial AI-enhanced future skills. Their work spans individual learners, team-academic collaborations, and institutional transformation (Gibson et al., 2023). Fostering boundary crossing and knowledge sharing across levels drives rapid, inclusive AI experience pioneering to prepare students for an AI-driven world.

Supporting academics grappling with disruption, learning designers catalyse insitutional change through their boundary crossing work. As education transforms, their role becomes pivotal, demanding continued collaboration and support to realize AI's potential in enhancing teaching and learning.

Keywords: Learning design, AI, change agents, partnerships.

What does learner-centered pedagogy look like in reimagining the digital classroom of the future?

Summary

Learning designers are emerging as crucial change agents for driving AI adoption in higher education amid disruptions. As third-space professionals, they leverage academic partnerships and co-design approaches to integrate AI into discipline-relevant learning experiences. Emphasizing equal partnership and shared values, the co-design approach positions learning designers ideally to harness academic relationships for pioneering inclusive AI experiences across individual, collaborative, and institutional levels. Their role in catalysing personalised, AI-enhanced education is pivotal as learning transforms.

References

Carvalho, L., Martinez-Maldonado, R., Tsai, Y. S., Markauskaite, L., & De Laat, M. (2022). How can we design for learning in an AI world? Computers and Education: Artificial Intelligence, 3, Article 100053. https://doi.org/10.1016/j.caeai.2022.100053

Gibson, D., Kovanovic, V., Ifenthaler, D., Dexter, S., & Feng, S. (2023). Learning theories for artificial intelligence promoting learning processes. British Journal of Educational Technology, 54, 1125–1146. https://doi.org/10.1111/bjet.13341

Huber, E. & Jacka, L. (2022). Co-Design of Higher Education. In C. Campbell, D. B. Porter, D. Logan-Fleming, and H. Jones (Eds.). Scanning the Ed Tech Horizon: The 2021-2022 Contextualising Horizon Report. (pp. 30-31). ASCILITE. https://ascilite.org/get-involved/contextualising-horizon/

Stubbs, S., & Nguyen, B. (2023). Co-Creating the Future: A Learning Design Team's Journey Fostering Institutional Change [Pecha Kucha Presentation]. Australasian Society for Computers in Learning in Tertiary Education Conference, Sydney, Australia. https://doi.org/10.14742/apubs.2023.645

Whitchurch, C. (2008). Shifting identities and blurring boundaries: The emergence of third space professionals in UK higher education. Higher Education Quarterly, 62(4), 377–396. https://doi.org/10.1111/j.1468-2273.2008.00387.x Books

OER-Codex: Harnessing OERs for Collaborative Online Learning

Giedrė Tamoliūnė[1], Aušra Rutkienė[2], Indrė Oleškevičienė[3]

[1 2 3] Vytautas Magnus University, Lithuania
[1] giedre.tamoliune@vdu.lt
[2] ausra.rutkiene@vdu.lt
[3] indre.oleskeviciene@vdu.lt

Correspondence: Giedrė Tamoliūnė: giedre.tamoliune@vdu.lt

Abstract:

This paper is based on the international Erasmus Capacity building project "OER-CODEX: Open Educational Resources for Collaborative Online & Distance Education and eXchange Context". The project aims to develop OER course modules that teach digital teaching and learning methods, including online collaborative learning, for educators in Higher Education. Online collaborative learning is important for blended and online learning, which is essential for imparting skills necessary for the 21st century. However, sometimes educators require assistance in sharing their expertise, and the lack of cross-institutional initiative further complicates this challenge. OER-CODEX tries to overcome this problem by creating online course modules structured along DigCompEdu, empowering educators, and fostering a self-sustaining OER repository.

Keywords: open educational resources, collaborative learning, online and blended learning, educators

Summary

Online collaborative learning is an effective approach to blended and online learning, which is an essential aspect of teaching and assessing Twenty-First Century Skills as identified by the OECD and its Programme for International Student Assessment (PISA). However, many higher education educators face several challenges in this regard. Educators who possess expertise in online and blended learning need support in sharing their knowledge with other educators. There is also a lack of international cross-institutional initiatives that aim to implement online and blended learning in a systematic and accessible manner by creating Open Educational Resources (OER) course modules for online collaborative learning and teaching based on the DigCompEdu framework. These courses will equip educators with the knowledge and skills needed to engage in blended learning activities at their institutions. In addition, the online course modules aim to create OER content with the participants, ensuring that educators acquire expertise in the courses and can apply their knowledge to develop OER content themselves. This OER content is published along with the online course modules, forming a self-sustaining OER pool for online collaborative learning and teaching methods.

OER-CODEX is an international Erasmus project, designed to equip educators with the skills, resources, and support needed to navigate the evolving landscape of digital education. In response to the challenges posed by rapid digitalization and the COVID-19 pandemic, OER-CODEX focuses on harnessing the power of Open Educational Resources (OER) to enhance collaborative online and distance learning experiences.

At its core, OER-CODEX aims to empower educators with the knowledge and proficiency required to excel in blended and online learning environments. By developing **nine** courses aligned with the DigCompEdu framework, the project ensures that educators improve their digital competencies. From introducing HE teachers to open educational resources (Tamoliune, et.al., 2023), and designing case studies for online collaborative learning (Ukhova, et.al., 2023) to leveraging learning analytics and conversational agent technology, these courses (see Fig. 1) cover various topics important for modern educators.

Cluster	Course	Title
Cluster 1: Open educational Resources for Collaborative Learning	**Course 1**	Digital Resources
	Course 2	Case Study Design
Cluster 2: Online Guidance and Facilitation	**Course 3**	Facilitating and Guiding Online Collaborative Learning
	Course 4	Learning Analytics
Cluster 3: Assessment and triggering self-reflection	**Course 5**	Assessment approaches with formative assessment
	Course 6	Assessing with Learning Analytics
	Course 7	Triggering reflection and self-reflection processes in students with the help of conversational agents
Cluster4: Advanced methods to encourage learning	**Course 8**	Gamification
	Course 9	Virtual Reality Environments for online collaborative learning

Fig. 1. The list of courses developed within the OER-Codex project framework.

Courses explore mentoring and guiding online collaboration, leveraging learning analytics, and fostering reflection through conversational agents. Educators also learn formative assessment techniques, gamification strategies, and the immersive potential of virtual reality environments. These courses foster a vibrant community of collaborative educators shaping the future of digital learning. However, OER-CODEX is not just about skill-building; it's about fostering a culture of collaboration and innovation within the education community. Through collaborative learning approaches, educators enhance their capabilities and contribute to a shared pool of knowledge and resources.

The outcomes of OER-CODEX are twofold: educators emerge with enhanced digital teaching skills and access to a wealth of OER content, while the initiative lays the groundwork for a self-sustaining ecosystem of OER and collaborative learning. This iterative process ensures that the OER-CODEX project remains relevant and impactful long into the future, shaping the landscape of digital education for years to come.

In essence, OER-CODEX represents a step towards a more collaborative, inclusive, and innovative approach to education. By empowering educators with the tools and resources they need to succeed in the digital age, the initiative is paving the way for a brighter future of teaching and learning.

Acknowledgments

This paper is being supported by the Erasmus+ Programme of the European Union (project "OER-CODEX - Open Educational Resources for Collaborative Online & Distance Education and eXchange", no. 2021-1-DE01-KA220-HED-000023196). All mentioned project results are available at https://www.oer-codex.eu/

This publication reflects the views only of the authors, and the European Commission cannot be held responsible for any use that may be made of the information contained therein.

References

Tamoliūnė, G., Rutkienė, A., Oleškevičienė, I. (2023). Digital Resources. *OER-Codex project training material.* https://www.oer-codex.eu/courses/

Ukhova, N., Heidmann, N., Schoop, E., Rutkienė, A., and Tamoliūnė, G. (2023). Case Study Design. *OER-Codex project training material.* https://www.oer-codex.eu/courses/

Bridging Knowledge and Building Trust: A Comprehensive Mentorship Journey in Artificial Intelligence (AI) and Machine Learning (ML)

Daniela Felipucci[1], Alfredo Soeiro[2]

[1] Straumann Group, Switzerland; dfelipucci@icloud.com
[2] Universidade do Porto, Portugal; soeiro.alfredo@gmail.com

Correspondence: Daniela Felipucci, dfelipucci@icloud.com

Abstract:

This case report examines a mentorship program in the rapidly evolving fields of AI and ML, with a focus on establishing a trusting and psychologically safe learning environment. The mentee aims to gain field literacy, receive expert guidance, form connections, and achieve relevance in AI and ML. The mentor, bringing over 30 years of experience in online teaching, training, and learning, contributes through a rich exchange of knowledge and insights. This paper highlights how open dialogue and constructive response facilitate exploration of online training and learning topics. The mentor's expertise in authoring papers, conducting webinars, and presenting at conferences is leveraged to transfer knowledge effectively to the mentee. Central to the study is the mentor's pursuit of new ideas and projects, indicating a commitment to continuous learning and innovation. This case underscores the significance of trust and rapport in effective mentorship, exploring key interactions, shared experiences, and dynamics that contribute to skill enhancement and knowledge acquisition. The paper presents an analysis of challenges faced, strategies employed to overcome them, and lessons learned from both the mentor and mentee perspectives. It concludes with reflections on the mentorship program's value, its impact on participants, and provides recommendations for enhancing similar future mentorship initiatives in AI and ML, thus contributing to the broader discourse on effective mentorship strategies in technical fields.

Keywords: AI, Mentoring, Dialogue, ML, Trust, Knowledge

Summary

In the landscape of AI and ML, **both upskilling and reskilling play pivotal roles in maintaining relevance and competitiveness**. Upskilling and reskilling can make employees more valuable to their current employers and more competitive in the job market. Moreover, **businesses that invest in these learning opportunities can retain top talent and attract new, motivated professionals** who value growth and development. **The CIGAR mentor model**, created by Green and Grant, is designed to be a **comprehensive and dynamic mentoring approach**. It stands for Coaching, Inquiry, Guidance, Advice, and Reflection.

From the **mentee perspective**, significant **gain in the literacy and knowledge** was achieved due the recommendation of papers, books and case studies about AI and ML. **Significant network has been built** since the beginning of the mentorship program, with concrete connections facilitated by the mentor. From the **mentor perspective** it is an **experience that enriches the pool of memories** related with **usefulness of dialogue and of reflection on an emerging issue**. Different perspectives and innovative possible paths bring broader conscience of the topics. It is in fact **a journey with new views and richer understanding**.

In the field of AI and ML, where technological evolution is rapid, **upskilling can help professionals keep pace with new developments and tools, while reskilling can be essential for those whose roles may be fundamentally altered or replaced by new technologies.** Both strategies are crucial for creating a workforce that is adaptable and prepared for the future of work. The authors appreciate the **EDEN DIGITAL LEARNING EUROPE** for the Mentorship opportunity.

References

Green, L. S., Oades, L. G., & Grant, A. M. (2003). Cognitive-behavioral, solution-focused life coaching: Enhancing goal striving, well-being, and hope. *The Journal of Positive Psychology*, 1(3), 142–149.

Integrating AI in Higher Education Curricula Through OERs: Scenarios and Experiences

Milena Stegner[1], Britta Lintfert[2], Jochen Ehrenreich[3], Regine Martschiske[4]

[1234] Abteilung Bildungsforschung, DHBW Heilbronn, Germany
[1] milena.stegner@heilbronn.dhbw.de
[2] britta.lintfert@heilbronn.dhbw.de
[3] jochen.ehrenreich@heilbronn.dhbw.de
[4] regine.martschiske@heilbronn.dhbw.de

Correspondence: Milena Stegner: milena.stegner@heilbronn.dhbw.de

Abstract:

Given the growing influence of AI on our daily lives and work environments, the necessity of its integration as a key qualification within higher education curricula is becoming increasingly evident. The AI Campus (https://ki-campus.org) offers a diverse portfolio of freely available online courses (OERs) about AI. These courses can facilitate the implementation of AI topics into higher education teaching in a low-threshold manner. This implementation has been actively pursued as part of an education research project at the State Cooperative University Baden-Württemberg (DHBW). We provide an insight into the experiences and discuss how this approach can also be put into practice at other educational institutions.

Keywords: AI, Higher Education, Future Skills, AICOMP, AI-Campus

Introduction

Due to the growing influence of AI on our living and working environments, the necessity of its integration as a key qualification in higher education is becoming increasingly apparent. As part of the AI-Campus Hub Baden-Württemberg, the DHBW Heilbronn and Karlsruhe provide Open Educational Resources (OER) from the AI Campus (https://ki-campus.org/) online courses and support university lecturers in integrating AI into their own courses. Beyond providing learning content, the aim is to offer solutions for technical and infrastructural issues as well as possibilities for didactic design in the low-threshold provision of digital learning resources.

Method

In order to further enhance the integration of AI Campus learning resources into university courses, the following steps are being pursued:

- Provision of a self-assessment tool for AI competencies based on the AICOMP model (Ehlers, 2023), which can help lecturers to identify the AI competencies relevant to their courses.
- Curating learning content from the AI Campus to enable individual and modularized integration into university teaching.
- Didactic and technical advice and support on integrating AI Campus learning content into teaching.
- Regular workshops, professional events and further training opportunities.

What digital transformations are needed for learning and teaching in the future?

- Evaluation, improvement and further development of course material in cooperation with lecturers.
- Evaluation, improvement and further development of micro credentials.

Conclusion

In order to realize the vision of an AI-competent society, teaching AI skills in higher education plays a central role. The results and experience gained by DHBW in this area can make an important contribution to promoting AI skills as key future skills at other universities.

References

Ehlers, U.-D. (2023). Kompetenzen für die KI-Welt. *managerSeminare 305*.

Ehlers, U.-D.; Schmidbauer, F. (2023). OER als Katalysator für innovative Bildung in Hochschule und Beruf. Paper presented at DHBW-Forschungstag, Baden-Württemberg. https://www.dhbw.de/fileadmin/user_upload/Dokumente/Forschung/Forschungstag_2023/DHBW_Forschungstag_2023_Digitaler_Tagungsband.pdf (Accessed: 14th of March 2024).

Flasdick, J. et al (2023). *Micro-credentials and micro-degrees. Current developments and potentials for educational practice based on the example of the AI Campus*. Discussion Paper. Berlin: AI Campus. Available at https://ki-campus.org/sites/default/files/2023-02/2023-02_Discussion_Paper_Micro-Credentials_Micro-Degrees_AI_Campus_EN.pdf (Accessed: 14th of March 2024).

A Breakthrough in the Application of Digital Skills in Education

Genutė Gedvilienė[1], Rasa Didžiulienė[2], Salomėja Karasevičiūtė[3], Romualdas Gedvilas[4]

[1] Education academy, Vytautas Magnus University, Lithuania; genute.gedviliene@vdu.lt
[2] Education academy, Vytautas Magnus University, Lithuania; rasa.didžiuliene@vdu.lt
[3] Kauno Kolegija, Lithuania; s.karaseviciute@gmail.com
[4] Kauno Technikos Kolegija, Lithuania; gedromas@gmail.com

Correspondence: Genutė Gedvilienė: genute.gedviliene@vdu.lt

Keywords: Breakthrough, competencies; digital skills; distance learning; Education institutions.

Introduction

The experience of the pandemic around the world has put unexpected additional pressures not only on students and their families, but also on teachers. In the fight against the COVID-19 pandemic, working at home has become the norm. The pandemic required school systems to move rapidly to distance education, leading to significant global changes in typical teaching practices (Salinas-Falquez et al., 2022). Teachers were tasked with rapidly implementing new teaching practices in a way that promoted student learning and ensured their safety. On the other hand, despite unexpected challenges, effective management of the stress caused by the demands of teaching led to teachers' professional resilience (Ott et al., 2017). Lithuanian educational institutions have replaced contact-based training with distance learning, following a Government Resolution, discovering training platforms, tools and teaching(si) methods for remote working in just a few weeks (Jusienė et al., 2021). It is important to pay attention to and analyse the psychological impact of training(s) in both pandemic and post-pandemic times, with a particular focus on the relationship between job demands, job resources, stress, resilience and occupational burnout (Sokal et al, 2020; Corrente et al, 2022).

Falloon (2020) states that digital literacy encompasses "aspects such as cybersecurity and the management of personal data and online presence, digital citizenship, ethics and decision-making, and the acquisition of knowledge from, and collaboration in, online networks and virtual environments". Janssen et al. (2013) (cited in Falloon, 2020) describe digital competence as "not only knowing how to use devices and applications", but also as inextricably linked to the ability to communicate using ICT, and information skills.

Taken together, the studies suggest that the pandemic quarantine caused stress (anxiety, depression and sleep disturbances) for teachers in most countries when it came to organising distance education at short notice (Besser et al., 2022). Teachers have become the main scriptwriters when implementing distance education. Negative work-related emotions became a cause of psychological exhaustion for most teachers (Kim and Asbury, 2020; Salinas-Falquez et al., 2022). Some studies have shown an increased risk of professional burnout among teachers when the consequences of teleworking became more stressful, not only in terms of IT management competences, familiarity and mastery of new teaching platforms, but also in terms of the digitisation of teaching materials, the etiquette of engaging with students in the virtual space, the subtleties of communication, the evaluation of teaching results in the virtual space, etc. On the other hand, the launch of distance learning also marked the beginning of a new phase of training, with a lot of work, workshops, and the introduction of new programmes, which is still going on today. The use of Digital Literacy in distance learning enables deep didactic learning, i.e. browse, analyze, collect and share information with others. Nevertheless, it is very important to encourage student participation in the learning process.

Methodology. Quantitative research methodology was applied. Educators of educational institutions (N-428) participated in the questionnaire survey. The average age of the teachers who participated in the survey was 50.1 ± 9.2. Their professional teaching experience ranged from 2 to 30 years. A quantitative research method was used to collect empirical data. The survey included both closed and open questions. Relevant literature was reviewed beforehand the items in the questionnaire were created. The questionnaire consisted of an introductory part, the respondent's consent to participate, a main part and part of sociodemographic questions. Statistical analysis was performed using SPSS 24. Research participants had the opportunity to fill out the questionnaire online at the freely available online survey portal www.apklausa.lt.

The research questions of this study are: How successful is the application of digital literacy in the pedagogical process? What are the dominant developments in digital competences in recent times?
The aim of the study is to identify teachers' digital literacy skills and application successes, highlighting the IT breakthrough in the pedagogical process.

Results

During the survey, respondents shared their opinions about professional resilience in the conditions of the COVID-19 pandemic. The responses were divided into two scales: Quality of communication (S–B = 0.81) and Readiness to work in a distance learning model (S–B = 0.84).

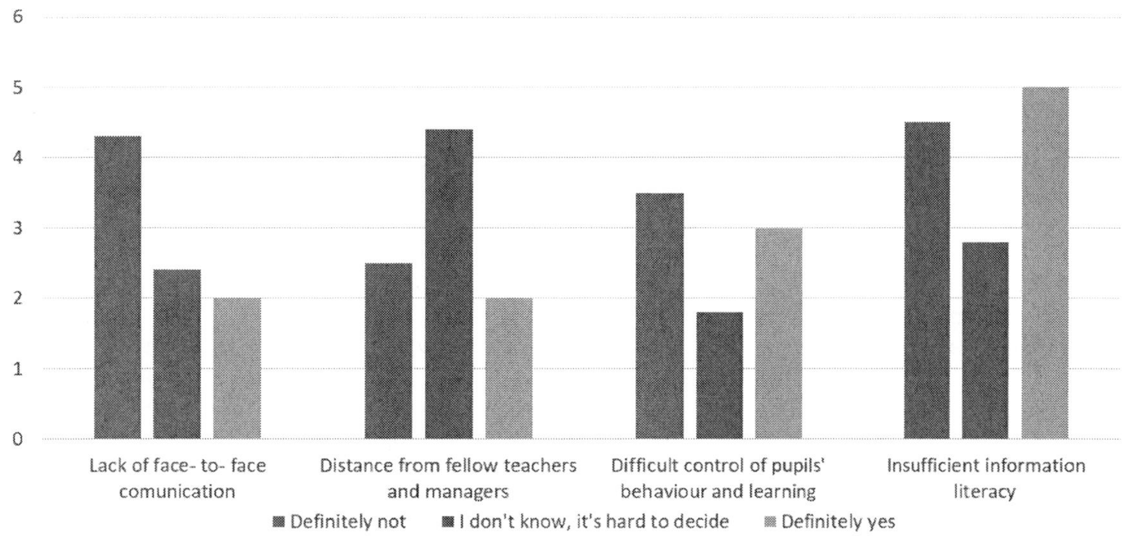

Figure 1. Teachers' inconvenience during the Covid-19 pandemic
when teaching students at a distance

Half of the teachers who took part in the study admitted that they were constantly stressed during the pandemic due to their insufficient information literacy (50%), and almost a third said that they had difficult control of pupils' the behaviour and learning (30%). Most teachers did not belong to such categories and said that they acted as Distance from fellow teachers and managers (42 percent); both lack of information literacy skills (27%) and lack of live communication (24%). However, it must be admitted that the other part of teachers, on the contrary, noted that they made excellent use of their digital literacy skills (45%), did not feel a lack of live communication (42%) and coped well with controlling pupils' behaviour and learning (36%).
In conclusion, the use of Digital Literacy in distance learning enables deep didactic learning, i.e. browse, analyze, collect and share information with others. Nevertheless, it is very important to encourage student participation in the learning process.

Conclusions

1. The analytical analysis of the sources shows that new digital technologies enable teachers to communicate with students and with each other. Digital technologies make a wide range of information available and provide universal learning opportunities.

What digital transformations are needed for learning and teaching in the future?

2. During the pandemic, teachers became the main scriptwriters in the planning and implementation of distance education. Although teachers felt emotionally unbalanced during the pandemic, they have improved their digital skills.

3. The quantitative study revealed teachers' positive attitudes towards the use of digital information retrieval in teaching and learning. It is therefore necessary to develop digital competences in distance learning classrooms and to create a constructivist learning environment with a creative approach to the learning process. In this way, the organization of learning would enrich the didactic process.

References

Besser, A., Lotem, S., & Zeigler-Hill, V. (2022). Psychological stress and vocal symptoms among university professors in Israel: implications of the shift to Online synchronous teaching during the COVID-19 pandemic. *Journal of Voice: official journal of the Voice Foundation, 36*(2), 291.e9–291.e16. DOI: 10.1016/j.jvoice.2020.05.028

Didžiulienė, R. (2023). *Subjective perception of professional happiness in the teaching community: gender comparison.* Doctoral Dissertation. Social Sciences, Education (S 007). 76-79.

Gedvilienė, G., & Vaičiūnienė, V. (2016). Distance learning at university from a lifelong learning perspective. *European scientific journal,* 12 (24), 46-59. Macedonia: European scientific institute, ISSN 1857-7881. doi:10.19044/esj.2016.v12n34p46.

Falloon, G. (2020). From digital literacy to digital competence: the teacher digital competency (TDC) framework. *Education Tech Research Dev.* Doi:10.1007/s11423-020-09767-4.

Kim, L. E., & Asbury, K. (2020). Like a rug had been pulled from under you: The impact of COVID-19 on teachers in England during the first six weeks of the UK lockdown. *Br. J. Educ. Psychol, 90,* 1062–1083. DOI: 10.1111/bjep.12381.

Ott, M., Hiebert, K., Rodger, S., & Leschiel, A. (2017). A well place to be: the intersection of Canadian school-based mental health policy with student and teacher resiliency. *Canadian Journal of Education, 40*(2), 1–30. Online available from: https://journals.sfu.ca/cje/index.php/cje-rce/article/view/2243/2422

Janssen, J., Stoyanov, S., Ferrari, A., Punie, Y., Pannekeet, K. & Sloep, P. (2013). Experts' views on digital competence: Commonalities and differences. *Computers & Education,* 68, 473–481.

Jusienė, R., Būdienė, V., Gintilienė, G., Girdzijauskienė, S., & Stonkuvienė, I. (2021). *Nuotolinis vaikų ugdymas pandemijos dėl COVID-19 metu: grėsmės ir galimybės ekosisteminiu požiūriu*. Vilnius: Vilniaus universitetas, 276 p. ISBN 978-609-07-0591-9

Salinas-Falquez, S., Roman-Lorente, C., Buzica, M., Álvarez, J., Gutiérrez, N., & Trigueros, R. (2022). Teachers' mental health and their involvement in educational inclusion. *Behavioral Sciences, 12,* 261. DOI: 10.3390/bs12080261.

Opening Horizons with the European Universities E^3UDRES^2

Radu Vasiu[1], Hannes Raffaseder[2], Vlad Mihaescu[3], Diana Andone [4]

[1] Politehnica University Timisoara, Romania, radu.vasiu@upt.ro
[2] St. Polten University of Applied Sciences, Austria, Hannes.Raffaseder@fhstp.ac.at
[3] Politehnica University Timisoara, Romania, vlad.mihaescu@upt.ro
[4] Politehnica University Timisoara, Romania, diana.andone@upt.ro

Correspondence: Diana Andone: diana.andone@upt.ro

Abstract:

E^3UDRES^2 stands for Engaged and Entrepreneurial European University as Driver for European Smart and Sustainable Regions, one of the "European Universities". E^3UDRES^2 builds on the complementary strengths of full partners from 9 countries of the existing alliance and further deepens, intensifies, and expands collaboration with members and related stakeholders, enhances the transformation processes towards a fully-fledged European University Alliance and demonstrates progress towards the alliance's long-term vision. The higher education institutions working together in E^3UDRES^2 aim to co-create outstanding ideas and concepts for future universities, set up formats and events introducing challenge-based education, bring together researchers for mission-oriented research, and serve as a platform for human-centered innovation. All these concepts are contributing to the vision of E^3UDRES^2 creating a multi-university campus across Europe.

Keywords: E3UDRES2, Entrepreneurial University, European University Alliance, Smart regions

Summary

E^3UDRES^2 stands for Engaged and Entrepreneurial European University as Driver for European Smart and Sustainable Regions, one of the "European Universities" (E^3UDRES^2, 2024) – a flagship initiative of the European Union that aims to build strong and long-lasting alliances between universities all over Europe. The higher education institutions working together in E^3UDRES^2 aim to co-create outstanding ideas and concepts for future universities, set up formats and events introducing challenge-based education, bring together researchers for mission-oriented research, and serve as a platform for human-centered innovation. All these concepts are contributing to the vision of E^3UDRES^2 creating a multi-university campus across Europe. E^3UDRES^2 aims to help small and medium-sized European cities turn into what we call "Smart & Sustainable Regions". These are regions that are future-proof, offer the best possible quality of life for its citizens, and stand for a progressive European society. Deeply embedded into those smart & sustainable regions, there's higher education institutions that also need to re-think the way they operate, how they educate their students, and what they stand for to be ready for the challenges the future holds - the Future Universities.

The universities are St. Pölten University of Applied Sciences, Austria, Hochschule Fulda-University of Applied Sciences, Germany, Instituto Politecnico de Sétubal, Portugal, JAMK University of Applied Sciences, Finland, Hungarian University of Agriculture and Life Sciences, Hungary, Saxion University of Applied Sciences, The Netherlands, UC Limburg, UC Leuven, Belgium, Politehnica University of Timisoara, Romania, Vidzeme University of Applied Sciences, Latvia.

E³UDRES² intends to pool expertise and resources for and with its members within four future-guiding Focus Areas: 1) Health, Wellbeing and Social Inclusion for Regions, 2) Digital Solutions and (Applied) Deep Tech for Regions, 3) Resilient Economy and Innovation for Regions, 4) Creative Industries for Region's Identity.

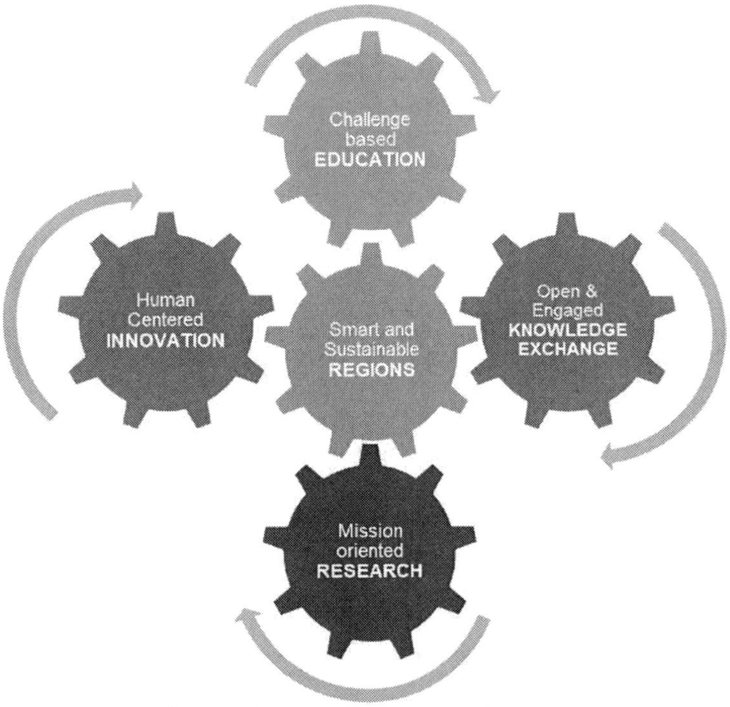

Figure 1: The E³UDRES² Smart region with education vision

Based on the alliance strategic core objectives we plan to enable Smart Learners to unfold talents as to serve as a platform for collaborative innovation to connect entrepreneurial minds (Ehlers, 2021). Our goal is to empower Ent-r-e-novators (entrepreneurs, researchers, educators and innovators) (Andone, 2024) to accelerate future universities in our quest for a shift to a fully-fledged European university to ensure excellent quality.

Closely related to the resonating innovation cycles, E³UDRES² establishes I-Living-Labs for future universities and smart and sustainable regions (Westerlund, 2018). The "I" stands for inspiring, innovative, intercultural, international, interdisciplinary, intersectoral, inclusive and intense. E³UDRES² adopts the concept of Living Labs for the development of "Future Universities" as well as for smart and sustainable regions (Andone, 2022). What makes the E³UDRES² I Living Labs stand out from more traditional Living Labs, is the definition of certain key components as well as the way these are linked with each other. Not only are all E3UDRES2 I Living Labs embedded in the curriculum, they also all have a strong focus on the acquisition of future skills. In addition, I-Living Labs make use of hybrid learning, which has an impact on the role of the student, the teacher and the regional stakeholders. The importance of inclusion in bringing European expertise into the local communities is a final key characteristic.

The E³UDRES² I-Living-Labs have been hosted on UniCampus, the open MOOC platform of the Politehnica University of Timisoara, where all students, teachers and administrators were able to co-learn, and which was one of the inspirations for the in-development E³UDRES² Arena, a joint digital environment which will attempt to integrate the multi-university campus, provide a digital unique-entry point for academics, staff, students and stakeholders to E³UDRES² digital tools and resources.

What digital transformations are needed for learning and teaching in the future?

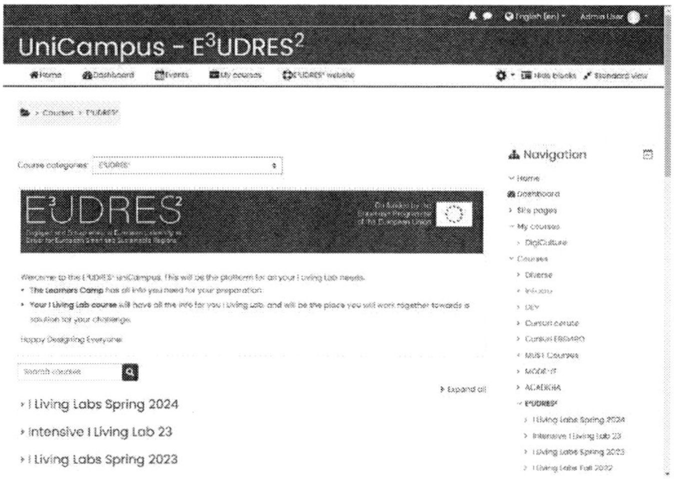

Figure 2: The E^{3}UDRES^2 area in UniCampus

Acknowledgements

The paper is based on research performed in the European Universities Project E3UDRES2 2.0 Engaged and Entrepreneurial European University as Driver for European Smart and Sustainable Regions. https://eudres.eu/

References

E^{3}UDRES^2, 2024 – Website https://eudres.eu/ Accessed 20 May 2024

U.-D. Ehlers and S. A. Kellermann, 'Future Skills: The future of learning and higher education', Karlsruhe, Mar. 2019. Accessed: Dec. 12, 2021. [Online]. Available: https://www.learntechlib.org/p/208249/Bannan-Ritland, B. (2003). The role of design in research: The integrative learning design framework. *Educational Researcher, 32*(1), 21-24. :10.3102/0013189X032001021

M. Westerlund, S. Leminen, and C. Habib, 'Key Constructs and a Definition of Living Labs as Innovation Platforms', Technol. Innov. Manag. Rev., vol. 8, no. 12, pp. 51–62, 2018, doi: http://doi.org/10.22215/timreview/1205.

Andone, D., Vasiu, R., Mihaescu, V., Vert, S., Ternauciuc, A., Mocofan, M. (2024, May). Opening Horizons for European Universities Alliances in Open Education. In 2024 IEEE Global Engineering Education Conference (EDUCON)

Andone, D., Vasiu, R., Bogdan, R., Mihaescu, V., Vert, S., Iovanovici, A., Ciupe, V., Dragan, F. (2022, March). International Innovative Labs–I-Living-Labs. In 2022 IEEE Global Engineering Education Conference (EDUCON) (pp. 1480-1489). IEEE. https://ieeexplore.ieee.org/document/9766823